360-degree
leadership

360-degree leadership

> **preaching** to transform congregations

michael j. quicke

BakerBooks
Grand Rapids, Michigan

© 2006 by Michael J. Quicke

Published by Baker Books
a division of Baker Publishing Group
P.O. Box 6287, Grand Rapids, MI 49516-6287
www.bakerbooks.com

Printed in the United States of America

Library of Congress Cataloging-in-Publication Data
Quicke, Michael J., 1945–
    360-degree leadership : preaching to transform congregations / Michael J. Quicke.
        p.   cm.
    Includes bibliographical references and index.
    ISBN 10: 0-8010-9188-8 (pbk.)
    ISBN 978-0-8010-9188-9 (pbk.)
    1. Pastoral theology. 2. Christian leadership. 3. Preaching. I. Title. II. Title: Three hundred sixty-degree leadership.
    BV4011.3.Q85 2006
    253—dc22   2006016385

To
my sons Simon and Robert—
with love and enormous admiration
for the people they have become

Contents

List of Figures   9
Foreword   11
Acknowledgments   13
Introduction   15

Part 1 The Critical Relationship between Preaching and Leading
1. A Great Divide   23
2. Together in Scripture   45
3. Both Need Each Other Today   61

Part 2 The Making of the Preacher/Leader
4. Fulfilling Vocation   77
5. Developing a Model   91
6. Learning Skills   103
7. Growing Character   125
8. Initiating Process   147

Appendix A: "Leadership 101"   173
Appendix B: Some Leadership Definitions   181
Appendix C: Personal Credo about Preachers as Leaders   185
Notes   189
Figure Credits   198
Index   199

Figures

1. A Triangular Model of Gospel-Culture Relationships   40
2. A Model of 360-Degree Preaching/Leading   52
3. Preacher/Leader Aptitudes and Levels of Leadership   81
4. Congregational Transformation Model   94
5. Models of American Evangelical Churches   113
6. Elements of Spiritual and Relational Vitality   128
7. The Preaching Swim and Leadership   165

Foreword

When we teach seminars on the topic of leading healthy congregational transformation, we often say that the pastor has a unique but not exclusive role in this process. So what does that mean in the day-to-day leadership of a church?

It means that the pastor has the specific biblical role of teaching, equipping, and leading the local body of believers. It means that God calls pastors into these roles and that we should not take this call lightly. It means that the pastor has far more opportunity than anyone else to influence the spiritual health and the strategic direction of the church. After all, who else is actively involved in the key decisions and also able to exhort the entire body each week?

Many books have described the role of pastor as leader, and others have taught the practices of effective preaching. What is lacking, however, are resources that integrate the practical aspects of pastoral leadership with a theological understanding of the office of "pastor and teacher." That is where Michael Quicke so ably steps into the gap. Quicke is both a practitioner and instructor, someone who understands the complexities and nuances of leadership through preaching. He rejects the notion that leadership and preaching can be divorced, and he accurately recognizes that this is exactly what many preachers and churches practice. He recognizes the traps of "thin-blooded preaching" into which many fall—traps that may result in smiles on the faces of congregants, despite how such preaching underestimates the transforming power of Scripture at the individual and corporate level. He also understands that leadership alone—without the guidance of the Holy Spirit and the foundation of Scripture—can quickly turn a church into just another club.

   To those who might think this sounds like hard work, we would respond that it most definitely is, but it is also work that is filled with
adventure, purpose, and joy. And for those who are concerned that adopting this approach is risky, we simply say that being a minister of the
gospel—the good news—has never been intended to be a safe journey.
Instead, we are called to be "Christ's ambassadors, as though God were
making his appeal through us" (2 Cor. 5:20 NIV) and "a workman who
does not need to be ashamed and who correctly handles the word of
truth" (2 Tim. 2:15 NIV). Surely this calls for excellence in preaching
and leading.
   As you open these pages, we encourage you to also open your mind.
Allow Michael Quicke to challenge and instruct you as you consider
how leadership through preaching can revolutionize your ministry and
your church.

Mike Bonem, Jim Herrington, and James H. Furr
coauthors of *Leading Congregational Change*

Acknowledgments

This book has emerged out of a long journey of personal involvement with leading through preaching. So many experiences in my own pastoral ministry and through reading and engaging with others have benefited and shaped me.

I am particularly grateful for the academic settings in which I have had opportunity to think aloud and gain valuable feedback from students and pastors. In particular, I thank the principal and faculty at Acadia Divinity College, Nova Scotia, for the initial outing of these ideas in the 2004 Simpson Lectures. Afterward several pastors commented that I was "scratching where they were itching." One said, "You have no idea how relevant your teaching has been to our situation. For years we have been steamrollered by leadership techniques, and we desperately needed you to reclaim the role of preaching." Another said, "You have touched a raw nerve."

Further lecturing opportunities have sharpened my understanding of the subject, including the 2005 William Conger Lectures at Beeson Divinity School, Birmingham, Alabama, and the 2005 Gladstone Festival Lectures at McMaster Divinity School, Hamilton, Ontario. In the last two years I have also engaged with pastors and doctoral students in other conferences and taught a Doctor of Ministry course on leadership through preaching, all of which have stimulated my thinking. Importantly, several preacher/leaders have granted me interviews and shared their ideas at some length, notably Ed Brown, Lynn Cheyney, Vic Gordon, Jim Nicodem, and Jon Stannard—to whom I express heartfelt thanks.

A few friends have taken trouble to read early drafts of this book, especially Noel Vose, and also John Armstrong, Lori Carrell, and Jim Stamoolis. For their insights and help I am extremely thankful, though no blame is attached to them for the convictions I express and the conclusions I draw. I also owe much to Baker Books—the support of Robert N. Hosack and the splendid editing skills of Paul Brinkerhoff.

Though I refer to several influential books, I chose one to be of particular significance: *Leading Congregational Change* by Jim Herrington, Mike Bonem, and James H. Furr. This workbook arose from fieldwork with one hundred local churches. In part 2 I use it as a basic text and owe much to its realism and wisdom. I am grateful to these authors for their encouragement to work with this model and for their gracious foreword to this book. I am also grateful to Jossey-Bass, their publisher, who generously gave permission.

Introduction

> It is Christ whom we proclaim, warning everyone and teaching everyone in all wisdom, so that we may present everyone mature in Christ. For this I toil and struggle with all the energy that he powerfully inspires within me.
>
> Colossians 1:28–29

Warnings

Various friends have expressed fears about this book project and warned me of the risks that I am taking. One person said: "I'm worried that some preachers will skim your book and just assume that you're placing them on even higher pedestals as leaders. It will only pump up their large egos. The last thing the church needs is more self-important and manipulative preachers!" Agreed. Please note, I have no intention of feeding any preacher's pride, least of all my own. This book is not an invitation to puff up self-aggrandizement of dominant preachers. In some places and cultures such preachers may already have unilateral control and receive adoration from the masses. What one of my African American students calls the "big dog syndrome" where the senior pastor rules with a rod of iron. I shall grieve if, by any misunderstanding, I add just one to their number.

Someone else expressed concern that by linking preaching with leadership I am in danger of diverting preaching from its primary task of proclaiming God's words and seeking his glory. To talk of leadership smacks of practical "how-to" projects focused on human glory, as biblical exposition about God's eternal truths loses out to short-term pragmatism. Of course, desire for human glory always lurks to ambush God's glory.

But when one preacher rebuked me: "I simply preach God's Word to his glory," I responded that there is nothing simple about exposing hearers to the power of God's Word so that his truth is applied practically within his church's mission. I believe that biblical preaching gives glory to God by its transformational power to change individuals and community, and that means taking leadership very seriously, ensuring that it does *not* focus on human glory.

Another pastor questioned whether this book was going to betray his pastoral role. "I see myself as a shepherd to my people," he said. "My main job is to feed the flock and care for them rather than to be their CEO." But Christian leadership is emphatically not about becoming Chief Executive Officers. Rather, it calls for skillful shepherding that addresses individual needs with their community consequences. In Scripture shepherds have very significant leadership roles. When Jesus claims: "I am the good shepherd" (John 10:11) he sums up his whole ministry purpose and he happens to be the world's greatest leader.

Another red flag assumed I was going to focus on "successful pastors" at the expense of average ones. "Oh, you will be telling stories of Bill Hybels at Willow Creek and Rick Warren at Saddleback, won't you? Already the average pastor feels inadequate but this will only make them feel worse." Sadly, "big names" can intimidate ordinary pastors whose struggles seem near hopeless when compared with (apparent) easy victories in larger churches. True, I shall mention both Hybels and Warren but most of my examples come from ordinary pastors whose names you will not know. I am passionate about God's calling and deployment of average pastors. Since most of us are average by definition we need encouragement about God's exciting possibilities for who and where *we* are. Much of my thinking has emerged out of my own story in smaller-scale ministry that has taught me how God promises to work anywhere that he has called preachers. You can read more of my story at the end of the book. God specializes in small scale as well as large. I write this book for average preachers whom God loves and uses.

Hopes

While these friends have been cautious about linking preaching with leadership, many others have cheered me on. One wrote: "How I wish our seminaries would make it very clear to the preachers we are sending out to pastor, that they will be plunged into the center of congregational transformation. Too often as preachers, we believe our only job is to preach and teach the Bible, when our calling is really to transform lives and transform churches by such preaching." Another said, "You have named what I have been trying to describe for many years. What you call thin-blooded preaching is ruining our churches and when you talk about full-blooded preaching I want to cheer!"

What drives this book is my hope that preachers rediscover leadership *through preaching*. In part 1 I shall describe how preaching and leading seem to operate in different spheres. This will involve me giving a survey and critique of leadership literature, quoting extensively from different sources. Chapter 1 analyzes their separation while chapter 2 examines what Scripture has to say about how they should belong together. Chapter 3 stresses the dangers if they continue to drift apart.

I believe that preachers must grasp the God-given leadership dimensions of preaching. Christian leadership belongs to preaching and preaching belongs to leadership because God's preachers are inevitably also his leaders. Of course preachers do not have exclusive claims to leadership. Many others are called to exercise Christian leadership both inside and outside the church. Yet, without diminishing these other leaders' roles, preacher/leaders need to discover their own responsibilities. I use this term *preacher/leader* in order to emphasize that I believe the preacher role should never be defined on its own. Rather, as I shall argue in this book, preachers are inevitably leaders because of their unique calling that inseparably combines preaching with leading. Because of their calling to speak God's transformational Word, preacher/leaders have a primary role. By Holy Spirit power, their preaching of God's Word should exercise leadership by envisioning, confronting, encouraging, stretching, releasing, and uniting the people of God to live out his will.

Recently, I spelled out a credo (included in full in appendix C):

> I believe that preaching is God's primary way of transforming individuals and communities because he empowers it.
>
> I believe that preachers have been leaders at every breakthrough in the Christian story.
>
> I believe that preachers as leaders arise out of God's calling and gifting.
>
> I believe that preaching needs to recover its prophetic voice today.
>
> I believe that preaching brings the whole church under God to see his vision and hear his Word for his mission.
>
> I believe that preachers have to reclaim the preaching/leading task with prayer, humility, energy, and collaboration.[1]

Just listing these convictions is likely to raise some people's blood pressure. How dare I make such big claims? Am I not writing as a self-interested dinosaur who has been preaching for thirty-five years, now earns his living as a preaching professor and itinerant preacher, and who simply doesn't seem to realize just how dull and irrelevant preaching has become in so many places? Yes I do realize, but I know God never intended it to be dull and irrelevant anywhere. I have already challenged the view that sees preaching as dry and useless. My book *360-Degree Preaching* claims that authentic preaching is empowered by nothing less than the spiritual dynamic of Father, Son, and Holy Spirit at work in the lives of speakers and hearers. I raise the stakes for biblical preaching, believing it to be prophetic, transformational, and incarnational: "Christian preaching, at its best, is a biblical speaking/listening/seeing/doing event that God empowers to form Christ-shaped people and communities."[2] Only those with seriously distorted experience from listening to sermons should call them dull and irrelevant.

My personal passion is to keep alive to God's high calling to preach and to sound out the trumpet to waken any sleepwalking preachers across my path. God has no more compelling way to form and transform people than when preacher/leaders hear God's Word for themselves and their people and declare it by his power, applying it by his Spirit. Through his preached Word God speaks contemporaneously to lead his people. Nowhere else can he be more clearly heard and by no other means can leadership have such authority.

Colossians 1:28–29 at the head of this introduction sums up this awesome task. Preaching is proclaiming Christ by warning and teaching. It is *inclusive*—everyone is to grow in wisdom so that everyone may be presented mature in Christ. It is *transformational* by helping whole church communities grow in maturity. The expression "in Christ" (*en Christō*; v. 28) is powerfully significant in the Pauline epistles. It often brings together the plural language of community—"you" (Col. 1:2)—into strong personal relationship with Christ. *En* has localizing force—"the place at which." So, Jesus Christ is the "place" where believers are and in whom salvation is. Believers belong together as a building (Eph. 2:21), temple (1 Cor. 3:16; 2 Cor. 6:16), and bride betrothed to God (2 Cor. 11:2), but the profoundest expression is as the body of Christ (Col. 1:18, 24). These corporate dimensions of being church have critical implications for preaching's task and will be addressed later in this book. Believers are on a journey together in Christ, with an outcome that presents "everyone perfect in Christ" (NIV), and preaching is given prime responsibility for making it happen by God's grace.

It is also *realistic*. Note how "toil" and "struggle" describe the preaching task. Preaching, as God designs it, demands so much hard work, discipline, and sheer dogged persistence. As James Black wrote of preaching, "Honest work is the great secret."[3] Yet pulsing through preachers' strenuous endeavors is God's energy "that he powerfully inspires within me." This great paradox about preaching, that it requires every ounce of human energy within God's mighty work, keeps preachers both fully stretched and humbly dependent.

While writing this book I was conscious of many pastors' situations. Two particularly impacted me. A senior pastor and his wife, who were shortly moving into a new church, visited me. I asked them about their new call, expecting some excitement. Instead, with frowning face, he described the pain of trying to deal with a problem person in his new church. He had yearned for the whole problem to be sorted out before he began. "Everyone acknowledges this person is difficult though he occupies an important leadership role and has been in the church for many years, but nobody has done anything about it," he said. Even before commencing his new ministry, he had already lost sleep over how to deal with this situation. Wearily, he lamented: "Well, I suppose that's leadership. You are never free of problems in leadership." That's true. We shall be confronted by the reality of conflict and the difficulties of dealing positively with it, which we will address later in this book. But the secret of Christian leadership is to place the unavoidably harsh facts of hard work, conflict, disagreement, and rank disappointment within the resources of God's energy "that he powerfully inspires in me." Conflict is inevitable because leadership means change, and change provokes resistance. If you are looking for a life free from conflict, make sure you don't become a leader or a preacher. Yet when God calls you to preach and to lead, remember, in the unavoidable pain, his promise of energy. This promise rings true in my experience and encourages me to pursue 360-degree leading.

Another conversation with a pastor has haunted me. He spoke transparently about his dilemma of no longer really understanding his calling. In his late forties, having spent over twenty years in the ministry, he found himself stuck on a plateau where so many of the things he was taught to do and had practiced with seeming effectiveness in the past no longer worked. As he put it: "Several of my lay leaders expect me to be more like their Christian heroes they see on TV, or whose books they read. To be strong and visionary. But I honestly do not know how. I thought God was calling me to preach and pastor. But it doesn't seem to be enough." This book is offered out of conviction that it *is* enough when such pastors rediscover how preaching leads. Yes, there are new developments in leadership that must be taken seriously but God's call to preach provides the framework—it is leadership through preaching.

One last warning must be given. Trying to research leadership literature for this book was like attempting to take a drink from a fire hydrant. I find it difficult enough keeping up with the flow of preaching volumes pumping out into my own teaching field. But it was impossible to do justice to the overwhelmingly vast resources available on leadership. Inevitably my limited reading and experience means many glaring gaps and oversimplifications. Yet, as I splash some broad brushstrokes across a vast canvas, I hope these next chapters will paint an interesting enough scene with sufficient details to stimulate readers to join me on the journey of discovering leadership through preaching. Much further reading, reflection, and engagement lies beyond these pages. So many stories need to be told—perhaps including yours! But at least let's make a start and dedicate ourselves to filling in more and more of God's picture for preacher/leaders in the twenty-first century.

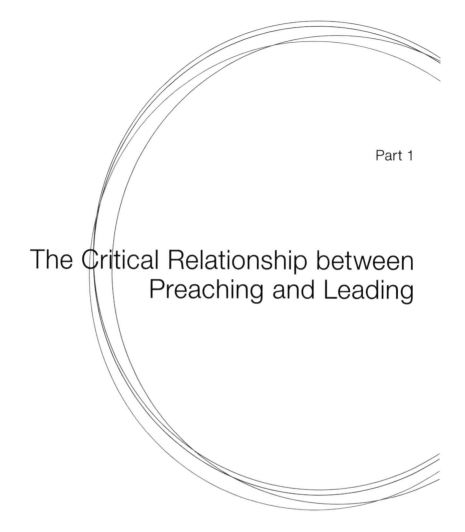

Part 1

The Critical Relationship between Preaching and Leading

1

A Great Divide

Preachers have lost the art of leadership through the proclaimed Word. There is too little courage and too much safe predictability, too little confrontation of evil by Christ's power and too much soothing of the already convinced. Fewer people can imagine that revival and renewal could ever come from preaching.

Michael J. Quicke, *360-Degree Preaching*[1]

When I first wrote that, it sounded rather dramatic, but I still believe it is true. A burden weighs heavily upon me. I grieve that two driving forces for good have become separated from each other: leadership from preaching and preaching from leadership. This broken relationship and my desire that they dialogue with each other in order to create a powerful working partnership dominate this book.

I picture them as two forceful personalities (the Old Testament provides a good precedent by personalizing wisdom as female in Proverbs 8). Male or female, preaching and leadership stand apart, like giants happily preoccupied with their own spheres of influence. Perhaps glancing at each other occasionally, they mostly focus on their own tasks, never thinking to meet and shake hands, let alone work together in partnership. Their characters are different. Preaching is theologically weighty and boasts long-term spiritual pedigree, giving it an assured place in the weekly cycles of church life. Perhaps it looks slightly smug with traces of irritation that another player has attracted so much attention. Leadership is a robust newcomer with a world of new ideas and language about how to work in the contemporary situation. Maybe it shows some impatience and touches of arrogance.

After all, leadership is well ahead in the popularity polls. Many people see the staple diet of Sunday sermons as solid unattractive necessities rather than magnetic opportunities. Many who were shocked by David Murrow's book *Why Men Hate Going to Church* nonetheless reluctantly agree with his conclusions that many men (and probably women too) are being bored out of churches.[2] But, on the other hand, leadership radiates excitement and action. For example, consider George Barna's definition of a Christian leader: "someone who is called by God to lead and possess virtuous character and [who] effectively motivates, mobilizes resources, and directs people toward the fulfillment of a jointly embraced vision from God."[3] How attractive and energetic that sounds compared with general perceptions about sermons! Leadership is red-hot, gaining loud applause from enthusiastic fans. Bill Hybels recently claimed: "I believe that the local church is the hope of the world and its future lies primarily in its leaders."[4] Sermons seem to lie cold and blue at the opposite end of the spectrum from dynamic leadership.

My picture of two personalities operating in different spheres of influence reminds me of a famous political relationship. In the cold war between West and East, two people eyed each other suspiciously in 1984—Margaret Thatcher, prime minister of Great Britain, and Mikhail Gorbachev, premier of the Soviet Union. However, in spite of many differences, when they met and began to talk a very significant thaw occurred, and Margaret Thatcher said famously, "This is a man that I can do business with." This was a turning point in relationships between West and East.

At present there seems little positive relationship between preaching and leadership, as this chapter describes. But the situation must change. Part 1 shows the need for developing partnership, and part 2 offers a model for a working relationship so preaching and leading can "do business" together. I believe that by doing business together, preaching/leading will transform local churches.

Local churches have been severely harmed by this non-relationship between preaching and leadership. God has designed local churches to spearhead his kingdom. I know how often they fall sadly short of God's ideal because they are full of unholy people like me. Christopher Idle likens denominations to characters in *Winnie the Pooh*.[5] Tigger is Pentecostal, Winnie the Pooh is Episcopalian, and Rabbit is undeniably Baptist because of the washings, the organizing of others by "rissolutions," and mostly his innumerable relations, who represent all the splits, persuasions, and separations. I am particularly aware of the failings of my own Baptist tradition. Supposedly, there are forty-seven Baptist denominational groupings in the United States, often not talking to each other. Yet in spite of all of this, by God's mysterious choosing, only local churches can flesh out the possibilities of grace as it works in forgiven men and women worshiping and living in their communities. Only in local churches can people belong under Christ's lordship as family. Only by local churches can whole communities be salted and lit up (Matt. 5:13–16) and missionaries be sent out to the world. Churches are part of God's cosmic master plan (Col. 1:18) and there is no plan B.

Personal Experience

As a Baptist pastor serving through the last thirty-plus years, three contrasting personal experiences illustrate my encounters with these two driving forces. The first was in my beginning pastorate, the second in my Cambridge ministry, and the third when I became principal of Spurgeon's College, London.

In 1972, between my call to the pastorate and my arrival in the Baptist church in Blackburn, Lancashire, I received dismal news that extensive dry rot had been discovered in the roof and walls, making the building unsafe. Courteously, the chair of the church management committee wrote inviting me to withdraw from the pastorate. After all, he said, who wants to begin ministry plagued by major building problems and no money?

However, I truly believed that God had called me for better for worse, for richer for poorer, in rot and in health. My first sermons declared: "In the beginning God" (Genesis 1), "In the beginning was the Word" (John 1:1), and "Jesus Invites You into His Kingdom" (Mark 1:14). Big themes! I knew that everything depended on God, and during seven years I preached my heart out weekly to a local church community that needed, with me, to grow in faith and vision through a building crisis into a mission for its neighborhood and beyond. Leadership studies were almost nonexistent. I wouldn't have recognized a mission or vision statement if it had come straight at me, announced what it was, and bitten me on my nose. Of course there were the usual Baptist church structures with deacons' boards, committees, and congregational meetings. But truthfully, preaching in worship, as worship, seemed central to all the ensuing events of church life and mission, which turned out to be exhilaratingly untidy and surprisingly eventful. I experienced, and my congregation with me, the mysterious fusion of the spiritual gift of leadership with preaching.

The title of John Killinger's 1969 book best summed up my ministry practice: *The Centrality of Preaching in the Total Task of the Ministry.*[6] I tasted something of full-blooded preaching. I have warmed to this expression, because *full-blooded* expresses the vital and invigorating task of being Christ's ambassadors staking the future on gospel truth—"if anyone is in Christ, there is a new creation . . . see, everything has become new!" (2 Cor. 5:17). As Walter Brueggemann strikingly describes it, the Bible world invites us into a contrasting reality as compared to surrounding culture, into "a counterstory about God, world, neighbor, and self."[7] How dramatically such preaching contrasts with anemic, thin-blooded preaching that offers no impelling counterstory. And right there, in Blackburn, Lancashire, I found my preaching was sounding out God's new way of living in a contrasting reality.

My second experience turned out to have immense impact on my development as a preacher/leader, though it began inauspiciously. Having resisted a call to become their pastor for two years (partly because so many positive things were happening at Blackburn), in 1980 I reluctantly found myself in a downtown church in Cambridge called St. Andrew's Street Baptist Church. The primary reason for my unwillingness to go to this church was obvious—it seemed to be in the last throes of terminal decline. Founded in 1721, boasting a proud history, the church building seated one thousand people, with a great track record of past members and preachers, but its numbers were reduced to a small group of elderly saints—seventy in the morning congregation and twenty in the evening. They mostly sat in the back pews so that, when the Fenland mist rolled in, I could hardly see them and, perhaps more to the point, they couldn't see me.

Nothing in my seven years of ministry had so far prepared me for this situation. All my experience at Blackburn had assumed a vibrant family community living within walking distance of the church buildings. But what was the mission of this downtown church? Its few members all lived a distance away and commuted in on Sundays. Indeed, some even wondered if it should have a mission. Someone suggested that perhaps I had been called to give the church a decent burial. "After all," they said, "there are enough churches in Cambridge. It is very important to help some churches die!" Another pastor told me he had declined the pastorate in the previous two years because it had no "mission patch" in the city. To some observers it simply didn't seem worth putting any more effort into it. Frankly, I wondered if anything I might say or do would make a scrap of difference. I knew that I was way out of my depth, with meager human resources and nothing in my past experience that I could see working here.

Rereading that last paragraph it might seem that I am exaggerating my sense of helplessness. But I really did feel completely overwhelmed. Questions like, What are we going to do? How will this ever work? plagued me. Yet what actually happened next proved to be the biggest surprise of my ministry. I learned, with this small and mostly elderly group, what it meant to pray and trust in God. To our amazement he worked out his counterstory, on the main street in Cambridge, through *us*. From 1980 to 1993 a story of congregational transformation unfolded. In this unlikely situation, I found myself practicing a series of principles about following God's guidance in prayer and faith which later on, to my utter amazement, lined up with the findings and conclusions that others propose in the leadership model that I shall introduce in part 2 of this book.

I shall share more of the story of what happened at St. Andrew's Street Baptist Church at the end of the book. But I want you to sense something of the powerful adventure that I, with the congregation, went through. My experience in that church changed my ministry and inspired me to think through what it means to be a preacher/leader. One person who knew the church well said to me later about the transformation, "If it could happen there, it could happen anywhere!" I am convinced that more and more congregations can experience transformation like that, when preachers lead.

During the 1990s, my ministry took a further turn as I left Cambridge to become principal of Spurgeon's College. It was here that I was introduced to my first business leadership book. A new college administrator thrust *Built to Last* by Jim Collins and Jerry Porras into my hand and urged me to read it. This classic business book analyzes eighteen world-beating companies compared with their closest, less successful rivals. I read it carefully with deepening fascination. It demolished myths of successful leadership and advocated accepting "both/and" choices rather than the "tyranny of the or." Successful organizations need a BHAG—a "big hairy audacious goal" (though why "hairy" I never understood). The book failed to mention God, yet I could relate so many of its principles to Christian leadership. After all, isn't the Great Commission (Matt. 28:19–20) the biggest BHAG? So much in the book made sense.

Since then I have read many such books and attended several conferences on Christian leadership. So have most pastors. A 2003 survey of U.S. pastors found that 94 percent of those surveyed had participated in some kind of leadership training or used leadership resources.[8] Over three decades, interest in leadership has gained ascendancy in the Western church.

Many positive results have flowed from this, as we shall see later. But there has been one disastrous consequence—the eclipse of the preacher/leader. The older model of the local church needed a preacher/leader within a complex organism focused around Sunday worship—Word and sacrament. Such public ministry both focused and initiated other church activity and community life. However, any organization structured on business principles has no critical need for preachers as leaders. Preachers still have a teaching role, but increasingly it is not deemed to be one of leadership. Their preaching has become thin-blooded, a sickly substitute for the real thing of being Christ's ambassadors of new creation.

Church Leadership without Preachers

Much of the extensive literature on church leadership has little or nothing good to say about preaching having a leadership role. Some authors even seem hostile. Thomas Bandy critiques traditional preaching for its wordiness, its precious ego, and its rejection of new technologies. Such preaching separates clergy from laity and acts like a CEO to stockholders and senior pastor to associates. In contrast, Bandy encourages the model of good coaching that relates as friend-to-friend, team-to-team, explorer to spiritual travelers, and mentor to apprentices. He looks for animation, synergy, and passion in his team-building model for the future church, but there seems to be no room for preaching.[9]

Many who write on leadership make scant reference to preaching. One of Kennon Callahan's *Twelve Keys to an Effective Church* is "corporate, dynamic worship." He describes five factors as important: warmth, music, preaching, liturgy, and seating. Preaching receives minimal attention. He briefly commends "preachers who are the shepherds, leaders, and prophets in their churches and community, . . . shepherds in caring and sharing, leaders with wisdom and judgment, prophets with thoughtful and insightful critique," but he gives no direct guidance about how preachers lead.[10] Similarly, Christian Schwarz identifies one of eight characteristics for "natural church growth" as "inspiring worship" yet fails to give preaching a primary place in strategy.[11] Leith Anderson also urges models of leadership without developing preaching's role.[12]

Sometimes books on spiritual leadership imply preaching in every chapter yet fail to name it explicitly. For example, Henry and Richard Blackaby's *Spiritual Leadership* has immensely helpful insights (which I shall draw on later). They stress God's call of the leader and the leader's responsibility to listen to God's agenda and communicate it. Page after page sounds as though it is especially about preachers yet, in their understandable desire to include other kinds of leaders, preachers end up as missing persons.[13]

Strangely, even gifted preacher/leaders seem to emphasize other aspects of leadership rather than the role of preaching itself. Rick Warren's *The Purpose Driven Church* is dedicated to bi-vocational pastors, and he briefly extols the "primacy of preaching" at the end of a chapter on "preaching to the unchurched." However, in much of the rest he fails to make clear just how much preachers are involved in the tasks of leadership as preachers. His programs such as "40 Days of Purpose" link small group work with daily readings of his book and viewing video films. He provides tools for preachers in order to mobilize church communities to form small groups and sustain the program, all the while presuming the leadership role of preachers but never spelling it out.[14]

Bill Hybels similarly presumes preaching's contribution to leadership and offers some examples, but he does not seem to develop a clear practical strategy for preaching/leading. Jim Herrington, Mike Bonem, and James Furr offer one of the most realistic models for congregational transformation, and I shall draw heavily on their work in part 2. But even they rarely mention the role that preaching uniquely has to play in terms of leadership.[15] Aubrey Malphurs's *Values-Driven Leadership* actually presupposes preaching but only addresses the significance of preacher/leaders briefly and late in his book.[16]

Explanations of how preachers might lead seem exasperatingly vague. *Leadership* magazine may highlight preachers who have made an impact and yet not actually talk about how their preaching led to transformation. In the "Community Transformation" issue, Bishop Vaughn McLaughlin is interviewed about the transformation of Jacksonville, Florida, by his message of economic empowerment. Yet nowhere is it made clear how he conveyed that message; presumably, he intentionally used preaching to lead his people.[17]

Intriguingly you would assume that an interview with John Maxwell in *Preaching* magazine on "Thinking, Leading, and Preaching" would bring together leadership and preaching. As a renowned motivational leadership speaker and preacher, Maxwell talks about his book *Thinking for a Change* and argues that successful people think differently from unsuccessful people. Successful people think realistically, creatively, and reflectively, and pastors need to do the same. Yet at no point does he speak about preaching's role in leadership. He comments: "I came out of college for my age as a good preacher. But I didn't connect with people. My definition of communication is very simple: the acid test of communication is connection."[18] True, connection is vital. But what about the potential transformational impact of Scripture as preaching's content?

Ironically, preaching's large body of literature lacks explicit reference to leadership. One notable exception is *The Roundtable Pulpit: Where Leadership and Preaching Meet* in which John McClure commends collaborative preaching that involves others in sermon preparation to develop participatory local church leadership. He contrasts the "sovereign preacher" whose autocratic leadership can hinder a congregation's empowerment with "dialogue and inductive preaching" by which a congregation learns to "talk itself into becoming a Christian community."[19] Over long experience he claims that such collaborative preaching develops congregational leadership that is mutual and participative. I shall refer to his ideas later.

In no way is this shotgun survey intended to denigrate the value of leadership literature. I recall recent conversations in which Christian leaders spoke enthusiastically about how certain books had helped them. One spoke of the impact of John Kotter's *Leading Change*.[20] Over dinner he explained how the eight-stage process of leading change had revolutionized his approach to leadership and helped to transform his organization. (Indeed, Kotter's process contributed to the leadership model that I shall advocate in part 2.) Another leader shared how *Visioneering* by Andy Stanley[21] had revolutionized his pattern of ministry.

My purpose is not to deny the worth of leadership literature to Christian leaders and certainly not to question the effectiveness of big-name preachers who have written about leadership. Rather, I am deeply concerned about the lack of explicit attention given to preaching's role in Christian leadership. Most writing on Christian leadership omits preaching, and most books on preaching leave out leadership. For many everyday pastors in ordinary churches this displacement of preaching has brought bewilderment and anxiety. The eclipse of preaching/leading has torn out the heart of the Christian ministry. Instead of the book title *The Centrality of Preaching in the Total Task of the Ministry* which summed up my experience in the 1970s, the situation today seems better described by *The Centrality of Leadership in the Total Task of the Ministry*. Much has changed over thirty years.

Indeed much has changed. Western culture has encouraged leadership's separation from preaching in evangelical churches by an increasing severance of the spiritual from the material, and of the private from the public.[22] Increasing secularism has undeniably helped to marginalize preaching's role as spiritual talk on the fringe of public values and action. Lesslie Newbigin's seminal work (out of which has flowed The Gospel and Our Culture Network)[23] has identified changes that dramatically affect the Western church's future. Based on Newbigin's analysis, George Hunsberger makes this judgment:

> The church's former privileged position in western societies under the Christendom model is now gone, and it will not be regained. The church, as a faith community, is relegated by the culture's frame of understanding to the private world of personal values, beliefs and opinions. By and large the church has willingly (if sometimes unknowingly) accommodated itself to that relegation and become a privatized, voluntary association for perpetuating its set of faith opinions.[24]

Thin-blooded preaching has accelerated this woeful accommodation in evangelical churches. Severely weakened, such preaching has primarily focused on spiritual and private concerns, deeming its task either to be solely *evangelistic*, offering individuals personal salvation by repenting and believing, or solely *teaching*, instructing individual Christians with right doctrine and about church commitment. Of course, preaching includes the vital tasks of teaching gospel truths for faith responses and of educating and nurturing individuals in their spiritual life, but this emphasis solely on evangelism and teaching severs preaching from its leadership role and plays straight into the private club mentality of many churches. Occasionally preachers may sally into community issues. Politics may enter the pulpit around election time as hearers are urged to "vote in line with their beliefs." Social issues such as abortion and euthanasia may be given pulpit time, especially when raised in public awareness as in the traumatic case of Terri Schiavo and the eventual removal of her feeding tube.[25] However, in general, personal spiritual issues dominate preaching time.

Interestingly, much Christian leadership literature seems to prefer the word *teaching* to *preaching*[26] perhaps because a didactic purpose more agreeably fits private worlds than talk of new creation and reconciliation. By majoring on teaching private beliefs and values, preaching has lost its power to lead communities of people to live out God's counterstory. Such preaching no longer dares to believe that God can use it to form individuals into his people.

Meanwhile leadership has forcefully entered center stage, thriving on the opportunities that secularism provides. At worst, some churches have even adopted the assumptions of business organizations, concentrating their leadership on the "bottom line"—the three "M's."[27] *Membership* (someone has claimed membership numbers are the most fraudulent statistics collected!), *maintenance* (budgets, committees, structures dedicated at least to maintain last year's figures), and, of course, *money* itself.[28] So absorbed are they in their pursuit of success defined in those terms, many churches have hungrily gobbled up secular leadership principles and practice. Indeed Henry and Richard Blackaby protest, "The trend among many Christian leaders has been for an almost indiscriminate and uncritical acceptance of secular leadership theory without measuring it against the timeless precepts of Scripture."[29] God-talk and spirituality are inevitably sidelined by leadership pragmatism when secular models exercise a hypnotic stranglehold on the church. It is hardly surprising that when churches use business models, little room is left for preaching to give significant leadership.

And what subtle influence secular thinking can have on Christian leadership! Many red flags must be waved about "uncritical acceptance." The tendency for secular leadership to focus exclusively on positives, playing to strengths and neglecting negatives, flies straight in the face of the Christian need for confession and dependence on God's grace. Certainly, fundamental biblical principles such as "strength in weakness" (which will be dealt with in chapter 3) cannot be flouted, yet what we need is biblical discernment.

George Barna waves several other red flags concerning misconceptions that Christians can have about leadership.[30] For example, leadership should not be confused with "influence." Influence majors on motivating people to do things without necessarily having any positively deep impact on their lives. After all, salespeople are classic influencers and yet salesmanship is an unhealthy gospel model. Similarly, Christian leadership must not be identified with "getting important things done efficiently." Barna associates efficiency more with managing people rather than leading them and asserts his research shows that "because leaders are focused on doing the right thing, they are often inefficient in their work—and yet, because of their transformational focus, their effectiveness is not hindered." Also, Christian leadership is not "based on controlling the decision-making apparatus through a consolidation of power and position." Control and power are so easily open to abuse, but great leaders empower and release others to share leadership.

As a useful exercise, consider the collection of leadership definitions in appendix A that are drawn from a variety of secular and Christian sources. See where the Christian perspective is strongest and choose which ones best represent your point of view. Mark your choices and later reevaluate those definitions based on your learning after reading this book.

Ironically, simultaneous with secular leadership's assault upon church thinking, many secular writers on leadership seem to be rediscovering spiritual values as witnessed in book titles such as *Leading with Soul: An Uncommon Journey of Spirit* by Lee Bolman and Terrence Deal,[31] *Leadership and Spirit: Breathing New Vitality and Energy into Individuals and Organizations* by Russ Moxley,[32] and *Spirited Leading and Learning: Process Wisdom for a New Age* by Peter Vaill.[33] In their wide survey of leadership literature, Robert Banks and Bernice Ledbetter observe that spiritual language crops up everywhere, citing Stephen Pattison's study that "much so-called secular thinking and writing about management displays a form of utopian religious faith."[34] Pattison sees four areas of such unrecognized beliefs and practices. First, many sell "faith, hope, and meaning" as much as specific knowledge or techniques, though couched in belief that human beings have a capacity to control the world, set goals, and achieve success. Second, many use mystical metaphors such as vision, mission, servant, or service. Third, organizations can develop ways of doing things that become similar to religious rituals having symbolic importance such as unquestionable belief in the "bottom line." Fourth, the business world and certain Christian groups can share assumptions such as "people are converted to the organization's aims, values, and practices."[35]

Religious expression ranges from humanistic "self-renewal" as in Stephen Covey's *The Seven Habits of Highly Effective People*[36] to belief in some higher power that permeates all life, with elements of New Age spirituality, on through to Christian faith itself. Banks and Ledbetter are impressed by the way some leadership literature uses common Judeo-Christian words such as *love, care, stewardship*, and *trust*, accompanied by Greek New Testament terms such as *koinōnia* (working in partnership), *diakonia* (humble service), and *metanoia* (radical change of mind).[37] They further examine several authors' substantial faith-based models such as Max Du Pree's Reformed Christian approach and Catherine Mowry LaCugna's *God for Us: The Trinity and Christian Life*.

Christian language turns up in surprising places. For example, Robert Quinn in *Deep Change* writes of leaders' need of moral power, to "surrender" control, and experience "the dark night of the soul."[38] Secular business life is peppered with talk of mission statements, covenants, and evangelists. In June 2004, Microsoft appointed an "Internet Explorer Evangelist." Research Machines UK has a "Product Evangelist" who "gives presentations to educationalists and key advisers to UK education . . . [which] include The Queen, Cabinet Ministers and the BBC." Macromedia has "Flash Evangelists" and "Flex Evangelists" on its staff—whatever that might mean!

Caught in the middle between churches devouring leadership concepts and secular leadership toying with spiritual language, many preachers find themselves in lose-lose situations. Restricted to teaching private spiritual concerns, their effectiveness is increasingly judged by material criteria. Commended for winning new members and keeping old members in profitable organizations, preachers are progressively more regarded as dispensable employees. Aubrey Malphurs complains that ministry is commonly practiced as a "hired-hand concept" rather than viewed as the spiritual gift of leadership, enabling the whole church to express ministry (Eph. 4:11–13). "Where did this hired-hand concept come from? It is primarily cultural. In fact, 85 to 90 percent of what the typical church does today is influenced by its culture . . . not the Bible."[39] One pastor wrote me an email: "Everything boils down to whether the local church views the pastor as employee or leader." Another pastor warned: "You'll never be able to bridge the gap between the pulpit and the board. I'm allowed to teach Bible truths. Other people run the church!" Preachers are employed to teach but others are to lead. Since the same leadership skills apply equally to churches and secular organizations, lay leaders argue that preachers should do their job while they practice leadership.

The Tragedy of Thin-Blooded Preaching

Sadly, therefore, preaching has become a small cog in the ecclesiastical machinery, turning in response to the driving momentum of larger leadership forces. Preaching is allowed to win sheep and keep them safely in the fold, but it cannot lead them out as a flock. It opens the door to faith and offers doctrinal morsels to chew on but does not mobilize sheep to see visions, obey God, and move into new pastures together. Anemic preaching addresses individuals but cannot lead them anywhere.

Nowhere is this assumption clearer than in George Barna's outburst in *Christianity Today* about the desperate lack of leaders in the church in North America. He comments:

> The people who fill the positions of leadership in churches today are, for the most part, teachers—good people, lovers of God, well educated, gifted communicators—but not leaders. They do not have or understand vision. They are incapable of motivating and mobilizing people around God's vision. They fail to direct people's energies and resources effectively and efficiently.[40]

Notice how Barna separates preachers, whom he sees as well-educated, gifted teachers, from leaders of vision. On one hand, preachers deal with teaching and evangelism. On the other hand, leaders motivate and mobilize people around God's vision, directing people's energies and resources as a community. A gloomy Barna sees few of the latter.

A 2003 survey of pastors and congregants discovered that 92 percent of pastors considered themselves as leaders and 94 percent of the congregants agreed.[41] However, the survey contrasted two types of preaching—teaching and exhortation (the latter defined as preaching to motivate change). Eighty percent said teaching was their spiritual gift, which doesn't leave many exhorters! So the majority defined their leadership as that of shepherding and bridge building with an emphasis on teaching and nurturing. When pastors were asked whether they saw themselves as "visionary" and "strategizing" the proportion dropped dramatically.

When congregants were asked about how they viewed their pastors' leadership qualities they often rated them lower: adaptable (72% pastors versus 48% congregants), team player (71% vs. 53%), flexible (65% vs. 46%), analytical (54% vs. 29%), practical (60% vs. 48%). Responding to these findings, Joseph Stowell suggests that many churches want strong leaders and "perhaps we have taken more the corporate model of leadership and imposed that into pastoral ministry as if Jack Welch (head of GE) were the premium pastor in America . . . (and) that is creating deep levels of frustration." Wayne Schmidt agrees and says of pastors pressured by church expectations: "I think because of that, quite frankly, we tend to overrate our leadership ability."[42]

Thin-blooded preaching describes a type of preaching that misses out on leadership. Attenuated gospel truth trickles out only half the story. It tells out good news of salvation but neglects the richness of God's vision for saved people—of growing his people into his counterstory of new creation. Such preaching has ten characteristics listed below, though several important cautions should be heard first.

Writing as a white male preacher, I recognize that other preaching traditions may be less susceptible to thin-blooded preaching. For example, in his dialogue with the black preacher E. K. Bailey, Warren Wiersbe notes two lessons he has learned as a white preacher. First, that the "whole person has to be in the pulpit. . . . The [white] tradition I was raised in didn't take that approach. You were a persona in the pulpit not a person."[43] Second, that the congregation comprises not just listeners but participants. "The main metaphor for most white preaching is that of a conduit or a conveyor belt. . . . He loads this conveyor belt with all kinds of stuff for their good. . . . But I've learned that people must be a part of the preaching process."[44] Certainly, much black preaching I have heard has a holistic community dimension and is much less likely to be lackluster.

Thinking about female leadership also challenges me. Rightly, Alice Mathews is cautious about gender stereotypes, but she claims research indicates "that the majority of women who lead have a more collegial leadership. . . . Men mentored by women in business have many of the traits of women's leadership style."[45] As a woman preacher she argues for leadership "from the middle" where "leading means enabling people to address their problems satisfactorily. . . . Leadership is the process of bringing people to a point of having to face their problems and to deal with them. *And that is what preaching is about*."[46] For her, preaching/leading requires realism about the contradiction between the values that people say they stand for and the daily realities of their lives. To bridge this gap between values and reality, she sees the need for preacher/leaders to design strategies for helping people change their attitudes, beliefs, or behavior.

> Leadership is about motivating people to face tough realities and deeply buried conflicts. . . . Leading people to maturity in Christ may mean letting go of some traditional notions of leadership and practicing some of the "feminine" leadership styles. When women lead, much of the focus is on listening to understand the issues and then educating in ways that transform situations.[47]

I shall illustrate this in chapter 8 by the story of Lynn Cheyney.

Bearing in mind therefore the limitations of my white male viewpoint, and with an element of parody (forgive me), I characterize thin-blooded preaching by these features.

1. Individualistic

Most obviously, thin-blooded preaching concentrates solely on the condition and needs of individuals. Of course, the gospel requires a personal response, but believers should always be made aware that they belong in deeper relationship together with other believers in Christ, *en Christō* (Col. 1:28). Hearers should never be able to walk away thinking Christ's challenge is all about "my life, my purpose, my future" instead of "our life, our purpose, our future." Dispensing with demanding kingdom and body of Christ language that stretches us beyond ourselves, such preaching comfortably settles for the unholy trinity of "me, myself, and I." One preacher responded sharply to me: "I've been preaching a series on healing the family recently. Would you call that individualistic?" I replied, "If you have concentrated on relationships between husbands, wives, parents, and children in nuclear families without challenging about the further dimensions of being church family before a watching world—yes!"

2. Aimed at Head or Heart but Rarely Both Together

At one extreme, anemic preaching specializes in lodging great slabs of words into heads. Sermons can be packed by cross-referenced biblical texts that multiply to fill the space so comprehensively that hearers are consumed by writing up notes and nodding contentedly, "That was a great series on 1 Corinthians!" Cerebral preachers love to use "The Blessed Treasury of Wonderful Bible Verses that will accompany your sermon text and fill up the space to stop you pursuing its specific consequences." One long-standing church member said to me of a preacher: "He just exhausts me with text after text. After forty minutes I feel mentally wiped out." But at the other extreme, thin-blooded preaching can touch only on emotions and bypass intellect (and biblical text) to focus on motivating "feel-good" outcomes for individuals. This is especially evident in "prosperity gospel" preaching that can miss completely the deeper implications of belonging in God's kingdom. One of my students attended a meeting of a well-known TV preacher. "He invited me to open my Bible at the beginning, but he didn't mention it once. He was lively and made me feel positive about myself, but afterwards I realized he had not referred to Scripture even once."

3. Spineless Theology

Sterile preaching suffers from a weak theology of preaching. Often Unitarian in practice, it acts as though there is no living Christ interceding and empowering, and no Holy Spirit bringing hearing and conviction. It cannot imagine that God—Father, Son, and Holy Spirit—can be actively involved in every part of the preaching process and prefers to treat sermon making as 90 percent human effort. Plenty of biblical texts may be quoted but mention of the Holy Spirit is rare. I recall a Pentecost sermon in which the preacher emphasized how we should repeat the early disciples' actions (Acts 2:42), yet referred only briefly to the Holy Spirit as an "it" that was additionally important. Not so, the divine person of the Spirit is all-important for the first and twenty-first centuries alike and preaching needs his power.

4. Generic Application

The favorite method by which debilitated preaching illustrates and applies its lessons is by homely generic examples, frequently drawn out of a preacher's personal life. Cheerful little stories about a preacher's sporting experience, family life, holidays, etc., are offered on a variation: "A funny thing happened to me on the way to preparing this sermon . . ." Such lightweight fare is supposed to support the greatest demands ever made on humankind—God's kingdom. The increase in generic sermon illustrations (aided and abetted by online resources) means a welter of all-purpose anecdotes that sometimes could have been preached unchanged fifty years earlier to any group of people, alive or dead. Actually, I think it is a good question to ask: Could this sermon have been preached fifty years ago? Thin-blooded preachers are specialists in sounding specific but manage always to be nonspecific and nonconfrontational about gospel transformation for community.

5. Avoids Conflict

The majority of preachers (in the survey mentioned earlier) preferred preaching that "nurtures and shepherds" people (often by individualistic, generic means) rather than "exhorting," with its possibilities of change and conflict. Thin-blooded preaching avoids conflict at all costs. Often bold in dealing with personal sins, it is silent about specific continuing sinful behavior such as crippling tension over worship, or disagreement between families. Texts that deal with handling disputes, such as Matthew 18:15–20, Acts 15, and Philippians 4:2–7, are never related to real conflict. Such preaching behaves as though tension is totally missing in church life. I recall someone commenting about a preacher, "He was like a lion in the pulpit, thundering about God's judgment on sinners and their need to repent, but he was a timid mouse when it came to dealing with conflict in the church. He ran away from confrontation."

6. Low Compliance

Thin-blooded preaching is wary of expecting much to be achieved. Certainly it welcomes positive comments about the sermon but does not anticipate that hearers will be measurably different because of it. Usefully, the leadership expert Peter Senge has sketched out the levels of response that people give when challenged by vision. At the highest level there is commitment when members want vision and will make it happen by deliberately choosing to change structures; second, genuine compliance sees the benefits of vision and does everything expected in the spirit of existing process; third, formal compliance also sees benefits but does the minimum; fourth, grudging compliance does not see the benefits but just does enough to identify; fifth, noncompliance does not see any benefits and has only apathy; sixth, apathy has no interest or energy for or against.[48] By pulling punches and selling out to generalities, thin-blooded preaching languishes at the lower levels by challenging no one to be or to do anything specifically different.

7. Absence of Process Issues

Pallid preaching leaves visions and strategic changes for others to talk about. For example, at a church service I visited, one of the lay leaders spoke enthusiastically about a fresh vision for establishing house groups to complement congregational gatherings. This was the Launch Sunday. Attenders were urged to sign up on lists in the church entrance for the group meeting nearest their home address. However, the preacher (who was senior pastor) failed to mention the vision even once. Though small groups have a significant role in Scripture and a sermon could have justifiably emphasized how God uses them (in Jesus's ministry and the early church), the impression was given that the vision was merely a church organizational plan. By omission, the preacher (intentionally or not) managed to relegate this church vision to a functional, second-order matter compared with what God really had to say in the sermon. Sadly, communication and implementation of genuine vision can be left entirely to organizational announcements outside the pulpit as thin-blooded preaching steers clear of applying Scripture to a process of congregational transformation.

8. Solo Role

Thin-blooded preachers generally consider themselves solo players with minimal need of collaboration and little overlap with other organizational aspects of church life. Maybe this was the reason why the senior pastor, just mentioned, failed to register the importance of the small group vision. Solo preachers are always likely to lose sight of the bigger picture within church life and to compartmentalize pious moments of individualistic biblical truth away from embracing the corporate life of the people of God. And then, sermons deteriorate into devotional extras on the sidelines of the real action.

9. Cowardice

I have already touched on lions and mice. Bluntly, pulpits can be cowards' castles. Together, this and the previous characteristics add up to loss of biblical nerve. Thin-blooded preaching plays safe, maintaining rather than initiating, concentrating on personal issues of faith rather than on organizational outcomes of faith. Safe pairs of hands operating within stable structures rather than big souls daring to live on the leading edge of God's new structures. Preaching as solely teaching and evangelizing has allowed itself to be detached from the task of leading congregational change. Preaching has forgotten the boldness of turning the world upside down—"These people who have been turning the world upside down have come here also" (Acts 17:6). Thin-blooded preachers have become understudies on the margins of leadership. Such preaching utterly fails to lead.

10. Missionally Defective

A "missional" church is one that knows it is both called and sent by God to live out Christly life as a missionary community. Sadly, many of the features listed above inevitably de-emphasize the vocation and missionary call of the people of God. Individualistic, generic, nonspecific, and cowardly preaching cannot lead a missionary people.

The rest of this book pursues full-blooded preaching that is corporate, holistic, trinitarian, specific in application, realistic about conflict, urges commitment, does justice to process issues, collaborates, is courageous, and is missionally effective. However, the last characteristic needs immediate attention.

Effective Missional Preaching

Missionally defective preaching leads to missionally defective people and utterly undoes the primary task of Christian leadership. Nothing is more important in church leadership than to enable a people to grow together while living under God's will and seeking first his kingdom in contrast with society in order to witness to the world. Local churches are God's called and sent people for the sake of a lost world and full-blooded preaching leads their mission.

Those who would lead through preaching therefore need to understand how preaching relates to the church's mission. Hunsberger has usefully summarized Newbigin's theology of culture by the model shown as figure 1, and though not designed for preacher/leaders, its dynamics flowing backwards and forwards within its three-cornered relationships have profound implications.[49] Indeed, they offer a test for whether or not preaching is full-blooded and leading transformation.

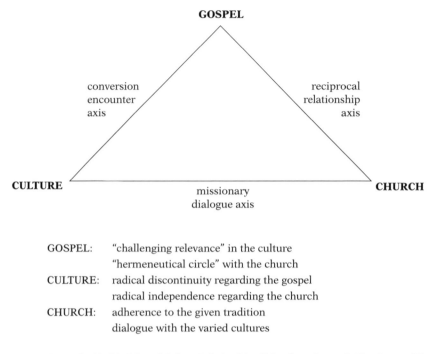

Fig. 1. A Triangular Model of Gospel-Culture Relationships. Taken from George R. Hunsberger, "The Newbigin Gauntlet: Developing a Domestic Missiology for North America," *Missiology* © 1991. Reprinted with permission of the American Society of Missiology.

Preaching faces in three directions. First, the *conversion encounter axis* lies between gospel and culture. This is the evangelistic message associated with classic *kēryssō* ("I herald") and *euangelizomai* ("I bring good news") New Testament preaching. Its core meaning of repentance from sin and of faith in Christ confronts hearers in their culture to change their lives. This axis means a "radical discontinuity regarding the gospel" for those living in any particular culture. However, new life in Christ cannot be totally disconnected from culture because, as Hunsberger explains, "the gospel and a person's response to it of necessity remain embodied in a particular culture's way of seeing, feeling and acting."[50] The ministry efforts of most evangelical churches major on this axis but focus almost exclusively on individuals making spiritual commitment to Christ. Such individualism often avoids calling individuals into conversion *within* God's new community to live out God's counterstory together.

Second, the *reciprocal relationship axis* lies between the gospel and church. Assuming personal conversion, this axis represents the challenge for believers to embody the outcomes of new life in Christ. It is called a reciprocal relationship because every church, no matter how short its history, inevitably reads Scripture out of its traditions. Each church interprets Scripture in the light of its experience, and its experience in the light of Scripture. This is the so-called "hermeneutical circle." In Hunsberger's words, "The community's tradition shapes its reading of the Bible, while its reading and rereading of the book further shape its self-understanding."[51] In New Testament preaching terms this is typically *didaskō* ("I teach"), with application of doctrine so believers may grow into maturity for works of ministry (Eph. 4:11–13). Preachers have vital responsibility to teach. Yet as with evangelism, if this teaching is individualistic without community relevance, hearers can very comfortably customize their faith into their culture. Values can derive uncritically from culture without being tested by biblical standards. Sadly, the gospel is "too often shot through with Western sentiments such as individualism, consumerism, security, personal happiness, and corporate success."[52]

Third is the *missionary dialogue axis* between church and its local culture. This axis assumes that a church community has been formed so that it can live out the gospel challenge in its own particular missionary context. Newbigin called for a relationship of true dialogue—a process of new converts (in community) being open to living out the unique implications of the gospel within the particularities of human cultures. This means that new converts (in community) have a relationship with local culture(s) that is not only in "radical discontinuity regarding the gospel" but also "radical independence regarding the church." Every church engaged in missionary dialogue is changing into something new as part of a continuing process. As noted earlier, this challenge issued to God's people to live out such missionary dialogue sums up Christian leadership's primary task—enabling a people to grow together while living under God's will and seeking first his kingdom in contradistinction to society in order to witness to the world.

In New Testament times this axis was lengthy as the early missionary church modeled new ways of love and purity in their relationships and behavior that strongly contrasted with culture. A communal emphasis on a called-out people sounds out through the Epistles (e.g., 1 Peter 2:9–12). However, with the "Christianizing" of society, most recently seen in modernity, society was presumed to share the same values as the church. In modern Western culture this sharing of values by society and church supposedly meant a much shorter missionary dialogue axis. But Stanley Hauerwas and William Willimon claim that modernity actually "tamed" the church—"as it went about congratulating itself for transforming the world, not noticing, that in fact the world has tamed the church."[53]

Today this third axis is again lengthy as the twenty-first-century church faces fresh challenges of modeling love and purity in our relationships and behavior. Preaching must recapture its full-blooded, first-century power so that believers are formed under God's Word by his Spirit to live *en Christō*. Living in missionary dialogue is poles apart from acting like a private club.

> The basic reality is the creation of a new being through the presence of the Holy Spirit. This new being is the common life (*koinonia*) in the Church. It is out of this new creation that both service and evangelism spring, and from it they receive their value. . . . These different acts have their relation to one another not in any logical scheme, but in the fact that they spring out of the one new reality.[54]

Preacher/leaders should be committed to living and telling out this new reality. Their aspiration should be to proclaim truth that is corporate as well as individual, specific in intent, and healthily honest about conflict. They should seek high commitment and collaborate with others as well as engage in process issues and show holy boldness. Sadly, too many preachers have lost leadership along each direction in this model and especially along the axis between church and culture. Preaching must rediscover its power to lead people together in a penetrating, life-altering way. The church's tri-directional dialogue should aim to disturb the world by the gospel message of radical discontinuity, to disturb the church lest it accommodate too easily to worldly culture, and to disturb the particular culture in which a church lives by the witness of its common life. For preachers this means nothing less than leading the missional church.

Because every church should see its nature and vocation as God's called and sent people, it should embody God's claims and promises by its worship and witness in its own context. Every relationship should speak authentically of disciples seeking to learn and grow together by Christ's grace. Instead of being generic congregations repeating standard formulae, they need to become communities of missionaries living out good news to a suspicious and sometimes hostile world. Such a missional church has many characteristics. Eddie Gibbs describes twelve empirical indicators: the missional church (1) proclaims the gospel, (2) is a community learning to be disciples, (3) has the Bible as normative, (4) understands itself as different from the world because it belongs to Christ, (5) seeks God's missional vocation for the entire community, (6) its members behave Christianly towards one another, (7) practices reconciliation, (8) holds its members accountable to one another in love, (9) practices hospitality, (10) has joyful, thankful worship central to its life, (11) has a vital public witness, and (12) "there is recognition that the church itself is an incomplete expression of the reign of God."[55] How important is that last characteristic. "Missional" means nothing less than "the church *being* in the world as a transforming presence."[56] This is the best possible outcome of Christian leadership.

Further pursuit of the implications of missional failure lie beyond the scope of this book, but the challenge to pursue missional success remains urgent for full-blooded preaching. A recent survey of suburban Midwest U.S. churches found that their outreach was successful in gaining members but "when asked to identify sermons . . . that showed risk taking, challenge to cultural structures and assumptions, and living counter-culturally, the boxes of the survey were surprisingly empty."[57] The third missional axis was missing. One pastor commented honestly:

> For years I think I lied to myself about being prophetic about culture. First we would get on our legs organizationally, then we would grow in our passion for following Jesus, then we would proclaim the scandal of the gospel with full throat. What does that strategy accomplish? It attracts and assimilates those who become used to hearing whispers in the area of social transformation instead of shouts. . . . Was it right for me to choose what I valued? I cannot know. But I'm sure God will talk with me about that at the Judgment. In the meantime I am beginning to shout . . . and my homiletic whispers are giving way to a clear proclamation of destroying the idols which bind and compromise us. Amazingly, the congregation has come to me and said, "It's about time! Don't let us off the hook in this area of our life."[58]

Full-blooded preaching is needed today as never before. Instead of the preacher's role being emasculated as chaplain to individual needs and cheerleader to organizational machismo, it must regain its God-given purpose, preaching in three directions to confront church and culture with the gospel.

2

Together in Scripture

> Preaching is the most important leadership task of the pastor. Every Sunday as I preach I see it as an act of leadership.
>
> Vic Gordon, interview with the author[1]

Some preachers will readily agree with Vic Gordon's assertion. I tell his story later in the book, as someone who has no doubt that leadership is part of his preaching, and who has proved it. But many other preachers do not seem so sure. Does Scripture support leading through preaching? We must apply some Berean diligence—"they received the message with great eagerness and examined the Scriptures every day to see if what Paul said was true" (Acts 17:11 NIV). Let's make four observations, of which the last is most important.

First, Scripture gives no simple blueprints for practice today. No direct parallels for our twenty-first-century church organizations and Sunday sermons can be found in the New Testament, let alone the Old Testament. Occasionally, the New Testament refers specifically to leaders. Believers are instructed: "Remember your leaders, those who spoke the word of God to you," and "Obey your leaders and submit to them, for they are keeping watch over your souls" (Heb. 13:7, 17). Judas Barsabbas and Silas are described as leaders (Acts 15:22). The apostle Paul speaks of a meeting with "acknowledged leaders" (Gal. 2:2). First Timothy 5:17 offers one closely studied text: "Let the elders who rule well be considered worthy of double honor, especially those who labor in preaching and teaching." Ralph Earle comments:

> Some have found here a distinction between ruling elders and teaching elders. But this is doubtful. Probably it means that some elders gave themselves to preaching and teaching in addition to their regular duties. Such was the case with Stephen and Philip as deacons (Acts 6–8).[2]

Not only does 1 Timothy 5:17 seem to combine responsibilities, but in 1 Timothy 3 leadership explicitly involves both teaching (v. 2) and taking care of God's church (v. 5).

Scripture does not provide verses to settle a knockout argument about how exactly preaching includes leading for the contemporary scene. Indeed, the explicit term *leader* is missing among a wealth of other images, such as *servant* and *shepherd*, which describe the powerful modeling of Jesus himself. Of course, many valuable insights and practical guidance from leadership principles can be gained for leadership as shown by such authors as Leighton Ford, *Transforming Leadership: Jesus' Way of Creating Vision, Shaping Values, and Empowering Change;*[3] David Baron, *Moses on Management: 50 Leadership Lessons from the Greatest Manager of All Time;*[4] and Laura Beth Jones, *Jesus CEO: Using Ancient Wisdom for Visionary Leadership.*[5] But Scripture's prime purpose is to reveal who God is in his-story and our story, and not pander to twenty-first-century pragmatism. Yet, as Scripture says much about the power of God's words and the role of his proclaimer/leaders, it does have profound bearing on contemporary leadership.

Second, Scripture endorses many kinds of leaders besides preacher/leaders. The Old Testament contains a roll call of judges, soldiers, kings, priests, and the wise, who lead the people of God. No one doubts, for example, King David's pivotal leadership role. The New Testament honors leaders in public government (1 Tim. 2:1–2; Titus 3:1) and occasionally refers to those in church government: "We have gifts that differ according to the grace given to us . . . the leader, in diligence" (Rom. 12:6, 8). Here *leader* (*proistamenon*) means "the one standing before" others, but the verse focuses on qualities of earnestness rather than the speaking role. Scripture shows many different kinds of leaders and, undeniably, God gifts nonpreachers to lead within his church, but they should function alongside preacher/leaders.

Third, leadership in Scripture begins in a very different place from secular leadership. In their survey of leadership literature, Warren Bennis and Burt Nanus apparently discovered over 850 definitions of leadership.[6] All of them attempt to encapsulate leadership's character and process, as with James MacGregor Burns's thoughtful definition:

"Leadership over human beings is exercised when persons with certain motives and purposes mobilize, in competition or conflict with others, institutional, political, psychological, and other resources so as to arouse, engage and satisfy the motives of followers."[7] But, in contrast, Scripture always begins with God and never with the motives of leaders and their followers. Christian leadership's source is God's vision and purpose and his call upon men and women to obey and speak out his will for his people. It is initiated by God's revealed will. Secular leaders develop visions within human possibilities; spiritual leaders develop visions beyond human possibilities. Secular leaders depend on their own strength; spiritual leaders depend on God's strength. Spiritual leading is initiated, directed, sustained, and is ultimately transformative because God involves himself from beginning to end. Spiritual leaders act differently. As the Blackabys put it: "Spiritual leaders work within a paradox, for God calls them to do something that, in fact, only God can do."[8]

Fourth, and critically important, is how Scripture sees the role of words. Words are essential for all leadership. As Warren Wilhelm claims in *The Leader of the Future*:

> At the core of effective leadership is the ability to communicate. All forms of communication must be mastered by the effective leader: written and oral, electronic and digital, communication by graphics and behavior, by art and music, by expressed emotion, and more. . . . The studied master of communication becomes a more effective leader.[9]

All leaders must use words. Agreed. All words have an ability to influence others. Agreed. But at this point, spiritual leadership emphatically parts company with secular leadership.

From Genesis 1 onwards, God's speaking means God's doing: "God said and it was so. . . . God said and it was so." His words make things happen. The Hebrew for *word* (*dabar*) means both word and event because when God speaks it is as good as done. He endows his words with energy. God's Word will not return to him empty but, as he says, "will accomplish what I desire and achieve the purpose for which I sent it" (Isa. 55:11 NIV). This power of words is especially seen in Scripture itself, the God-breathed writings that reveal truth by God's Spirit, which are powerful and sharper than a two-edged sword piercing through (Heb. 4:12). By Scripture God gives conviction, vision, and direction to transform his people. God leads by word.

The conviction that God's power works through his words forges a transformational role for preaching/leading. For when God calls people to speak his words, they inevitably share in his power to change others. Speaking God's words inexorably means transformational leadership.

This power of God's Word in Scripture therefore sanctions preaching to be the primary means by which God shapes his people to his will. Whenever people obey God's call to tell out his Word they become his leader whether they realize it initially or not. That's why the Blackabys are right when they assert that "according to the Bible, God is not necessarily looking for leaders, at least not in the sense we generally think of leaders. He is looking for servants (Isa. 59:16; Ezek. 22:30)."[10] He is looking for servants of the Word.

Whoever God calls to be a servant of the Word, speaking Scripture truth on his behalf, is also called to be a leader. New Testament lists of leadership gifts (Romans 12; 1 Corinthians 12; Ephesians 4) cluster ministries that take precedence. Ephesians 4:11, for example, lists five leadership gifts: apostles, prophets, evangelists, pastors, and teachers. We can debate over some of the distinctions between these gifts, especially about the linkage between pastors and teachers. But clearly they all involve speaking words. Key leaders are those called to proclaim God's Word; those called to proclaim God's Word are key leaders. Bluntly, you cannot proclaim God's Word without leading his people. Preachers cannot detach themselves from the outcome of God's message as though they are Teflon-proofed channels delivering transformational words without personal engagement. By definition preachers cannot be neutral or indifferent to the leadership consequences of God's Word.

Because God promises to empower his Word, spoken by spiritual leaders to change people and to make things happen, preacher/leaders work in dramatically different ways. *Secular leaders speak their own words to make an impact by skillful use. Preachers speak God's words to make an impact by God's power and grace.* Secular leaders may well quote Scripture (as does the devil, incidentally) but often for their own ends rather than God's. Scripture claims God's unique power is at work whenever people speak for him and his glory.

Throughout Scripture God's spokespeople therefore play a vital role because as servants of his Word they inevitably lead others.

Two Prime Examples

Scripture records a succession of men and women who demonstrate this combination of leading with proclaiming. Moses is the best Old Testament model whose very reluctance at the beginning of his call underlines how important words are to God. God commands him to speak to the people (Exod. 3:15–22). Famously he refuses to be God's spokesman. Among his reasons, he excuses himself because of an anticipated poor response: "But suppose they do not believe me or listen to me, but say, 'The LORD did not appear to you'" (Exod. 4:1). And then in desperation: "O my Lord, I have never been eloquent, neither in the past nor even now . . . but I am slow of speech and slow of tongue" (Exod. 4:10). God rebukes him with the reminder that remains classic for all preacher/leaders:

> Who gives speech to mortals? Who makes them mute or deaf, seeing or blind? Is it not I, the LORD? Now go, and I will be with your mouth and teach you what you are to speak.
>
> Exodus 4:11–12

As Moses still refuses, God nominates Aaron to the speaking task. However, as the story gathers momentum, Moses does become dominant as God's authoritative speaker. His story underlines how spiritual leadership never begins with the motives of leaders and their followers but always with God's vision and purpose. Moses's leadership begins differently—in God's revealed will. Rather than grasping visions within human possibilities he must develop visions beyond human possibilities. He must not depend on his own strength but on God's. He must not speak his own words but God's. God's methodology employs spoken words—by these he initiates, directs, implements, sustains, and transforms. Moses, speaking God's Word, not only confronts Pharaoh's might but shapes a new people in their religious, legal, moral, political, social, and martial responsibilities. "Never since has there arisen a prophet in Israel like Moses, whom the LORD knew face to face" (Deut. 34:10). Moses demonstrates graphically how God fuses speaking with leadership.

In the New Testament, Christian leadership finds its greatest example in Jesus. Any roll call of world leaders should include Jesus Christ. John Adair's review of great leaders in history begins with the Greek philosopher Socrates as a leader of ideas: "Leadership is tied to situations and depends largely upon the leader having the appropriate knowledge."[11] His list also includes Alexander the Great, Alfred the Great, Abraham Lincoln, Winston Churchill, and Mahatma Gandhi. Vitally, he includes Jesus. "Many people—not only Christians—would argue that Jesus was the greatest transformational leader in history."[12] Jesus changes how we understand leadership forever by what he says and does.

Yet on his mission to the cross, Jesus is primarily a preacher. All other roles such as leader and healer are predicated upon his principal role as preacher. This is the Synoptic Gospels' claim. Mark 1:14 records a summary of Jesus's mission: "Jesus came . . . proclaiming" (see Matt. 4:23; 9:35). Luke shows that Jesus begins with preaching (Luke 4:43), continues preaching (Luke 8:1), three years later is still preaching (Luke 20:1), and as risen Lord continues to preach (Luke 24). Jesus is first and foremost the proclaimer! He is Word made flesh (John 1:14). No one else in human history has been able to reveal words with power like Jesus: "I am the way, the truth, and the life" (John 14:6).

Jesus leads as a preacher by his preaching; he preaches as a leader. By his preaching the extraordinary consequences of the kingdom of God break into humanity, eternal destiny opens up through his ransom on the cross (Mark 10:45) and blazes the trail for the church (Matt. 16:18) to change forever the course of human existence. He combines words and deeds as no one else has. He is the supreme preacher/leader. In Jesus the message and messenger are one.

Distinctively, Jesus models a new kind of leadership. He demonstrates powerfully what leadership is not. In Mark 10:35–45 James and John presume that belonging to Jesus fits into traditional hierarchy—the closer they are to him, then the higher is their status. Dramatically, Jesus offers an entirely new way—power, authority, and ambition do not motivate his leadership (vv. 42–43). Rather he leads by serving. In this power-hungry situation, note the powerful use of different words relating to service: *diakonos* (servant) in verse 42, *doulos* (slave) in verse 43, and *diakonēsai* (to serve) in verse 45. Jesus's leadership is not status-driven but service-driven, upending conventional wisdom by the principle that "whoever wishes to be first among you must be slave of all" (v. 44). This is strikingly modeled by Jesus himself in the foot washing incident in John 13:1–17. Adair claims that this event is the most extraordinary scene in the history of leadership. Jesus offers the profoundest model for preacher/leaders. As the Blackabys emphasize,

> Jesus' life is so profound and so beyond our common experience that we must continually reexamine it. . . . Jesus did not develop a plan nor did he cast a vision. He sought his Father's will. He had a vision for himself and for his disciples but it came from his Father.[13]

Many other examples of preaching/leading could be added. Acts 6 provides an early indication of how preaching is fused with leadership. As problems compound within the church organization over the neglect of widows, the twelve apostles recognize their responsibility for the core task: "It would not be right for us to neglect the ministry of the word of God in order to wait on tables" (Acts 6:2 NIV). By appointing seven others "full of the Holy Spirit and wisdom" so that the apostles might "give our attention to prayer and the ministry of the word," they show a priority of preaching with prayer but also demonstrate leadership as they direct others into new tasks. As "point persons" their leadership delegates tasks to safeguard their core values. In the developing story other significant preacher/leaders emerge, particularly the apostle Paul, whom Robert Banks considers "the biblical benchmark" for leadership, since he "led a parachurch mission team and organization and set up local congregations in various cultural contexts."[14]

Proclamation belongs at the center of God's work in history, and at its every turn those who proclaim God's words are also God's leaders. So biblical understanding of preaching as words empowered by God inescapably results in preacher/leaders.

360-Degree Leading

In *360-Degree Preaching* I concluded that

> preaching is most effective when several factors positively combine: Scripture, words (combined with images), God (the Father, Son, and Holy Spirit), the person of the preacher, the listener, and the worship context. All these aspects belong and work together as the trinitarian God empowers the preacher's words and the hearers' responses.[15]

In contrast, 180-degree preaching arcs between Scripture on one side and hearers on the other side, making the preacher responsible for bridging the gap. Unwittingly, it can portray a dynamic that, while recognizing Scripture's inspiration and God's involvement, places too much emphasis on the preacher's gifting and energy. Instead of a simple 180-degree "bridge," I contend that a strong trinitarian theology places preaching within a 360-degree dynamic empowered by God's returning Word. God the Father reveals truth through Scripture and by his Son, Jesus, the Word, who is central to every gathering of believers, and through the Holy Spirit the preached Word inspires, convicts, and renews. As Jesus says: "The Spirit gives life; the flesh counts for nothing. The words I have spoken to you are spirit and they are life" (John 6:63 NIV).

My 360-degree preaching model involves preacher and hearers in a vortex of hearing, speaking, and living out God's Word together. It attempts to express a trinitarian theology and places in preaching a premium on God shaping his people to his will by his Word. Its outcome is a different kind of living, a missional living of worship and witness.

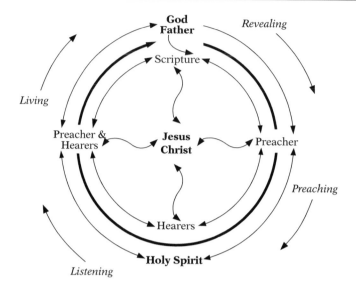

Fig. 2. A Model of 360-Degree Preaching/Leading. Taken from Michael J. Quicke, *360-Degree Preaching* © 2003. Reprinted with permission of Baker Academic, a division of Baker Publishing Group.

All aspects of church life and mission require that preachers and hearers listen to God's Word and respond obediently as he initiates, directs, implements, sustains, and transforms. Where else do visions and directions come from? And since Christian leadership depends so unreservedly on God's Word, preachers have a pivotal role. Because they have prime responsibility to discern, embody, and proclaim God's will they necessarily stand in vital leadership positions. Indeed, preachers can only avoid leadership responsibility by denying that God's Word can change lives.

This model, with its emphasis on our trinitarian God making things happen, should therefore include leading. Full-blooded preaching must expand beyond teaching individual salvation to embrace the bigger purposes of leading saved people into God's new reality. He is not just concerned that people are saved but that we are saved together, in order to live in his new ways. As I mentioned earlier, my own preaching experience in downtown Cambridge opened my eyes to preaching/leading. I discovered how, in a seemingly dire situation, God had a purpose of growing a missional people who would have an impact on the wider community in which they lived. My earlier definition of Christian preaching must expand to include leading.

Christian preaching, at its best, is a biblical speaking/listening/seeing/doing event that God empowers to lead and form Christ-shaped people and communities.[16]

Such preaching connects powerfully along all three directions of gospel, culture, and church shown earlier in figure 1. Instead of claiming that leadership is supremely important and that preaching supports it, let's assert that preaching is supremely important and leadership flows out of it.

This 360-degree leading approach resonates with other leadership definitions that consciously exclude preaching. For example, George Barna's popular definition:

> Leadership is the process of motivating, mobilizing, resourcing, and directing people to passionately and strategically pursue a vision from God that a group jointly embraces.[17]

Isn't this what 360-degree leading does by God's Word returning in power through the action and life of his people? Every time preachers open Scripture and preach out God's challenge, they should motivate, mobilize, resource, and direct people, because God's Word is the source and God's power is the energy for fulfilling any divine vision. Who else can fulfill this charge to be passionate and strategic? Where do Christians believe vision, resources, and passion come from unless from God?

Consider also Henry and Richard Blackaby's understanding of spiritual leadership as "moving people onto God's agenda." They argue that since God's will and purpose is primary, leadership should be understood first and foremost in terms of responding to God. They prefer to speak of vision in terms of "understanding God's revelation." Spiritual leaders therefore need to be prayerful people of integrity who encounter God, depend on the Holy Spirit, interpret God's will in Scripture, and communicate it effectively. The Blackabys' review of biblical examples of spiritual leadership shows how godly communication is key to such leaders influencing others by "spiritual means" (Moses and Jesus are given plenty of coverage).

> Spiritual leaders don't sell vision; they share what God has revealed to them and trust that the Holy Spirit will confirm that same vision in the hearts of their people.
>
> You cannot be a poor communicator and a good leader. Spiritual leaders . . . rehearse what God has done, they relate what God is doing, and they share what God has promised to do. . . . Leaders cannot grow weary of bearing witness to God's activity.[18]

Doesn't that sound as close to preaching as you can get without actually mentioning it? "Moving people onto God's agenda" resonates with 360-degree leading dynamics that give preachers a key role in God's purpose. Whenever the Word of God is heard and obeyed, people are moved onto God's agenda.

God's Leading Word

Scripture is foundational to 360-degree leading, with innate power that makes a practical impact (2 Tim. 3:16), fulfills promises (Isa. 55:11), sees visions (Prov. 29:18 KJV), and *says* and *does* things. "All Scripture is inspired by God" (2 Tim. 3:16), and the word *inspired* (translated "God-breathed" in the NIV) evokes powerful images of blowing wind (Gen. 1:2) and moving Spirit (John 3:3–8). By Scripture and through his Son, God takes the initiative in revelation and relationships with humankind. Scripture makes a profound impact. It sources preaching/leading through lively exegesis and interpretation, and it engenders passion for prophetic relevance and visionary purpose. But God's Word also confronts issues of power, wisdom, and building community.

Lively Exegesis and Interpretation

Scripture's most famous self-claim says that it is "useful for teaching, for reproof, for correction, and for training in righteousness" (2 Tim. 3:16). However precisely these four functions are understood, they undeniably concern how Scripture transforms whole persons and entire communities to live differently. "Teaching" leads to right understanding of truth, "reproof" challenges a person's old way of thinking and living, "correction" opens up to new ways of living, and "training in righteousness" emphasizes how right living with God is a continual process of learning and practice. Scripture has its own practical agenda to create long-lasting change, and whenever you engage with it intentionally it moves you further away from old life into new.

Exegesis and interpretation therefore never deal with flat inert text but instead deal with God's living Word which personalizes transformation. Scripture does not illustrate other leadership principles, react to other ideas, and offer generic concepts; rather it reveals and generates God's purposes that are utterly unlike any others for particular communities. Preacher/leaders do not bring urgency to Scripture but release urgency from within Scripture. However upbeat contemporary leadership ideas may sound, Scripture long ago anticipated and preempted them. As we shall see in chapter 6, leadership skills such as "generating and sustaining creative tension" only describe what Scripture does best. It out-energizes, out-dynamites any other method of moving people known to humankind. It *is* God's Word.

Rather than sleepwalking through a text, plodding through exegesis, interpretation, and design, preachers should immerse themselves in Scripture's dynamic that continuously leads people forward. Preaching Scripture is like plunging into a fast-flowing river. Instead of generic catchall sermons that can anesthetize Scripture's challenge and smother its creativity, preachers must engage in lively exegesis and interpretation for their own situations. No more dulled two-edged swords! Preachers do not have to import leadership notions into the text but rather to respond to God's leadership power already within the text. This theme will be developed later.

Prophetic Relevance

Today's preachers follow in the long line of prophets and apostles who claim to speak God's Word which is also his deed.[19] When Christian preachers respond to Scripture, as Old Testament prophets did when they heard the Word of the Lord, they stand under God's authority, speaking God's Word that it might be God's deed. "Whoever speaks must do so as one speaking the very words of God" (1 Peter 4:11).

Old Testament prophets presented a distinctively subversive challenge for the people of God. "They join[ed] together the holiness of God, the moral quality of historical reality, and a counter-future for the world."[20] They read the signs of the times and addressed them in the light of God's revealed will. They spoke of God's alternative community, a people belonging to the Holy God of Israel, warning complacent people about false successes and offering exiled people "a new thing" (Isa. 43:19–21). Evocative hope was never far away but neither was God's judgment. They spoke of peace but rigorously rejected false substitutes (Jer. 23:9–40). With passion and boldness, theirs was an uncomfortably disturbing role recalling the community of faith to God's will. They were God's disturbers of human status quo. "Like poets of all ages," suggests Richard Skylba,

> they saw reality at its deepest level. They took a long loving look at that reality and either saw God or the absence of God. From that divine epicenter moved waves of tenderness or anger as yet unexperienced by the merchants and farmers of Israel or Judah. Prophets knew the vitality of God and spoke accordingly.[21]

Discerning God's character and purpose, Old Testament prophets declared how God's people should live within current events and culture. The power of God's Word continues forcefully in the New Testament, particularly in the preaching of Jesus (Luke 4:16–30) and the apostles (Acts 17:6). This prophetic task is vital to the missional church and the challenges of the reciprocal relationship axis and missionary dialogue axis (see fig. 1) by changing people in community. God's Word cannot help but lead.

Visionary Purpose

Memorably, Proverbs 29:18 declares: "Where there is no vision the people perish" (KJV); it can be understood as: "Where there is no revelation of God the people cut loose." Without a controlling vision there is an uncontrolled people. Scripture provides discerning preacher/leaders with vision that they must express in order to be God's "controlled people." God summed up for Moses the vision in the burning bush: "The LORD, the God of your ancestors . . . has appeared to me, saying: . . . I declare that I will bring you up out of the misery of Egypt, to the land of the Canaanites, . . . a land flowing with milk and honey" (Exod. 3:16–17). Jesus's vision is succinctly summarized: "The time is fulfilled, and the kingdom of God has come near; repent, and believe in the good news" (Mark 1:15). Part 2 of this book will examine how preacher/leaders can help churches to understand and express their mission and vision. Preaching Scripture remains foundational to this process.

Ambiguity of Power

Of all the factors complicating leadership, appropriate use of power is the most complex. A retired pastor sadly commented to me, looking back on his different pastorates: "The one constant factor in all my churches was power struggles. I always seemed to be in situations where a small group of people wanted to run the church." Tragically power struggles can so easily bedevil local churches and undermine worthy Christian leadership. John Stott reminds us how "the three major human ambitions (the pursuit of money, fame, and influence) are all concealed drives for power."[22]

Scripture faces this reality head-on by calling leaders to live out the extraordinary paradox of "power in weakness," which forms a central theme in 1 Corinthians 1. First Corinthians 1:18–2:5 mentions power several times but always as power through weakness. Though the gospel appears utterly weak to the world since the cross lies at its center, this is God's power (1:17–25). The Corinthian church was also weak and vulnerable yet God chooses weak people to shame the strong (1:6–31). Paul's own approach was one of weakness but "with a demonstration of the Spirit's power" (2:4 NIV; see 2:1–5). Humility and dependence on God are peculiarly powerful in God's hands. "All God's giants have been weak people," remarked Hudson Taylor.[23] But as Stott comments:

It is not an invitation to suppress our God-given personality, to pretend we feel weak when we do not or to cultivate a fake frailty. Nor is it an exhortation to renounce arguments. . . . Here then is an honest, humble acknowledgement that human beings cannot save souls.[24]

And we must add, human beings cannot build Christ's body or lead his people in their own strength either. Scripture reinterprets power in leadership to show that men and women need total dependence on Christ, "because apart from me you can do nothing" (John 15:5). Christian leaders should never stop learning how to live out the radical implications of Christ's different kind of power.

Spiritual Wisdom in Foolishness

First Corinthians also focuses on a further astonishing paradox for Christian leadership. First Corinthians 2:6–16 teaches about wisdom from the Spirit as compared with worldly wisdom, "the wisdom of this age or of the rulers of this age" (v. 6 NIV). In contrast with the wisdom of university, government, law court, and media is "God's secret wisdom, a wisdom that has been hidden and that God destined for our glory before time began" (v. 7 NIV). The apostle comments bluntly that the church possesses few intellectual heavyweights (1:26) skilled in worldly wisdom. But spiritual wisdom is a gift in relationship—"God has revealed it to us by his Spirit" (2:10 NIV).

John Stott helpfully describes four stages of the Holy Spirit's ministry as agent of divine revelation. First he *searches* the depths of God and knows the deep things of God (vv. 10–11). "The Holy Spirit has a unique understanding of God because he is himself God. . . . Since only he knows God, only he can make him known."[25] Second, he *reveals* the gift of salvation that God has freely given to those who believe (vv. 10, 12). Third, he *inspires* the preaching of the apostles "not in words taught us by human wisdom but in words taught by the Spirit" (v. 13 NIV).

The same Holy Spirit who searches the depths of God and knows the thoughts of God, and who revealed his findings to the apostles, went on to communicate them to others through the apostles in words which he gave them. He spoke his words through their words, so that their words were simultaneously his.[26]

Fourth, he *enlightens* (vv. 13–16). "The Holy Spirit was working at both ends of the communication process—inspiring the apostles and enlightening their hearers and readers."[27] There is all the difference in the world therefore between "those who are unspiritual," who reject gifts of God's Spirit because they seem foolish, and those who accept these gifts—"those who are spiritual discern all things" (vv. 14–15). God makes it possible for Christian leaders to think differently because they are numbered among "those who are spiritual." But this is not a solitary exercise.

Building Community

In Scripture God continually addresses individuals within community. His covenant promise forms his people in the Old Testament. Addressed to Abram it is expressed in a promised future nation: "I will make you into a great nation and I will bless you" (Gen. 12:2 NIV). This promise is frequently confirmed in the people of God's developing story, as when Moses dramatically expresses covenant by sprinkling half of the sacrificial blood on the altar and half on the people: "This is the blood of the covenant that the LORD has made with you" (Exod. 24:8 NIV). Echoing famously in Jeremiah 31:31, the new covenant's sealing is made explicit in the Lord's Supper: "This cup is the new covenant in my blood; do this, whenever you [plural] drink it, in remembrance of me" (1 Cor. 11:25 NIV).

Corporate images fill Scripture. Nowhere is this clearer than in images of the church. The church is described as a building (Eph. 2:21), temple (1 Cor. 3:16), bride (2 Cor. 11:2), the body of Christ (Col. 1:18, 24; Eph. 1:23). We have already noted the significance of belonging together *en Christō*, but this is profoundly connected with the New Testament understanding of *sōma* (body) and the contrast between being one in Adam and one in Christ (Rom. 5:12–19). Deeply rooted in Old Testament and early Jewish thinking is the concept of "corporate personality" when one person represents the whole community. Adam is the representative figure bringing in sin, condemnation, and death, and Christ by voluntary identification as Lord for the body, *sōmati* (1 Cor. 6:13), reverses these by grace, justification, and life through his obedience, death, and resurrection. Christians therefore belong to the body of Christ (Rom. 12:4–5; 1 Cor. 12:12) with the intense solidarity of Christian community as new creation. A premium is put upon its unity—"Once you were not a people, but now you are the people of God" (1 Peter 2:10 NIV). No wonder that the plural use of *you* (*humeis*) peppers the New Testament, as people are addressed collectively. This us-ness of the gospel does not allow believers to respond individualistically and evade faith's corporate dimensions.

In particular, Christian leaders have to come to terms with the surprising claim in 1 Corinthians 2:16. Referencing Isaiah 40:13, that nobody can know the mind of the Lord, the apostle boldly states: "But we have the mind of Christ." Because believers belong *en Christō*, in the body of Christ, *together* they have possibilities of discernment and spiritual knowledge as though they were Christ himself. Spiritual individuals may be gifted with spiritual wisdom, but spiritual wisdom is supremely a corporate phenomenon, discerned together as the body of Christ. This bold claim is set within the weakness and vulnerability of the church community

As the Holy Spirit breathes upon the early church, emboldening Simon Peter to be a preacher/leader (Acts 2), there is a growing recognition of God's gift of spiritual wisdom. Matthias prayerfully fills the apostolic vacancy caused by Judas Iscariot's betrayal and demise (Acts 1:24, 26). As we noted earlier, to safeguard their main tasks of prayer and the ministry of the Word (Acts 6:4) the apostles chose deacons who were "full of the Holy Spirit and wisdom" (Acts 6:2–3 NIV). All decisions and actions must be in accordance with the Holy Spirit. This is explicit when resolving the major church dispute for the first Christians: "It seemed good to the Holy Spirit and to us" (Acts 15:28 NIV). As the early church community developed, leadership gifts were exercised for the sake of the body. Always such gifts are "to prepare God's people for works of service, so that the body of Christ may be built up until we all reach unity in the faith and in the knowledge of the Son of God and become mature, attaining to the whole measure of the fullness of Christ" (Eph. 4:12–13 NIV).

Christian leadership depends on Christ, the Head of the body (Eph. 4:15), directing individuals within his community. The more his presence, his mind, and his personality is experienced, then the more mature and effective Christian leadership will be. Viewed as a diagram, 360-degree preaching/leading (see fig. 2) depicts the Holy Spirit as being involved at every point—"in the revealing, preaching, listening, and living. Minds, hearts, mouths, ears, individual lives, and communities are all within his influence."[28]

God Continues to Invest Himself in Preacher/Leaders

Scripture commands those who speak God's words to lead. It propels preacher/leaders to the forefront of Christian leadership. Flat generic exegesis and interpretation, dulled prophetic relevance, misplaced visionary purpose, missed paradoxes of power in weakness and spiritual wisdom in foolishness, and neglected community building are inexcusable for those who take Scripture seriously.

Rather, Scripture authorizes preachers to exhort, teach, and evangelize within deeper visions of living out God's will for his community.

God-empowered, full-blooded preaching always brings people into *corporate* visions and dimensions of community. It is *holistic*, avoiding extremes of both cerebral and emotional preaching. It has *theological spine*, expressing the power of God—Father, Son, and Holy Spirit. It is *specific*, grounded in a particular congregation's transformation, not some generic fit-all program. It is *real*—facing conflict, healthily aware of the consequences of God's counterstory, and calling for commitment. It reinforces the *process* of transformation as people learn to do God's Word together, and it is *courageous* because the preacher is first exposed to God's challenge and then dares to tell out what it means. It is also *missional*, challenging people to be and live as missionary communities.

You can lead without preaching (Rom. 12:8) but you cannot preach biblically without leading. There are striking examples of those within the body of Christ who have led without preaching. But for every one person like that there are nine others whose first call is to preach and thereby to lead. Church history shows that the majority of those called to be leaders have also been preachers,[29] because leading is not found *outside* God's Word but *within* it. Effective church life and mission has always burgeoned when preaching has been powerful. In the complicated tasks of leading the people of God in twenty-first-century life and mission, God continues to need his principal truth-tellers. He calls for a new generation of full-blooded preacher/leaders.

3

Both Need Each Other Today

Backward Christian soldiers, fleeing from the fight
With the cross of Jesus nearly out of sight. . . .
Sit here then ye people, join our useless throng
Blend with ours your voices in a feeble song.
Blessings, ease and comfort, ask from Christ the King
With our modern thinking, we won't do a thing.

Anonymous

Someone's satire of "Onward, Christian Soldiers" hits home rather too close for comfort and sadly reflects the outcome of much thin-blooded preaching. Urgently, leadership and preaching need to join together within the same 360-degree spiritual dynamic so that God's Word transforms "useless throngs" into missional people, banishing feebleness and inaction.

The two forceful giants, preaching and leadership, must see how they need each other. Earlier I pictured them working apart, perhaps glancing occasionally at each other but refusing to shake hands, let alone offer friendship and enter dialogue. I hinted that like all personalities they could suffer from jealousy, pride, suspicion, and immaturity. Enough! Looking at each other with openness, preaching must do business with leadership and vice versa. One brings theological weight and long-term spiritual pedigree and the other a world of new ideas and terms about how to work in the contemporary situation. They must bury suspicion, smugness, irritation, impatience, arrogance, and whatever else separates them and get on with doing gospel business together. They both need each other.

Leadership Needs Preaching

Leadership left to its own devices can lose spiritual footing in several ways. Separation from preaching increases the dangers of leadership degenerating into humanistic advice, becoming devoid of the Holy Spirit, empty of spiritual understanding, and predisposed to puffed up pride.

First, leadership principles practiced apart from preaching can *foster humanistic models*. After all, it is argued: Does it really matter that secular leadership books fail to mention God, when after all they advocate such obvious good advice? Surely, practical matters of organizational efficiency don't always need to begin with Scripture, do they? But God's people, utterly unlike any other group, owe their existence entirely to God's grace, revealed only in Christ and Scripture.

Jesus's name cannot be used to endorse other models. He offers the only starting point and mode for being Christian. Salvation history turns on the death and resurrection of Jesus Christ, who is the new Adam. "Therefore just as one man's trespass led to condemnation for all, so one man's act of righteousness leads to justification and life for all" (Rom. 5:18). Christ's new humanity is totally unlike any other way of living. Jesus broke into the world scene inviting people to enter his kingdom. He initiated an organic fellowship, identified in New Testament epistles as his body, restored by resurrection, growing by grace, nourished by love, and consumed with mission. Churches should never be regarded as just another kind of human organization but as complex mixtures of human and divine. God is uniquely at work, transforming his people by his mission. His leaders have no direct equivalents anywhere else.

Second, reliance on human organizational skills leads to another serious danger of *dispensing with the Holy Spirit*. Whenever local churches are successful through their own wisdom and energy they neglect the Holy Spirit. Human efficiency receives the glory rather than God. Who really needs prayer, for example, when a motivational program accomplishes results? To misquote Zechariah 4:6: "It *is* by might, by power and not by Spirit," says the church almighty. Some leadership models do not require God to do anything. In fact, it would complicate matters unnecessarily if God became too active! Leadership principles, especially in the hands of highly motivational persuaders, can become the ultimate natural tools displacing any need to trust in God's presence and power.

Leadership programs often work by the spirit of the world rather than the Holy Spirit, who blows wherever he wills.

The spirit of the world has little time for spiritual wisdom. Yes, it stresses team building, vision, and focus groups, with an emphasis on casting vision, planning strategy, and communicating it to followers. Yet, by so doing, it downgrades spiritual wisdom as the more powerful way of discerning God's will. As noted earlier, the world's wisdom deems such claims foolish (1 Cor. 2:6–16). Preaching must keep confronting the church with the priorities of prayer and spiritual discernment, reminding believers that taught by the Spirit they "have the mind of Christ" (1 Cor. 2:16). Primarily, the church as a body belongs corporately in Christ (*en Christō*), under his headship, with the Spirit giving both unity and guidance so his people can together say, "It seemed good to the Holy Spirit and to us" (Acts 15:28 NIV). "No one comprehends what is truly God's except the Spirit of God. Now we have received not the spirit of the world, but the Spirit that is from God" (1 Cor. 2:11–12).

Business models can mislead churches into becoming marketing organizations that measure their success primarily in terms of numbers and finances. Such progress achieved by clear thinking and solid action appeals to human nature. However, preaching ensures that God's Word by God's power guides and shapes his people—"like living stones . . . being built into a spiritual house to be a holy priesthood, offering spiritual sacrifices acceptable to God through Jesus Christ" (1 Peter 2:5 NIV). All too quickly a church can be sidetracked onto easier but lesser goals. Preaching must keep it on track.

Third, leadership principles without preaching can *distort theology and flatten spiritual paradoxes*. Preaching offers salvation, emphasizing the destructive reality of sin, the need of a Savior, the power of forgiveness, and the miracle of grace in the counterculture of God's new community. But secular leadership begins elsewhere and has no need for talk of sin, salvation, forgiveness, and conversion by grace through faith. It puts plans into operation with no attention to the problem of sin. Unsurprisingly, though leadership speaks boldly of planning successful outcomes, results rarely turn out exactly as envisaged. Preachers, however, know that downright sinfulness and inexplicable grace complicate all community life. For the church everything depends on God's grace and purpose: "But you are a chosen race, a royal priesthood, a holy nation, God's own people, in order that you may proclaim the mighty acts of him who called you out of darkness into his marvelous light" (1 Peter 2:9).

Christian theology makes all the difference. A church leader described to me a session he had led during which a congregation had received back a previous leader who had failed morally. After accepting discipline, receiving counseling, and seeking reconciliation (Matt. 18:15), he was accepted back by the community at a special service. The session leader said, "No other organization in the world deals with failures like the church does, when God gives second chances to sinners. Isn't the church amazing when it works well?"

Secular leadership is bemused by biblical claims such as "those who wait for the LORD shall renew their strength, they shall mount up with wings like eagles" (Isa. 40:31). What waiting and what eagles? The Beatitudes (Matt. 5:1–12) are deemed to be inspirational poetry rather than practical principles, as are Jesus's claims that the greatest shall be as the least, the leader is servant, the poor are somehow rich, along with Paul's claim that "these three remain: faith, hope and love. But the greatest of these is love" (1 Cor 13:13 NIV). Secular leadership finds paradoxes such as power in weakness idealized and impractical. Indeed, worship itself is seen as a by-product rather than an end itself.

Leadership jargon with its relentless pragmatism and optimism often lives uneasily with Bible language and Christian experience. Even when sympathetic, leadership can too easily make simplistic connections with biblical texts and risk reducing Moses and Jesus to endorsers of current business models. Jesus did not spend his three years' ministry writing a leadership manual but initiating disciples into full-blooded kingdom living.

Fourth, at their worst, leadership plans can puff up *pride*. Dietrich Bonhoeffer chillingly warned about the way that Christians can have dreams which they then enforce:

> By sheer grace, God will not permit us to live even for a brief period in a dream world . . . every human wish dream that is injected into the Christian community is a hindrance to genuine community and must be banished. . . . God hates visionary dreaming; it makes the dreamer proud and pretentious. The man who fashions a visionary ideal of community demands that it be realized by God, by others and by himself. . . . He acts as if he is the creator of the Christian community, as if his dream binds men together. When things do not go his way, he calls the effort a failure.[1]

Bonhoeffer called for community living not as an ideal but as a divine reality won in humble love by God's grace. Christian leaders who imbibe too many secular principles are in danger of fashioning their own visionary ideal of community and acting as if *they* are "creators of the Christian community."

John Stott writes that for over thirty-five years he has been privileged to visit churches in many countries and observe their leadership.

> As a result, it is my firm conviction that there is too much autocracy in the leaders of the Christian community, in defiance of the teaching

of Jesus . . . and not enough love and gentleness. Too many behave as if they believed not in the priesthood of all believers but in the papacy of all pastors. Our model of leadership is often shaped more by culture than by Christ.[2]

Preachers need to confront pride in themselves and their congregations at every turn. Only by living out Christ's call to humility can preachers and churches grow beyond the destructive vortex of pride.

Yet, even as we hear warnings that leadership without preaching is in danger, preaching without leadership is in desperate trouble too. Preaching is dangerously flawed if it neglects fundamental leadership ideas and terms.

Preaching Needs Leadership

Without understanding leadership, preaching becomes woolly in its piety, naïve in its application, and guilty on all counts of thin-bloodedness. Leadership brings much-needed realism and knowledge into the preaching task. Preaching urgently needs to learn from leadership about critical issues such as change, conflict, the need for intentionality, and understanding process.

Change

Leadership studies are ruthlessly realistic about the nature and need for change and its rapid rate and turbulent discontinuities in current culture. Alvin Toffler was the first to write of "future shock" caused by the accelerating rate of change. In his book titled *Future Shock*[3] he claims that the majority of material goods used in daily life have only been developed in the present eight-hundredth lifetime of human existence. Leonard Sweet likens cultural changes to tsunamis creating world sea changes as modernity is overwhelmed by postmodernity.[4] The horrific tsunami of December 26, 2004, now imprints unforgettable images about the scale of change envisioned by Sweet. Successive generations reflect these cultural changes: Pre-Boomers (born 1927–1945), Boomers (born 1946–1964), Post-Boomers or Generation Xers (born 1965–1981), and Millennials or Generation Y (born since 1981). Leaders must wrestle with the implications of change for their organizations. As Jim Herrington, Mike Bonem, and James Furr comment, "Leaders bear a disproportionate share of the responsibility for leading change."[5] Dramatically, Robert Quinn says that today's choice is "between making deep change or accepting slow death."[6]

In contrast, many preachers seem blissfully unaware of how huge these changes are and continue to specialize in general themes for no one in particular. Characteristics of thin-blooded preaching such as individualism, generic applications, and low compliance reinforce impressions of inert preachers going through tired motions. Some assume that we only need to find energy to go on doing what we have done in the past. But no one should underestimate the significance of dealing with change in new ways. "Church leaders of the past could be successful by gradually improving on what their predecessors had done. . . . The current setting for ministry demands continuous learning."[7] As Herrington, Bonem, and Furr challenge: "If you keep doing what you've been doing, you'll keep getting what you've been getting."[8]

Ironically, by job description gospel preachers are consistently required to preach change, to urge new birth, new life, and new creation. But they can inappropriately "spiritualize" change by restricting it to inner individual changes of heart and mind through repentance and faith and so evade its leadership challenge. Even while talking boldly of spiritual revolution, such preachers can organize churches to protect their cultural presumptions and avoid the "missionary dialogue axis" (see fig. 1). Incongruously, churches can become highly protective environments, minimizing change and sponsoring sacred cows. Safe havens of status quo, they boast future dreams but indefinitely postpone them by long-range plans organized by tiny, incremental, nonthreatening steps. The satirical version of the hymn "Onward, Christian Soldiers" at the beginning of this chapter rings too true. Many preachers need leadership's challenge about the implications of change.

Conflict

Remember how thin-blooded preaching wants to avoid conflict at all costs? Leadership studies are ruthlessly honest about conflict's inevitability and helpfully face its consequences, emphasizing the need for conflict management and offering various styles of resolving tension. While conflict can be destructive when people lose sight of common vision, it possesses life-giving possibilities when through healthy tension new understandings emerge. Thin-blooded preaching assumes that it needs to pacify awkward people and defuse potential conflict. We empathize with the bewildered pastor who said, "All my life, I've judged my success by how happy everyone in the church was. You are telling me that if I'm really on mission with God, one sign of my success will be the presence of conflict."[9] Preachers sometimes fall into the old trap of preaching peace when there is no peace (Jer. 6:13–14; 7:4). True peace does not paper over difficulties but emerges through conflict in honest new health.

Preachers have much to learn if they are to avoid naïveté. Lyle Schaller cites a salutary case study of a senior pastor leading a nineteen-hundred-member church into developing small study groups. (Incidentally, initiating and sustaining small group ministry remains one of the commonest leadership tasks in local churches.) The associate pastor, charged with planning and leading these new groups, began by training new members who showed high commitment and responded well to lay training. Group studies took a main theme: "What does it mean to be the church in today's world?"

Forty-one months after the date that the first study group had been initiated, however, the new group of vocal lay leaders had gained such prominence that at the church council meeting they asked for the senior pastor's resignation. After a stormy session both the senior pastor and associate pastor were forced to resign. Ironically, some change-oriented Christian leaders had become "victims rather than facilitators of their own acts." They had cut their own throats. They made a series of mistakes such as choosing a study theme that inevitably stoked up discontentment, providing no constructive outlet, and failing to integrate new members within older structures. And, most seriously, Schaller concludes that both ministers overlooked the doctrine of original sin and "failed to recognize the almost irresistible temptation that often entices laymen to play one minister against the other in a multiple staff situation. . . . The key question is . . . How stupid can a pair of ministers be and still serve the Lord?"[10]

Intentionality

Leadership studies teach how to intervene proactively in different situations. By evaluation and through vision they show how to initiate processes to bring about desired change with positive outcomes. Understandably, some pastors feel trapped in a weary, unending cycle of other people's expectations. As I described in *360-Degree Preaching*, much church life can be summed up in saying, "The wheel is turning but the hamster is dead." Herrington, Bonem, and Furr quote one pastor who said, "I'm working harder than I've ever worked, for less results than I've ever gotten. My health is failing and my family is falling apart. . . . One thing is clear to me. Working harder at what we've been doing is simply not the answer."[11] But leadership must reject hand-wringing and arm-flailing and commit to intentional processes that develop and implement fresh mission and vision strategies to make a difference. Preacher/leaders need to commit themselves to processes of change to flesh out God's will and purpose.

Positive expectations are important too. Leaders are challenged to build expectations for win-win outcomes rather than induce guilt. Frankly, many preachers find this difficult, as Paul Borden confesses:

I find that as a preacher negativity and guilt rolls out of me like sweat on a hot day. I don't have to work at that but being positive is something I must work at. . . . For people to buy into a vision that is bigger than themselves, is larger than the church, there has to be communication from a positive perspective—the assumption that people want to serve God, . . . that sanctification has put within people the desire and the ability . . . to serve God.[12]

Understanding Process

Within process, preacher/leaders must particularly understand the role of evaluation and the meaning of values, mission, and vision.

EVALUATION

Leadership studies take analysis very seriously. Their search for hard facts eschews woolly assessments. The leadership model that I shall use later in this book (from Herrington, Bonem, and Furr) emerged from a defining moment of starkly honest analysis. Membership, attendance, and giving trends from 1950 to 1989 were analyzed for a group of churches. At first glance the results were broadly encouraging, showing growth everywhere. But when trend lines for the city's growth were laid alongside, a significant gap opened up between community and church growth every year of the survey. "In business terms, we had been losing market share for forty years."[13] Shock from this courageous audit propelled leadership forward with fresh urgency.

Self-interest can often falsify facts. A friend undertook some sabbatical research to visit pastors of growing churches in the United Kingdom. "I've noticed," he said, "that on every single occasion the preacher exaggerated the size of the congregation to several tens larger than the number actually present." Realism about church statistics compared with their contexts is vital, because the mainstream Western church has been in continuous decline over the last forty years. Gibbs quotes some researchers who are "predicting that if present trends continue, sixty percent of all existing Christian congregations in America will disappear before the year 2050."[14] Somberly, he adds: "Any church is potentially just one generation away from extinction."[15] Evaluation brings sober facts to light, and preacher/leaders need large doses of such realism.

VALUES

Several terms in leadership's vocabulary are significant for Christian life and can sharpen the preacher's task. For example, *core values* identify an organization's beliefs and values, answering the question of *why* an organization does what it does. Organizations define their core values in order to express corporate identity—the stories, expectations, norms, symbols, rewards, and worth that tie a people together with a sense of belonging. Aubrey Malphurs summarizes core values as "the way we do things around here."[16] Values look to the present and the past. Malphurs contrasts values with other issues such as principles, strategies, and doctrinal statements that should flow out of core values. He defines a Christian organization's core values "as the constant, passionate, biblical core beliefs that drive its ministry."[17]

> The organization's central beliefs are the driver sitting behind the wheel of the ministry car. While a ministry is vision-focused, it is values-driven. The primary beliefs are the ministry's shaping force.[18]

MISSION

Alongside values, an organization's *mission*, *vision*, and *visionpath* answer the question of *what* an organization is going to do. Mission needs to be distinguished from vision and visionpath, and Herrington, Bonem, and Furr helpfully define each.[19] Mission describes the broad sweep of an organization's purpose by one or two sentences that set out the framework and boundaries for vision. When applied to the church it expresses God's eternal purpose and answers the question "for what purpose did God establish the church?" Mission statements sum up an organization's broad-brush inspirational purposes.

VISION

Vision describes a more specific picture of what an organization proposes to do over the next three to five years. Couched in several sentences or paragraphs, it sets out more specific objectives within the broad mission. Herrington, Bonem, and Furr define vision for churches as "a clear, shared and compelling picture of the preferred future to which God is calling the congregation."[20] Visions can only be effective when they are clear, unifying, and motivational. But of supreme importance for a church's vision is that its leaders discern what *God* wants them to do next. It is his "preferred future," moving a congregation on his mission, that gives vision validity. Preachers find it relatively easy to speak in general terms of God revealing his will in Scripture, but particular details can seem very elusive and difficult to articulate for a local church. We need to remember Bonhoeffer's judgment on visionary dreamers who run ahead of God's plan for community, while giving attention to leadership studies that can provide clarity and help for pursuing God's plans. All leaders unite in stating vision's importance. As Wilhelm comments:

A core characteristic of all effective leaders is the ability to have a vision of where they are trying to go and to articulate it clearly to potential followers so that they know their personal role in achieving that vision.[21]

Preacher/leaders have responsibility to respond to God's vision, or "understanding God's revelation" as the Blackabys term it, in order to help others see it and know their role in achieving it.

VISIONPATH

Visions need to be broken down into smaller steps, specific issues, often set within a one-year time frame, that contribute towards implementing the bigger vision. A pastor shared with me his concern: "I know that we need a vision for us to grow as a church—something to stir people up. We need to extend our parking lot but that's not much of a soul-stirring vision. The trouble is that I just don't know what else the vision is supposed to be." This dejected pastor was trapped at the specific level of visionpath. Parking lots can be very important but only as part of the wider mission and vision that must come first.

There is much else that preachers can learn from leadership. For example, James MacGregor Burns's seminal work in 1978 was the first to draw a contrast between *transactional* and *transformational* leaders.[22] Transactional leadership is based on transactions or exchanges between leaders and followers motivated by mutual self-advantage. People have certain needs, which Abraham Maslow has expressed well in terms of physical and emotional security.[23] Transactional leaders influence situations in order that everybody wins out with mutual basic self-interests fulfilled. In a church situation a leader can work for increased membership, stable maintenance, and healthy finances so that its members can enjoy a sense of pride in their organization and gain others' admiration. For this a leader may be rewarded financially, with flattery, and with loyalty. However, such leadership inevitably tends to maintain status quo with high comfort levels.

In contrast, transformational leadership "helps followers embrace a vision of a preferred future. Leaders inspire and empower followers to achieve new levels of personal and corporate performance. . . . Followers gladly commit to a future they help to create."[24] It hardly needs emphasizing that full-blooded Christian leadership should be about transformation, living by faith, taking godly risks, and moving out of comfort zones. Yet, too often preaching veers toward transaction, anesthetizing rather than energizing. Fear of change and conflict reinforces a bias towards keeping people happy in the status quo.

Another helpful though controversial distinction is drawn between managers and leaders, based on research by Warren Bennis and Burt

Nanus in the 1980s. "Managers are people who do things right and leaders are people who do the right things."[25] Earlier we noted how a church survey shocked leaders about the true situation of decline in their community and propelled them into new vision. But when new plans were implemented, churches only showed improvement while outside consultants were working with them. As soon as these consultants left, pastors no longer appeared to know what to do. The provocative conclusion drawn was that most pastors are trained to manage rather than to lead. "They approached their work from the question 'How do I improve the programs and ministries we are currently doing?' Few had been trained to ask 'Are the things we are doing the most faithful and effective means of reaching our community with the Gospel?'"[26] Thin-blooded preaching always prefers managing to leading.

Other important research has focused on stages of commitment. Peter Senge's levels of response in an organization were mentioned earlier when describing low compliance as a characteristic of thin-blooded preaching. Transformational leaders also need to learn about mental models, team learning, and systems thinking. Helpfully, whatever new terms and ideas leadership studies introduce, they all agree that leadership skills can be learned given both time and effort. Preachers must persist in learning how to integrate the practice of leadership with preaching, and part 2 will develop the making of the preacher/leader.

Both Need Each Other

Instead of operating independently, eyeing each other suspiciously, preaching and leadership must embrace and do gospel business together. Preaching needs leadership as much as Christian leadership needs preaching. When Jesus Christ calls preachers he creates unique leaders for his church—those who declare his Word today so that by the grace of God people and communities are transformed. "We proclaim him, admonishing and teaching everyone with all wisdom, so that we may present everyone perfect in Christ" (Col. 1:28 NIV). God desires preacher/leaders. No one is more visible, more spiritually empowered, with higher profile and quality corporate time to develop relationships along the missionary dialogue axis than the preacher/leader. A church's mission and vision should be most clearly articulated in worship through preaching. Preachers have God-given responsibility to lead.

Bill Hybels perceives a modern-day tragedy in churches.

> All over the world people have never been led. They've been preached to and taught. They've been fellowshipped and Bible-studied. But with no

one to inspire them, to mobilize them, their desire to make a difference for Christ has been completely frustrated. I believe that the great tragedy of the church in our time has been its failure to recognize the importance of the spiritual gift of leadership. It appears to me that only a fraction of pastors world-wide are exercising the spiritual gift of leadership.[27]

It is time to confront this tragedy by reconciling preaching and leading. One pastor told me his own story:

> I now realize that I had mistakenly created a dichotomy in my pastoral ministry. Effectively, I was separating leading the church from preaching to the church. In my modern mind, I had treated the leading component of pastoral ministry as if I were leading a business organization: chart the course, equip the leaders, stay the course, evaluate the outcomes. Thus leading, I thought, was what happened "behind the scenes" that people see during Sunday worship services. Preaching, on the other hand, was my opportunity to serve as a spiritual guide to the flock in which God has entrusted me. I always took the God-given opportunity to preach as a way to spiritually shepherd my congregation. I lead and I preach, but I had functionally missed the interrelatedness of these two responsibilities. I now recognize and am beginning to utilize the God-given opportunity to lead through preaching. I desire to move beyond teaching through preaching. I desire to provide more than counseling through preaching. I desire to engage leadership through preaching.

Too few preachers appear to see how widely the gap has opened up between preaching and leading. Paul Borden comments on contemporary church discussion about change: "Whether they're coming from Barna or Hybels or Leadership Network or whatever, no one is really discussing what is the leader's role as a preacher fitting into this new paradigm."[28] He contends that pastors are often deemed "chaplains" who focus inwards rather than leaders concerned about mission, vision, and reaching an unchurched culture. Pleading for churches to be missional in changing times, he urges that preacher/leaders "ask the 'so what?' questions of the passage or the idea of the text, and they answer it in the plural not in the individual."[29]

Jim Nicodem, senior pastor of Christ Community Church, St. Charles, Illinois, is another preacher/leader who is concerned about the gap between preaching and leading. Called in the early 1980s by a core of six families to plant a new church in St. Charles, he now leads a congregation of over four thousand, with holistic ministry that involves its members in commitment together as well as to its community. Significantly, he recognizes his preaching as the priority in the story of the church's growth. As the key gifting in his spiritual inventory it forms the basis and core of his work as leader. In a message titled "Preaching with a Leader's Heart,"[30] he addresses the false dichotomy between preaching and leading, warning that continual emphasis on leadership in contemporary church culture subtly leads to two dangers. First, it diminishes the importance of preaching since it is assumed you cannot do both things well. Since leadership appears to be the more significant and urgent activity, preaching is inevitably given second or third place. Second, too great a stress on leadership activity can lead to a neglect of God's Word. Practical schemes can take precedence over obedience to God. He claims that in his own experience most leading takes place through preaching, and motivating God's people is best done by preaching. Unsurprisingly, in the light of earlier distinctions between teacher preachers and exhorters, he sees himself primarily as an exhorter.

Jack Hayford agrees that the pastor's task comprises both leading and feeding and warns how people much prefer feeding to being led. "They like to learn. They like to have freshness, things that warm their soul . . . but when you start to say, 'Folks, it's time for us to move, not just feed,' you'll recognize the flock will begin to grumble and mumble, because the sheep would rather just bed down and eat there for a long time."[31] He comments:

> I do believe every pastor has a leadership responsibility. He cannot simply be a chameleon reflection of what he thinks the people want and the elders mandate. . . . You can get into all kinds of potential political problems, and maybe even lose your job, but there are times where a pastor needs to raise his voice.[32]

Too true! As a matter of fact, 360-degree leading is the most awesome, demanding, daunting, and exhilarating task in the church. Nowhere else is God's will so pointedly exposed than in the person and the words of the preacher. Let's restate it: you can lead without preaching but you cannot preach biblically without leading.

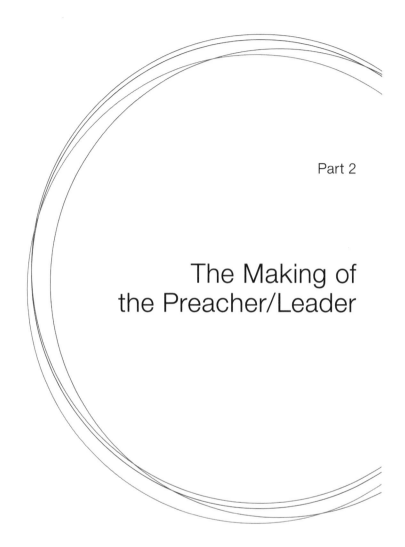

Part 2

The Making of
the Preacher/Leader

4

Fulfilling Vocation

The congregation looks at the person behind the pulpit as the leader of the church whether or not it is true. Consequently, the sermon is a primary vehicle that the leadership uses to cast its beliefs and dreams.

Aubrey Malphurs, *Values-Driven Leadership*[1]

On January 14, 2005, the Huygens space probe landed on Saturn's largest moon, Titan. It was a remarkable journey taking seven years to complete. A number of scientific instruments were carried on board. One of them, designed to measure wind velocity on Titan's surface, took inventor David Atkinson, of the University of Idaho, eighteen years to develop. When amazing pictures of Titan's surface were successfully transmitted, Atkinson's team waited for its data to come back. It never has. The scientist commented sadly: "The story is actually fairly gruesome. It was human error—the command to turn the instrument on was forgotten."

Part 1 claimed that too many preachers have forgotten their God-given responsibility to lead. It should be happening but in too many places it isn't. And it's fairly gruesome human error. But how is this to change? How can preachers lead again? Instead of eyeing leadership suspiciously, at a distance, preaching must take the initiative to reach out and enter into genuine dialogue—a dialogue that means openness to learn with a willingness to change into something stronger and more full-blooded.

While thin-blooded preachers will ignore the challenges of leadership, those who long to be preacher/leaders of transformation must work through how leadership impacts every part of the preaching task. Part 2 of this book pursues key aspects of the making of the preacher/leader. This chapter deals with vocation as God calls potential preachers into leadership. Chapter 5 introduces a leadership model. Chapter 6 outlines the skills required of the preacher/leader, while chapter 7 looks at particular character issues required. Finally, chapter 8 describes the process by which preacher/leaders enable congregational transformation to occur. I am not aware of any author who has taken a leadership model and analyzed its meaning specifically for preaching. Yet nothing will change for the better unless preachers dare to dialogue with leadership in practical ways to learn what should never have been forgotten about their biblical task of leading.

First, and crucial for everything else, is God's call upon preachers to be leaders. Nothing can be accomplished without God's call upon particular persons who respond with their gifting, personality, and relationships. Scripture records how God calls a variety of people in unique ways, such as Moses (Exodus 3); Joshua (Deut. 34:9); Deborah (Judg. 4:4); David (1 Sam. 16:13); Isaiah (Isaiah 6); Jeremiah (Jer. 1:4–10); Simon, Andrew, James, and John (Mark 1:16–20); Matthias (Acts 1:26); Saul (Acts 9:1–18); Barnabas and Saul (Acts 13:2–3); and Priscilla and Aquila (Acts 18:2–3). Each time, God perceives a person's heart (1 Sam. 16:7) and, by calling that person, gifts him or her to a speaking/leading role. George Barna's advice given to leaders applies equally to preachers: "First you must understand God's calling on your life. He has called some people to be leaders, and most others he has not. This is an issue of discernment. You cannot force God's calling, nor can you experience a significant life by dismissing or denying his call."[2] And when God calls people to be preachers he also calls them to be leaders. This is foundational for everything else.

Incidentally, leadership books can also stress vocation in business life. William Diehl, for example, surveyed the character quality of "faithfulness" among almost two hundred Lutheran CEOs. In contrast with Thomas Peters and Robert Waterman who chose "excellence,"[3] Diehl decided on the quality of faithfulness. Using various indicators of faithfulness such as spiritual growth, active prayer life, commitment to community, and financial stewardship, he found 30 percent consistently scored much higher than the rest. In further statistical research he identified one element common to this 30 percent.[4] Commenting on Diehl's conclusions, Banks and Ledbetter reiterate what made the difference: "They all shared a sense of call, meaning they felt they were in the place God wanted them to be."[5]

Vocation concerns the "who," "how," and "where" of a person's life response to God. Preachers matter because of who they are with their people. Thin-blooded preachers downgrade their personal involvement, by seeing preaching as walking backwards and forwards between study and pulpit, offering individualistic informational gospel sound bites. But communities cannot be transformed that way. Rather, God calls preacher/leaders to develop distinctive leadership gifts and to recognize different levels of influence as well as to be people whose quality of character leads as "ethos givers" (see chap. 7). Also preacher/leaders should be convicted that God employs the "foolishness of preaching" to change individuals and communities. Unless they have this confidence they had better not begin. God calls preacher/leaders to be obedient so that the "where" of their calling locates them in God's right place—they have beautiful feet (Rom. 10:15). Preachers must wrestle with the implications of incarnation, of words becoming flesh through their lives. For when they seek to personify God's message humbly and openly, to prepare the entire body for works of service (Eph. 4:11–12), they inevitably lead.

Vocation is essential. In my first pastorate I placed these words upon my desk: "God called me here for his glory." Every word reminded me powerfully that I was in Blackburn because it was God's will for *me* and that I was to be concerned about seeking his glory not mine. While other pastors might appear to have easier tasks in greener pastures with better outcomes, I needed to keep recognizing my call and role in this particular place. It is human nature for pastors who consider themselves average to wish they had more gifts. One pastor said to me: "I wish I was more like Rick Warren—he's such a leader!" Such wishing is profitless (though we should never stop learning from others). Far more valuable is taking Jesus's teaching about talents seriously and recognizing that each of us is of equal worth to God if we use our talents to the full, whether we are gifted with one, two, or five (Matt. 25:14–30). Most of us are one- or two-talent people and that's how God has made us. God loves average pastors and he has made many of them not that they will be less successful, but that they will fulfill exactly what is useful for his glory where they are. Average pastors can accomplish what no one else is called to do because they are called where they are.

Sadly, "big names" and their stories can often intimidate preacher/ leaders into thinking that only high profile leadership is effective, directing at superior levels in spectacular ways. Indeed, retelling success stories can give the impression that the only way forward is for others to attempt to copy great leaders. Not so. There are many kinds of preacher/leaders and they need to recognize carefully that their differences are due to varying personalities, giftings, and situations. Never forget—God loves average preachers and is pleased when they give him their best. But God expects all preachers to be leaders, his change agents.

Lyle Schaller popularized the notion of "change agents,"[6] arguing that change provokes three main reactions. *Denial* means both leaders and people pretend that nothing has changed. Tragically, some preachers and congregations live in massive denial, seemingly oblivious to their decline. *Resistance* to change consciously rejects all innovation and immersion, preferring instead to live in nostalgia. *Commitment* to change means openness to its opportunities and risks. "Some people are passive agents of change, others are negative agents of change, and an increasing number are becoming affirmative agents of change."[7]

Scripture demands the third option. Openness in obedience to God's calling marks the story of God's people. From Abraham onwards, the response of faith means moving forward on spiritual (and sometimes physical) journeys. At times lessons on waiting are required until God reveals the next step (Acts 1:4), but such waiting always leads to fresh energy for new directions. In response to Scripture, preacher/leaders have prime responsibility to become "affirmative agents of change." Such a claim deepens understanding of God's call and gifting.

Too many preachers think of their vocation in limited terms. Perhaps they get as far as considering which kind of preacher they most typically are, but they are never stretched to ask about what sorts of leadership God calls them into. The rest of this chapter invites preachers to ask probing questions of themselves about their leading.

Different Kinds of Preacher/Leaders

In *360-Degree Preaching* I identified four kinds of preaching. Now I must add different leadership insights to tease out various kinds of preacher/leaders. Figure 3 combines types of preaching and leading with diverse aptitudes and contrasting levels of leadership. Instead of one monochrome pattern of preaching/leading, a complex diversity of options emerges, each of which will be considered in turn.

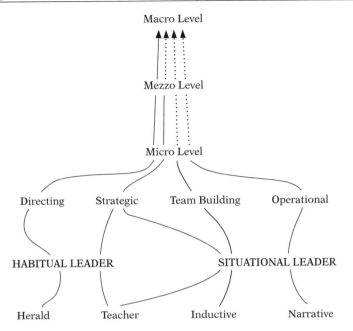

Fig. 3. Preacher/Leader Aptitudes and Levels of Leadership. The dotted lines show the aspirations of situational leaders who progress beyond the micro level.

Four Types of Preachers

At the bottom of figure 3 are four types of biblical preaching that I identified in *360-Degree Preaching*.[8] Obviously, throughout Christian history, a diverse range of individuals has expressed unique personalities and gift inventories because of different experiences and theologies. However, without denying their unique traits (and composite practice), I define certain common categories of style that are legitimated by scriptural differences of genre and by preachers' personalities and temperaments.

First, *herald preachers* have a defining belief that God empowers both Scripture and the preaching event itself. Though such preaching shares deductive and propositional characteristics in common with teaching, it sounds very different. Often dramatic in style, herald preachers build their appeal with large building blocks, presenting a text's challenge with fewer details and greater appeal to right-brained congregations. The emotional content is likely to be higher with illustrations, stories, and evocative language all playing a major part.

Second, *teacher preachers* have a defining belief that hearers should understand Scripture. They have a high view of Scripture, stay close to

the text, and explain its meaning deductively. Typically doctrinal and in-
structional, didactic preaching examines verses in logical order so as to
"get information across." Teacher preachers prefer to build convincing
arguments going verse-by-verse and paying close attention to historical-
grammatical issues. They build using many small bricks as "left-brained"
personalities with a bent towards logical deductive reasoning. Such preaching is particularly appropriate for the Epistles, especially when it takes the
form of teaching sermons, with tightly packed arguments and applications.
But many other parts of Scripture can benefit from the teacher preacher's
grasp of points and subpoints and the use of clear teaching structures.
Teacher preachers have a foundational responsibility for safeguarding
truth, paying close attention to the text, and sustaining biblical literacy
and doctrinal knowledge among congregations. Their exegesis, exposition,
and application offer the bread-and-butter method of preaching.

Third, *inductive preachers* have a defining belief that hearers' needs are
most important and that preaching must be relevant to them. In marked
contrast with the deductive preaching of teachers and heralds where the
preaching dynamic goes from Scripture to hearers, this preaching has an
inductive dynamic that begins with the hearers and moves to Scripture in
order to find appropriate texts. Inductive preaching may have many stimuli
such as evangelism (beginning with "felt needs"), apology (defending Christianity from attack), pastoral care (dealing with issues within congregation
or society), or political concern (addressing current topics).

Fourth, *narrative preachers* have a defining belief that sermons should
have a story *form* that catches listeners up into an experience of God's
truth. Though most preachers use stories, this kind of preaching pays
particular attention to hearers' listening patterns and plans sermons
accordingly. With its roots in the literary and rhetorical patterns of
Scripture's narrative, especially Jesus's parables, it has recently gained
popularity. Sermons are structured carefully to work like narratives so
that hearers are taken on a journey to experience both the tensions that
the gospel creates and the resolutions that the gospel brings.

Two Types of Leader

At the next level up in the diagram, leadership insights are directly
related to various sorts of preachers. From two decades of leadership research, George Barna has concluded that there are two kinds of leaders. A
small proportion, about one in eight people, are "habitual leaders" who are
called and gifted by God and cannot help but lead because of their strong
directing personalities. These are the "natural born" leaders who emerge
from any group as irrepressible front-runners. For Barna, "habitual leaders
who are Christian innately seek to provide direction that guides people to

God's desired outcomes by facilitating life transformation and obedience to God."[9] Leadership is in their spiritual DNA, for they know intuitively and discern incisively appropriate courses of action—and they *do* it.

Many characters in Scripture are habitual leaders. For example, Simon Peter and the apostle Paul are natural leaders whose gifting is sharpened by God's call. Never has a habitual leader made a sharper about-turn than Saul's leading role against Christ transformed on the Damascus Road (Acts 9) into Paul's leading missionary role for Christ. This man could not help but make a difference one way or another! And when such habitual leaders are also preachers, they become major "movers and shakers" as God empowers their words with his energy and direction.

John Adair's *Great Leaders*, from Socrates to Mahatma Gandhi, lists habitual leaders. The roll call of habitual leaders through church history includes great names such as John Chrysostom, Augustine of Hippo, Martin Luther, John Calvin, John Wesley, Charles Finney, and Charles Haddon Spurgeon. All of these would have excelled in any other walk of life—university, politics, business, military service, or whatever. Praise God, they chose to serve him and his church by obeying and fulfilling their unique callings and giftings from God for ministry. Someone commented to me about Bill Hybels in regard to his Willow Creek fame: "You know whatever he had chosen to do he would have been at the top. He's a born leader." God uses born leaders.

However, Barna claims that the rest of the population, seven out of eight people, often find themselves in positions that force them into leadership. He terms these types "situational leaders" because their situations demand leadership in spite of their inadequacies. Often they can feel like "fish out of water" because they have little natural talent for what is therefore an unnatural and uncomfortable struggle. Indeed, some situational leaders spend all their time just trying to survive, counting the avoidance of failure as their best success. A weary pastor once said to me: "I only have eight years to go before I retire." But Barna is convinced that Christian situational leaders can develop skills to lead God's people and can even grow to enjoy their responsibility as such. Since the majority of preacher/leaders are statistically likely to be situational leaders, this is good news. While many such preachers feel ill-prepared for leadership, God promises strength to learn necessary skills. Remember his repeated call to Joshua: "Be strong and courageous" (Josh. 1:6; see 1:1–9).

Four Leadership Aptitudes

The diagram's third level up introduces leadership aptitude, defined as "a relatively predictable set of abilities and perspectives that enables the leaders to deliver one dimension of leadership with excellence."[10] Barna's research identified four primary aptitudes as directing, strategic, team building, and operational. Each refers to a cluster of issues about how a leader thinks, uses information, and relates to others. He also claims that with very few exceptions each leader possesses just *one* of these aptitudes, and he commends using tests to discover skills inventories, such as the online Christian Leader Profile.[11]

Preacher/leaders therefore not only preach in different ways but also have various aptitudes. Is it possible that there is a link between particular preaching styles and leadership aptitudes? Attempting to make connections between the two is likely to be highly speculative, but it is worth some effort.

The *directing leader* is most easily identified with the "strong leader" who successfully draws others into vision. By stimulating imagination and motivating others, such leaders are effective public speakers, making decisions easily and often demonstrating an intuitive sense of the right course of action. Their conviction gives courage and confidence to others. They bear all the hallmarks of "habitual leaders." On the negative side they are often impatient with working through the details of implementing a vision. Indeed, they "tend to be restless, have short attention spans, favor action over reflection. . . . They genuinely love people but they typically cause chaos when they attempt to organize people around the vision, goals and strategies that they have promoted. . . . Their interest is in making good things happen—now!"[12] The directing leader connects well with the herald preacher whose emotional engagement with people conveys compelling biblical vision with excitement and passion. Herald preachers have ability to direct others with courage and confidence. Those preachers who are "habitual leaders" are also likely to be heralds in the pulpit, exhorting people with spiritual conviction. C. H. Spurgeon is a good example of a herald who as directing leader spearheaded phenomenal vision in his church planting, orphanages, and seminary.

In contrast, the *strategic leader* works by amassing much information and thinking through which are the best possible choices. Here cerebral activity is elevated with a desire to work out concepts logically. Strategic leaders specialize not so much in conceiving vision as in developing its consequences. They tend to be thorough, ask the hard questions, and take great pains in their preparations. Sometimes emotionally detached, they are firmly committed to communicating truth with precision and completeness, though they tend to be perfectionists, taking a long time to reach decisions. The strategic leader connects well with the teacher preacher whose cerebral approach gives much attention to detail with great capacity to be a vision developer and shaper. John Stott is an excellent example of a teacher preacher whose ability to strategize has had worldwide impact. Of course such leaders are often "habitual" too.

Third, the *team-building leader* has ability to draw others to work together in teams, using intuition about how people will complement each other in pursuing vision. Team builders

> identify and pursue the appropriate people, determine their gifts and abilities, knit them into complementary work units, and provide the emotional energy that keeps them going. . . . Being with people energizes them, and people are energized by their presence. . . . After spending time with a team-building leader you most likely feel as if you have been heard, understood, and loved by a trusted friend.[13]

However, team builders are sometimes less able to cope with details of process. This aptitude seems to have parallels with inductive preaching with its concern to listen to and relate to people in their needs and in discovering their potential. Inductive preachers should perhaps have an ability to build teams. The roundtable model of preaching developed by John McClure, which employs successive teams of church members to participate in sermon preparation, illustrates this kind of preacher.

The *operational leader* has ability to master process, "developing systems around the vision, resources, and opportunities available, creating new routines that maximize whatever they have to work with, in light of where they want to go."[14] They provide the organizational structures to fulfill mission with an eye to fresh opportunities and new solutions. As concrete thinkers, they devote more time to practical details than the other three types, though they tend to dislike conflict and can behave more like managers than leaders. Perhaps because of their concern to integrate practical challenge into stories, narrative preachers are likely to be able to develop structures to lead hearers on the gospel journey. Earlier, Alice Mathews's description of leadership "from the middle" stressed the need to bring people to a point of facing problems in order to deal with them practically. This approach has similarities with operational leadership.

Such matching of preaching style with leadership aptitude is admittedly exploratory and patchy at best, but it prods preachers to reflect on who they are as change agents. Instead of trying to put other preachers' names to these different options, each preacher should identify which style and aptitude most adequately sums up his or her type of leadership. As Barna summarizes:

> It was God who called you to be a leader. He chose your leadership aptitude and you cannot do anything about it—nor should you want to, since it's the approach to leadership that will deliver the greatest joy and fulfillment to you and the people whom he allows you to lead.[15]

Of course, since each preacher/leader typically has only one aptitude, the need to work with others is essential. Barna describes how a "dream team" can combine each of the leadership aptitudes to complement one another. "A team that blends these four aptitudes is one that has the potential to accomplish great things for the kingdom, with excellence, efficacy, and efficiency."[16] However, when aptitudes fail to harmonize with each other, they can destabilize ministry as different leader types find themselves at odds over the same issue.

Three Levels of Leadership

One further aspect of leadership needs consideration—its different levels of influence. The lowest, the micro level, concentrates on individual needs in the local context. Situational leaders operate most happily at this stage since they cope more easily with smaller scale issues. The next level is mezzo, which influences a wider group of people with broader community implications. This level provides critical proving ground before leadership moves up to the macro level, which is the most demanding of all, having responsibility for people regionally, nationally, or even internationally. Barna notes that while similar, basic leadership elements are found at each level, their intensity changes dramatically from level to level. So, for example, the need for vision remains vital at each level. For situational leaders the vision is:

> Seeking to bring glory to God by fostering obedience to biblical principles, empowering his people to pursue his vision for their lives, and enabling lives to be spiritually transformed.[17]

Barna calls this the "default vision," but as leadership develops through mezzo and macro levels, the responsibilities of identifying and working through vision become increasingly demanding. Again, as with certain other leadership definitions we have encountered, this statement of vision sounds remarkably like a working definition of preaching/leading!

Each level has significance for preacher/leaders. Because the majority are situational leaders, they inevitably concentrate on the *micro level*. Much traditional seminary training focuses on developing potential pastors' knowledge, skills, and character in order to care for local congregations. After all, as noted at the outset, the local church is essential to God's cosmic master plan. However, micro-level leadership can focus exclusively on needs *of* individuals rather than building community *with* individuals. Indeed, micro-leadership can aid and abet thin-blooded preaching by its individualistic nature and its willingness to settle for grudging compliance rather than full commitment. Any preacher who expends energy on nurturing individuals is always in danger of missing out on the wider courageous responsibilities of preaching/leadership.

At the *mezzo level*, focus moves from individuals to community. It offers preacher/leaders opportunity to lead believers together to embody outcomes of new life in Christ. In terms of the missiological model (see fig. 1), this level operates along two axes: the *reciprocal relationship axis* between gospel and church, so that the local church community develops communal responsibilities, and the *missionary dialogue axis* between church and its local culture. Such mezzo-leadership deals with a congregation's missional responsibility to model God's truth in the face of an ambivalent and sometimes hostile local culture. It leads people to worship, witness, and serve together in contrast with the world. The opposite scenario, missional failure, results in a church of individual believers who acculturate to culture, having no discernible contrast with their surroundings. Since micro-leadership likely misses the challenge of countercultural living, preacher/leaders should always be aspiring to mezzo-level influence.

At the *macro level*, leadership exercises much wider influence by mobilizing people whose greater diversity covers a considerably broader geographical area. By their speaking and writing, such leaders may make national or international impact. Obviously, with leadership in their DNA, habitual leaders are able to operate at this level much more easily than situational leaders, often developing innate skills learned from experience as they progressed upward from micro through mezzo levels.

Even though the majority of preachers are situational leaders, they are the key discerners and communicators of God's vision and purpose for their churches. Though most comfortable at the micro level, especially those who relish pastoral ministry, they should face the challenges of moving up to the mezzo level. Growing beyond comfort zones into new leadership opportunities requires the hard work of reading, listening, learning from others, and practicing new skills. Barna claims situational leaders need several strategies to develop skills in these areas: teamwork, defining God's vision, godly character, nurturing effective followers, creating conflict to make progress, spiritual renewal, and understanding life cycles of organizations. Of these, probably situational preacher/leaders find the creative use of conflict the most difficult skill of all. Recall how thin-blooded preachers desire to avoid conflict at all costs! Yet Barna bluntly asserts: "When you strip it all away, leaders do just two things: they create conflict and they resolve conflict."[18] Using conflict positively lies poles apart from the pastor's specialty of bringing comfort. Barna's list requires much new learning by preacher/leaders, and the next chapters will work through some of the implications.

Figure 3 suggests a variety of paths open to preacher/leaders. At the left, the herald preacher with directing style represents a predictable picture of preacher/leader. Habitual leaders by gifting, heralds are the "big names" in church history as well as contemporary church life. Actually, habitual leaders may also use strategizing and the teaching style—indeed we noted earlier the preferred use of the word *teaching* in much Christian leadership material. Because such leaders move more easily to the macro level, they have a public profile through books, conferences, and a variety of audiovisual resources.

Unwittingly, herald preachers may give the impression that theirs is the only successful style, as though the choice is between being a five-talent person or nothing (see Matt. 25:14–30). But the other three tracks in figure 3 offer equally valid and valuable options for preaching/leading according to different personalities, giftings, and situations. Preachers who are primarily teachers, inductive, or narrative in style must also identify whether their way of leading is by strategy, team building, operational process, or even by directing. Figure 3 describes different options rather than prescribes limits. My challenge is to ask all preachers about how they lead. Perhaps knowing that they do not possess directing skills, they have assumed they have no leadership skills at all. Not so. All preacher/leaders should find themselves somewhere on this diagram. Average pastors can accomplish exactly what God wants them to do when with aptitude they push beyond the micro level.

Turning the World Upside Down

It is easy to use the word *preachers* pejoratively. For example, Peter Drucker tells one such story:

> [Assigned] a high school term project on World War I, one of my fellow students said: "Everyone of these books says that the Great War was a war of total military incompetence. *Why was it?*" Our teacher did not hesitate a second but shot right back, "Because not enough generals were killed; they stayed behind the lines and let others do the fighting and dying . . . effective leaders are not preachers but *doers*."

Here *preachers* come off badly as all talk and no action—talkers whose (cheap) words allow them to stay behind the front line and avoid costly action. As Drucker sums up:

> Effective leaders are not preachers but *doers*. . . . Effective leaders delegate a good many things, . . . but they do not delegate the one thing that only they can do with excellence, the one thing that will make a difference, the one thing that will set standards, the one thing they want to be remembered for. *They do it*.[19]

Frankly, in spite of figure 3, many may still regard preachers talking about leadership as so much hot air—posturing about differences they can make without actually making any.

It is time for preachers to fulfill their vocation as God's change agents. Preaching involves not only saying words but also *doing* God's Word. Jesus's challenge to be like the wise man that built his house on the rock is literally translated: "Everyone who hears all these words of mine and does them" (Matt. 7:24). Instead of mealy-mouthed, thin-blooded posturing, preachers have to embrace the consequences of their calling and make differences for God.

One of the greatest compliments given Christian preacher/leaders was paid in Thessalonica (Acts 17:1–8). In reaction against the preaching of Paul and Silas, jealous Jewish leaders stirred up a riot and rushed to where they were staying—at Jason's house. Finding Paul and Silas absent, they brought Jason before the city officials and paid their unintentional compliment: "These people who have been turning the world upside down have come here also" (Acts 17:6). Literally translated: "The ones of the inhabited earth having turned upside down—they're here."

This "turning the world upside down" faith (or turning the world the right way up) was not just a matter of adopting new ideas, joining a new organization, and signing up for a new vision. Nor was it primarily a matter of fresh experience. Rather it was an uprooting and upending of conventional structures of life, as they knew it, to live in a new way in Christ. As T. R. Glover declared about the early church: "The Christian 'out-lived' the pagan, 'out-died' him and 'out-thought' him. . . . He beat him hollow in living."[20] Preaching opens up new ways of living and dying. This compliment unintentionally expresses how preacher/leaders should be seen—as spiritual agitators, subversive pastors, un-settlers of old ways, and embodiers of the new Way.

So Jesus summons preacher/leaders today. By his teaching, by modeling a new way of leadership, by breathing his Spirit, the greatest transformational leader in history continues to do it his way! There is no more critical place for transformation than the local church in which no one has a more significant role than preachers as change agents. Of course, preacher/leaders have limitations like any other leader, but their daily walk with their people and their weekly exposition of God's Word remain the most focused source of power by which lives can be changed and communities formed and by which the world is turned upside down.

5

Developing a Model

If you were on trial for being a Christian leader, would there be enough evidence to convict you?

A seminary colleague of mine is presently engaged in "cross-over" research between hip-hop culture and adult learning processes. Though these two topics may at first sight seem to have little in common, he argues several significant links between them benefit adult learning. Bringing together two such dissimilar areas of knowledge and experience has charged his fresh creative thinking.

Of course, I have made a case from the beginning that preaching and leadership should not be regarded as dissimilar but actually need each other. Already, in the previous chapter, I integrated leadership styles, aptitudes, and levels of influence into the preacher's vocation. But now it is vital to engage in "cross-over" thinking between preaching and a practical leadership model. Admittedly less startling than bringing together hip-hop and education, it is nonetheless unusual for a preacher to analyze a practical leadership model for the sake of understanding preaching better. The rest of this book therefore works through a specific model to charge fresh creative thinking about what qualities, skills, and processes preachers must learn to develop and use.

Out of tens of leadership books considered, I have chosen *Leading Congregational Change: A Practical Guide for the Transformational Journey*[1] by Jim Herrington, Mike Bonem, and James H. Furr. Why this book? True, it rarely mentions preaching directly, yet every page resonates with my convictions about preaching/leading. In response to my inquiry, the authors have graciously encouraged me to look at their ideas from a preacher/leader's perspective. Rather than attempt a comprehensive restatement of their research and conclusions (which would wastefully duplicate much of their foundational work that should be read in its own right), I shall identify key principles that preacher/leaders must learn from their research. Committed to spiritual transformation, they use the best secular insights, develop practical principles with disarming honesty, and develop a realistic model of leadership. Much of what follows flows out of their work. When I write "they" it will most often refer to these authors in regard to their book.

A Leadership Model That Can Preach

Rather than maintaining churches continuing in decline—"if you keep doing what you've been doing, you'll keep getting what you've been getting"—they urge spiritual transformation: "Do not be conformed to this world, but be transformed by the renewing of your minds" (Rom. 12:2). Working with over a hundred churches in Houston, Texas, they pursued one question: "How do we transform declining congregations into Christ-like bodies that display the power of the Gospel in our communities?"[2] Rejecting the latest "quick-fix answers," they labored through a lengthy process marked by prayer, obedience, and passion. Scripture and spiritual vitality permeate their work's tone and spirit. At so many points the preacher can only shout "Alleluia!"

They also draw helpfully on a wide variety of insights from Christian and secular leadership books. Rick Warren and Bill Hybels are influential on their work as well as Henry Blackaby and Claude King's *Experiencing God*,[3] which seeks to identify God's activity within a congregation's situation and then to "make the personal and congregational adjustments needed to join him in that activity."[4] Also important are John Kotter's *Leading Change* and Peter Senge's *The Fifth Discipline: The Art and Practice of the Learning Organization*. Kotter focuses on leaders embedding fundamental change and on how his eight steps greatly impact the "change process" leaders adopt. Senge's book particularly challenges readers about learning organizations and the use of systems thinking.

Further, the work Herrington, Bonem, and Furr have done is realistic, tried, and tested. Sharing over fifty years of practical experience, the three authors worked long-term with some typically ordinary congregations, many of which were long established and in decline. The resulting wide range of experiences and personal stories adds bite to their conclusions. They are remarkably honest about their own vulnerability when inevitable conflict and unpleasantness arose. "We learned as much from our failures as we did from our successes. We experienced conflict at many different levels. The process was both humbling and rewarding."[5] Unsurprisingly, they urge patience about the length of time required for congregations to change (at least five to seven years). Eschewing narrow "how-to" prescriptions, they focus on principles and concepts but always with "ordinary" churches (and preachers) in mind.

Of all the different leadership models I have studied, I found this to be the most realistic and workable model for preacher/leaders. Many practitioners, including Vic Gordon, whose experience is included in chapter 8, speak of this model's effectiveness in their local churches. Other teaching colleagues testify to its usefulness in the leadership field. Rather than working with leadership ideas that risk fostering humanistic models and tend to dispense with Holy Spirit power, this model places spiritual growth at a premium. Instead of distorting theology and flattening spiritual paradoxes, this model encourages thoughtful theology that is full of surprises. And, very importantly, instead of aiding and abetting human pride, this model presumes human weakness and conflict, and stresses the need to depend completely on God's grace for transformation.

Central to the book is a three-part model (see fig. 4) that summarizes the many complex issues involved in leading congregational change by integrating three interdependent and interactive components. Every preacher/leader needs both to understand and also to take responsibilities in all three parts. First, "spiritual and relational vitality" is critical as the driving force for congregational change. "A congregation that is not committed to following God or that is experiencing serious discord within the body will find it virtually impossible to follow the difficult path of transformation."[6] Second, four "learning disciplines" are required in order to lead an effective process of change for congregations. Third, a tried and tested eight-stage process is the means recommended for bringing about change.

What hugely complicates this model is the way that all three elements interact simultaneously for congregational transformation. Instead of following a neat sequence of actions, its parts jumble together in exhilarating ways that the authors liken to whitewater rafting. Having all the right equipment and a map of the river cannot guarantee what actually happens when the raft takes to the water's surging torrents. Any missing element spells disaster. Enthusiastic commitment to spiritual vitality without a clear map and skills to negotiate the journey means calamity, as does possessing skills and a map yet lacking spiritual vitality. These three elements depend utterly on God's grace to achieve anything of eternal value.

This fits well with my own analogy of the "preaching swim" that places the preacher in the exhilarating dynamic of God's working his purpose through local churches. That's one reason why 360-degree leading—"at its best, a biblical speaking/listening/seeing/doing event that God empowers to lead and form Christ-shaped people and communities"—lies central to integrating and developing the three components of congregational transformation. God especially calls preacher/leaders to take responsibility for a congregation's spiritual and relational vitality. How else does a church become spiritually alive unless under God's Word and by his Spirit? Remove preaching and you eliminate God's best means and method. But miss out on *any* part of the model and preaching can be reduced to trickles of thin-bloodedness.

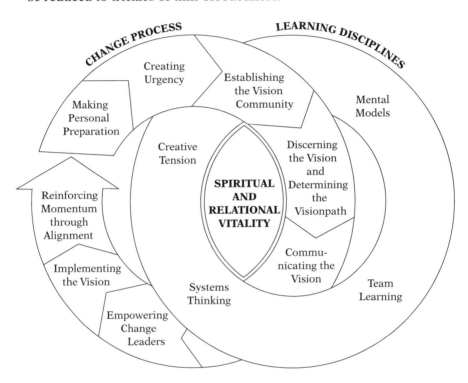

Fig. 4. Congregational Transformation Model. Taken from Jim Herrington, Mike Bonem, and James H. Furr, *Leading Congregational Change* © 2000. Reprinted with permission of John Wiley & Sons, Inc.

An Untidy Process

Behind this model lies a fascinating story of blood, sweat, and tears, coupled with the Holy Spirit's working in local churches. The *change process* was first to emerge, forced by the churches' decline and an urgent need for new leadership styles. Then, *spiritual and relational vitality* was spurred on by the need to resolve conflict. And last, *learning disciplines* emerged out of the failure of leadership in churches.

Initially, two issues prodded development of the eight-stage *change process*. First came jolting church surveys that showed continuous decline over forty years in a large sample of churches in comparison with their communities' population growth in Houston, Texas. Instead of complacency, church leaders were forced to act in order to stop the hemorrhage. Also, pastors expressed concern that older leadership styles no longer seemed to be working. Former traditional long-range planning, based on standard denominational programs, measured progress against previous years and assumed that little steps of incremental change would bring growth. But now pastors were saying that, despite their best efforts, these programs were failing to stem decline, and they needed somehow to lead in new ways. Therefore, thrust into having to learn about shifts in leadership styles, Herrington, Bonem, and Furr found themselves immersed in "generative learning" with much personal stress.

> Our own image of leadership made it difficult to be in the role of learner. There is a certain vulnerability that comes from acknowledging that we don't know what we need to know to succeed. Yet in today's rapidly changing environment, leaders are increasingly required to be learners.[7]

With hindsight they recognized that they underwent a "paradigm shift" in understanding leadership. Instead of seeing change as something slow and incremental, they had to come to terms with the nature of contemporary change as rapid and discontinuous. Former assumptions no longer worked.

With urgency they began developing a different sort of "change process" for the churches. Every preacher/leader who engages with the eight stages for bringing about desired change will see multiple connections with the weekly preaching task. Chapter 8 deals with these stages in greater detail, but even a preliminary glance lets us see how vital is the preacher/leader's role, especially at stages 1, 2, and 5.

Stage 1, *making personal preparation*, carefully lays the groundwork for change by "carving out the time and space to discern God's voice and direction for the leader's own ministry and for the church."[8] Honest analysis of the current situation asks questions such as: "Exactly what do you want me to be *willing* to do about this situation, Lord?" Spiritual leadership always begins with God's vision and call rather than with human motives. While secular leaders develop visions within human possibilities, spiritual leaders develop vision beyond human possibilities. The only way by which authentic full-blooded preaching leads is by its preachers' discerning, obeying, and preaching God's will for the whole community, beginning with themselves.

Stage 2, *creating urgency*, recognizes that leaders need to undertake the difficult task of creating energy for change. Only masochists welcome tough personal changes with open arms. The majority always votes for the status quo and resists any deeper structural change. The standard not-in-my-backyard reaction says, "I'm all for change—for other people." Change provokes a thousand faces of resistance, including denial, nonco-operation, and downright conflict. Yet, as we have seen, Christian leaders by definition preach new life. Gospel salvation contrasts the before/after of life, calling people to cross the gap between safe knowns to the risky unknowns of the kingdom of God. Belonging to Christ shifts disciples away from their (less desirable) present situation towards God's future vision. While thin-blooded preaching aims for low compliance, letting hearers off the hook, full-blooded preaching declares God's vision clearly, raising tension creatively to stimulate spiritual urgency that propels people forward into God's preferred future.

Stage 5, *communicating the vision*, offers the most obvious connection with the act of preaching. Undeniably, a church's preacher and sermon remain primary vehicles by which a church glimpses God's plans. Though church communication uses other written and visual means (which should be imaginatively employed), there is no substitute for preaching. As we have seen, God gives unique authority to preaching biblical words in 360-degree leading, and there is no more powerful way for people to hear and respond.

Preaching also connects well with the other stages in the change process such as *establishing the vision community, discerning the vision and determining the visionpath,* and *empowering change leaders.* All of the stages will be considered in chapter 8.

The model's second part, *spiritual and relational vitality,* arose largely from initial failures among ten pilot projects. In spite of early enthu-siasm, nine churches quickly degenerated into conflict that wrecked further progress. It is easy to speak about "creating urgency" (stage 2 above) in theory, but in practice the conflict such efforts stir up can be harshly destructive. Most of these local church leaders failed to cope. This brought about a massive reality check in regard to conflict and the need for leaders to be prepared for facing it. "As we reviewed the biblical patterns, every time—without exception—the people of God began to make adjustments to join God in his activity, conflict emerged."[9] Though such conflict is inevitable, they grew to realize that it could be handled in two contrasting ways.

Negatively, conflict can be *life-threatening* when people lose sight of God's vision, as when the people complained after the exodus (see

Exod. 15:24; 16:2; 17:3, 7). Such discord can easily spiral out of control and destroy community life or even life itself. In contrast, *life-giving* conflict leads to spiritual growth as people gain deeper understanding and commitment even through resolving discord. For example, Acts 6:1 honestly describes discord over unfair food distribution, yet the leaders deal openly with the problem, without endangering priorities, so that "what they said pleased the whole community" (v. 5). Acts 15 also shows a negative situation described as "no small dissension" (v. 2), with a church divided by some Judaizers' demands that circumcision was essential for salvation. Through debate the church reached newer, deeper levels of mutual agreement—"for it has seemed good to the Holy Spirit and to us to impose on you no further burden" than the four items mentioned (v. 28). Congregations facing conflict can either break apart or grow together more strongly. Much depends on how well their leaders have helped them mature in spiritual and relational vitality.

All this emphasizes the immense importance of developing spiritual and relational vitality, which lies at the bull's-eye of the preaching/leading task. It is central to who preacher/leaders are and what they do in weekly preaching. Unless a congregation experiences spiritual transformation, nothing spiritually positive can happen. Indeed, "developing a congregation's spiritual and relational vitality" defines preaching's core task. Full-blooded preaching proclaims God's big picture of men and women reconciled in Christ's new creation, incarnated in local communities of disciples drawn into deeper love for him and costlier mission towards others.

Such spiritual and relational vitality that is strong enough to cope healthily with conflict is defined as "the life-giving power that faithful people experience together as they passionately pursue God's vision for their lives."[10] Here, high-quality leadership is essential, for "leaders bear a disproportionate share of the responsibility for leading change. It follows that the spiritual and relational vitality of the leader or leaders is foundational to the change journey."[11] Unless leaders are growing spiritually in their relationship with God and each other there is little hope for long-term congregational transformation. Much patience and wisdom is required. Pastoral leaders need lengthier pastorates to grow with their people into more mature love and understanding so that, by God's grace, when conflict arises it may become life-giving, not life-threatening. Indeed, one litmus test of a leader's maturity is how well he or she responds to censure and conflict. Nothing proves the presence or absence of maturity quicker than how a leader deals with criticism.

Chapter 7 will emphasize that preacher/leaders, by calling and gifting, are to be the *ethos givers* for this spiritual and relational vitality.

Four learning disciplines, the model's third element, also emerged out of leadership failure in local churches. Herrington, Bonem, and Furr noticed that initially outside consultants brought successful change, but after they left and pastors resumed responsibility, progress stalled. They concluded that much of this failure resulted from these pastors being managers rather than leaders. Remember the distinction: "managers are people who do things right and leaders are people who do the right things." Probably most pastors by training and temperament are happier *managing* their congregations, assuming that their best efforts can sustain and even improve on current programs. But faced with the need to *lead* the change process in a context of rapid change and continuous learning, many pastors unhappily proved inadequate.

For pastors to thrive they need to develop skills. Head knowledge about change process and spiritual and relational vitality is not enough. Using Peter Senge's work on leadership as "mastering a set of disciplines that leaders must use to guide an organization through turbulent times,"[12] pastors can develop these four key disciplines, which are identified in the model as crucial to making the other parts work.

Each discipline has vital implications for preacher/leaders. For example, the first, *generating and sustaining creative tension*, concerns how a preacher/leader responds to Scripture and actually conveys God's mission and vision for a congregation. Connecting directly with stage 2 of the change process about "creating urgency," this discipline forges across the gap between current reality and God's future vision. Thin-blooded preaching misses out on this skill more than any other because it tends towards managing people, minimizing tension, and avoiding challenge. However, full-blooded preaching primarily works by this skill, presenting vision creatively to enable hearers to grow through tension into new possibilities. The major difference between these two kinds of preaching relates to whether or not the preacher has learned the leadership skill of generating and sustaining creative tension.

Similarly, the other three disciplines matter a great deal to full-blooded preaching: *harnessing the power of mental models*, *enabling team learning*, and *practicing systems thinking*. Because they have a fundamental impact on preaching practice, I shall deal with them next in chapter 6.

This brief examination already reveals how each of the model's three elements sizzles with significance for preacher/leaders. Yet the model's greatest challenge lies in the complex ways by which its three aspects interact, both circles moving simultaneously with their complicated dynamics grounded in shared spiritual vitality. Preachers dialoguing with this leadership model need particularly to wrestle with how their role relates to how the three parts work together. As I have studied this model, I increasingly believe that preacher/leaders have a major responsibility to integrate all three leadership elements. By this bold statement I do not claim omnicompetence for preacher/leaders. Far from it. Most of them are situational leaders who have lifelong struggles trying to learn the four disciplines. All of them need to work with other leaders. But their preaching responsibility for the congregation's spiritual growth makes them pivotal to the process of congregational change that should involve exercising leadership disciplines. By God's calling and gifting, preacher/leaders are plunged into the center of congregational transformation and therefore touch its every part.

The Greatest Example

Before delving into practical implications of this model in the next chapters we should consider whether it resonates with the practice of Jesus Christ, the world's supreme transformational leader. I believe that this model does connect with the Gospel record, as in, for example, Luke 4:42–5:11.

> At daybreak he [Jesus] departed and went into a deserted place. And the crowds were looking for him; and when they reached him, they wanted to prevent him from leaving them. But he said to them, "I must proclaim the good news of the kingdom of God to the other cities also; for I was sent for this purpose." So he continued proclaiming the message in the synagogues of Judea.
>
> Once while Jesus was standing beside the lake of Gennesaret, and the crowd was pressing in on him to hear the word of God, he saw two boats there at the shore of the lake; the fishermen had gone out of them and were washing their nets. He got into one of the boats, the one belonging to Simon, and asked him to put out a little way from the shore. Then he sat down and taught the crowds from the boat. When he had finished speaking, he said to Simon, "Put out into the deep water and let down your nets for a catch." Simon answered, "Master, we have worked all night long but have caught nothing. Yet if you say so, I will let down the nets." When they had done this, they caught so many fish that their nets were beginning to break. So they signaled to their partners in the other boat to come and help them. And they came and filled both boats, so that they began to sink. But when Simon Peter saw it, he fell down at Jesus' knees, saying, "Go away from me, Lord, for I am a sinful man!" For he and all who were with him were amazed at the catch of fish that they had taken; and so also were James and John, sons of Zebedee, who were partners with Simon. Then Jesus said to Simon, "Do not be afraid; from now on you will be catching people." When they had brought their boats to shore, they left everything and followed him.

Through this text Jesus Christ continues to exert leadership over preachers. Anyone called to be a leader for him must pay serious attention to the pulse and rhythm of his leadership, and there are many intriguing leadership issues in the congregational transformation model that connect within this text.

First, note prayer's strategic importance. Jesus's pattern of leadership begins in the solitary place (Luke 4:42), and Luke especially notes how regularly Jesus precedes action by prayer (Luke 3:21; 6:12; 9:18; 11:1). Human action presumes that thought and muscle power are all-important, but God's people recognize the priority of a prayer relationship with God, by which he reveals his will and through which he gives his power. Jesus's pattern of dependent prayer remains foundational. Nothing worthwhile for God is accomplished without prayer, and Christian leadership skills must not be exercised independently of prayer. The model rightly stresses the continual importance of spiritual and relational vitality and the leader's personal preparation.

Second, recognize that the specific details of this situation matter. Luke 5 describes weary fishermen who have worked unsuccessfully all night, have pulled up their boats and are washing their nets. Christian leadership must be practiced in real situations and not be conceived abstractly. Jesus's leadership realistically takes their fishing failure to move disciples forward in mission. The congregational transformation model insists on honest evaluation of the current situation so that people sense the urgency of moving towards God's vision.

Third, Jesus's personal vision centers on preaching. When crowds want to prevent him from leaving, he sums up his mission in the strongest terms: "I must [emphatic] proclaim the good news of the kingdom of God to the other cities also; for I was sent for this purpose" (Luke 4:43). Preaching is Jesus's preferred leadership method. He continues proclaiming (Luke 4:44; 5:1, 4); by preaching he initiates and sustains his mission, prepares his disciples, sends them out (Luke 9–10), and moves single-mindedly towards Jerusalem (Luke 9:51). He believes in finishing towers (Luke 14:28–30) and lives out the preacher's life to the fullest, beyond the cross, on the Emmaus road (Luke 24:27), and in the upper room (Luke 24:35). What a significant confirmation of the role that preaching plays in leading.

Fourth, Jesus's mission vision focuses on the "kingdom of God." "I must preach the good news of the kingdom of God" (Luke 4:43 NIV). This vision looks way beyond boats and nets to new ways of living, now mysteriously present in him yet not fully consummated in the present/future kingdom. As we shall see, congregational transformation needs leaders to think "mental models" and develop "systems thinking." "Kingdom" is, in effect, Jesus's powerful "mental model" by which he inspiringly sums up the complex, corporate reality of a new people living for deeper purposes and in greater ways. Ever since, preacher/leaders can never be content with the language of human organizations but should dare to proclaim and live by the kingdom's big picture.

Fifth, Jesus initiates change. His command "Put out into the deep water" (Luke 5:4) has huge leadership significance. In leadership language, it challenges disciples to enter a "change process." Clearly, Jesus uses fishing as a metaphor for the kingdom of God, a mission into which he is calling them. But, literally, unless they push out into deep water and let down their nets, they cannot learn lessons of faith and obedience in God's surprise response. Here Jesus demonstrates dynamic principles for preacher/leaders and their people—their need to move and change with him. Deep water speaks both of opportunity and risk. When Simon moves in trust and obedience, and only when he moves, can God initiate change with him and through him.

Sixth, Jesus involves others. Jesus is in the boat as Simon lets down the nets but Simon cannot accomplish the task on his own. He needs to signal to James and John for help (Luke 5:7). The congregational transformation model stresses how vital teams are for Christian leadership. Jesus believes in team working, identifying twelve disciples as his core group (Luke 6:13–16) and laboring with them over three years' ministry.

Seventh, because Simon puts out into deep water, led by Jesus, there is a unique "God happening" in the large catch (Luke 5:6). This emphasizes the paradox that Christian leaders work towards outcomes that ultimately only God can produce. Simon's consequent worship on his knees (Luke 5:8) forcefully reminds all preacher/leaders of God's awesome holiness, especially when he acts in our lives. As we shall see, the model makes holiness an important foundational feature of spiritual and relational vitality. Christian leadership anticipates ultimately impossible-to-manipulate outcomes that only God can deliver. And when he does, he propels believers to new experiences of worship. Encountering God remains central to spiritual transformation.

This significant story of Jesus's preaching/leading has much to teach us and many echoes will be heard in the next chapters. I include a sermon, preached in a local church setting, titled "Leadership 101" (appendix A) that draws out some of its principles further.

So with mounting excitement that this three-part model does justice to many of the substantial issues involved in preaching/leading, the next chapters identify some of its practical implications, beginning with the skills that preacher/leaders must develop.

6

Learning Skills

Leaders are not really in charge. Church leaders are followers of the living God who directs their lives through the Holy Spirit. They are, however, called to initiate transformation in the corporate life of the congregation where they serve.

Jim Herrington, Mike Bonem, and James H. Furr,
Leading Congregational Change[1]

Rick Warren wants to dispel several myths that circulate about growing churches, one of which is: "If you are dedicated enough your church will grow."[2] A favorite at pastors' conferences, this statement asserts that if only a preacher keeps praying and preaching the Word with doctrinal correctness, then growth is guaranteed. Warren is infuriated because of the harm this myth causes godly pastors when their faithful service only seems to result in decline. "It takes more than dedication to lead a church to grow; it takes *skill*. . . . both elements, God's power and man's skilled effort, must be present. We cannot do it *without God* but he has decided not to do it *without us!*"[3]

Many preachers seem hostage to this myth, like this thirty-seven-year-old pastor: "I need help. I'm not sure exactly what to ask. I thought I had the right education. I know I can preach and care for people in crisis.

But when it comes to getting the whole congregation mobilized to reach the community, I'm clueless."[4] Many pastors seem satisfied with their preaching ability and pastoral gifts but confess inadequacy about their leadership skills. As noted earlier, George Barna reckons that seven out of eight people are not instinctively natural leaders but rather are "situational leaders," and since the majority of preachers are among their number, it is imperative that they learn preaching/leading skills. Only thin-blooded preachers can be satisfied with blasé claims that they are good at preaching yet clueless about leading.

In contrast, full-blooded preachers want to be better at both. Dependent on divine power yet needing to use the best human skills, their preaching/leading is imbued with a sense of urgency and vision. They reject sermons that merely tread water or meetings that aimlessly mark time. Rather, they feel everything should be intentionally committed for God's high purposes. A great strength of the congregational transformation model (see fig. 4) is its emphasis on a leader's continual need to master learning disciplines *at the same time* as fostering spiritual and relational vitality and leading the change process.

Necessary Preaching/Leading Skills

Preachers who wish to be better leaders need all four skills in different parts of their ministry. First, *generating and sustaining creative tension* addresses much-needed realism and urgency in sermon preparation and content. Second, *harnessing the power of mental models* challenges the preacher/leader's mindset. Third, *enabling team learning* asks key questions about the preacher's working relationships. And fourth, *practicing systems thinking* asks big questions about how a preacher views the whole church body. Whenever preachers apply these skills they improve their *leading*.

Provocatively, these skills challenge preaching's traditional preparation. Commonly divided between time spent in the study and pulpit, the preacher exegetes and interprets texts, designs sermons that are faithful to this hard work, and publicly delivers them in Sunday worship. Tragically this process has too often resulted in thin-blooded preaching with characteristics noted earlier. Full-blooded preaching develops traditional skills into another dimension that ensures both faithfulness to Scripture and commitment to transformational leadership. Preacher/leaders have to learn how to build fresh disciplines into everyday ministry so that *every sermon matters*, a litany that I reiterate throughout this chapter.

1. Generating and Sustaining Creative Tension

This single most important skill goes to the heart of 360-degree leading. For dynamic leadership must both *generate* tension between an honest picture of present reality and a compelling vision of God's future and *sustain* such tension as a godly force for change. Such tension is healthily creative when a congregation comes to recognize that it falls short of a vision that it wants to grow into. Skilled leadership therefore avoids guilt or overkill. It does not depress about the present nor manipulate about the future. Rather, it positively keeps vision alive with bearable tension so people are motivated to develop through the pains of change. Some of us have suffered from quickly constructed, local church, master plans drawn up with suspiciously little prayer or even thought beforehand. A call has gone out, for example, to double the size of church membership within the next ten years. But instead of inspiring people, it seems only to make for increasingly desperate preachers wearing out dispirited people.

In contrast, this skill of generating and sustaining creative tension proceeds from a full-blooded preaching that brings the best out of people and is used in several ways: by realistic evaluation, by articulating vision both personally and corporately, by directing congregational prayer, and by dealing healthily with conflict.

REALISTIC EVALUATION

Every preacher/leader needs a clear picture of current reality. Nobody can change for the better without recognizing truth about the present, though it takes considerable skill to paint an honest picture of "how things really are." Defensiveness and blame-throwing lurk just beneath the surface whenever leaders and communities analyze strengths, weaknesses, opportunities, and threats. One lay leader shared with me how surprised she was when everything turned sour. At first her church enthusiastically underwent an intensive congregational survey. However, certain negative aspects in the final report fueled so much criticism that blame was unfairly heaped on the senior pastor, who was then forced to leave. Of course, realistic evaluations should puncture complacency, but they need also to be grounded in upbeat trust in God's continuing vision and purpose. Avoid nostalgia, false optimism, and carping criticism like the plague.

Leadership books offer a range of practical programs to audit the health of a local congregation within its wider community.[5] Preacher/leaders need to engage in such realistic evaluation so they can understand and portray current reality helpfully as the context for vision. We noted how nets, boats, and past failure form the basis for fresh happenings with Jesus, as shown in Luke 4:42–5:11. Preacher/leaders begin honestly in their own situations.

VISION

Like a mantra, every leadership book stresses the importance of vision. For churches, vision is defined as "a clear, shared, and compelling picture of the preferred future to which God is calling the congregation."[6] Such vision expresses what "really matters" for individuals and communities as they face the future. It motivates by giving the reason why faith and hard work is going to be worthwhile. Reflecting on twenty years of church research, Barna comments:

> There is a direct correlation between the impact of an individual or an organization and the presence of God's vision as the driving force behind the activity that brought such influence.[7]

However, Barna found that most senior pastors of smaller U.S. churches have no sense of God's vision—"in fact, fewer than 10% of all Protestant senior pastors in the nation can articulate God's vision for their church."[8] What tragedy! Sadly, talk about vision seems to belong to a different world from that of creating weekly sermons. Traditional sermon preparation apparently operates in a separate compartment. Yet no one should be more aware of the importance of personal and corporate vision than the preacher/leader.

Stephen Covey's first habit of highly effective people involves the principle of personal vision, instructing them: "Be proactive." Covey advises leaders not merely to react to circumstances but by combining creativity and resourcefulness to create a proactive culture for their organization.[9] Barna advises writing down a brief statement that encapsulates the core substance of personal vision.[10]

The remaining 90 percent alluded to above who cannot articulate God's vision for their church need first to spend time on their personal vision of preaching itself. God does not call preachers to be reactive to surroundings but proactive for his kingdom. Some preachers have written out their preaching vision. For example, Covey directly influenced Jim Nicodem, pastor of Christ Community Church in St. Charles, Illinois. After reading Covey, Nicodem made time to pray through and eventually write down his personal vision for preaching: "To impact as many lives as possible, through the private and public teaching of God's Word so that others are able to understand it, led to believe it, motivated to love and obey it, and equipped to study it on their own." In conversation he readily repeats this memorized personal vision because it lies at the core of his ministry.

My personal vision for preaching takes a different form—part commission and part prayer. At my ordination in 1972 I wrote myself a kind of vision statement for my eyes only. Now on a worn and tattered piece of paper, it was intended to generate and sustain creative tension—to inspire my preaching in the rough and tumble of routines and anticipated discouragement.

Your task on Sunday will be the most important ever given mortal man. For the words of the Living God will come alive again through you. The purposes of the Living God will become clear through you. Words of challenge will be heard from you. Words of comfort will be said by you. No greater task has ever been given anyone.

Prepare for it with all that the Lord your God has given you.

With the Holy Spirit who will guide you into all truth, whose conviction and boldness will inspire, correct, rebuke.

With the friendship of Jesus Christ who will walk with you as he did with the first fishers of men.

With the experience of the past when the goodness of God has upheld you and strengthened you as you were about to fall.

With the evidence of his past working through your words.

Prepare for preaching with eagerness to give the best of your:

Time—not left hurriedly to the end of a tiring week but the support to all else undertaken.

Mind—not trite repetitions of others' experiences or the easy way that reduces God's thoughts to your thoughts, but the profoundest way possible.

Personality—not something of the head only but reaching up through the wholeness of body, mind and spirit with humor, with compassion, with deep understanding of being human beings in today's world.

Dear Lord, help me to resist the Devil who would have me preach non-essentials, inanities, comfortable words of soothing medicine when souls are dying. Stir me up that I shall give the best of myself to be your preacher. In Jesus' name, Amen.

I confess I have used this erratically. Indeed, at one period of my ministry, involving a move to a new house, I mislaid the prayer for many months. Yet during much of the last thirty years its high sense of urgency has sustained my preaching vision. I encourage my doctoral students, all of whom are experienced preachers, to reflect on their call and preaching task by asking: What is God's will for me as preacher? What difference does being a preacher make to my living day-by-day and week-by-week? How can I best express my preaching task? Then I urge them to write up a personal vision statement. High personal vision makes for proactive preacher/leaders.

But beyond such personal vision, every preacher/leader should also be able to discern and describe a shared vision for their community in God's name. "Understanding God's revelation" is how Blackaby terms it, so that every member of the community might see how they belong together in God's preferred future. Remember the three sides of the missional triangle (see fig. 1). This is God's big picture for the whole congregation's living! Random makeweight sermons or pointless conversations are inexcusable, for everything done and said should be on message for God's vision.

Developing such shared vision belongs within the change process, and will be detailed in chapter 8. Obviously, practicalities vary greatly from church to church depending on organizational structure and history. As we shall see, in some congregations preacher/leaders can convene a smaller representative group of people into a "vision community" to work prayerfully through ideas that the whole church eventually embraces. Whatever process is used the preacher/leader must not only participate responsibly but also learn how to open up preaching to express God's will and motivate response. Since God gives vision through his Word, every sermon has a part to play in the process as the preacher/leader discerns, and then generates and sustains creative tension by preaching it.

Alongside Jim Nicodem's personal vision, mentioned earlier, he shares Christ Community Church's big mission: "To Know Christ and To Make Christ Known." This is expressed by vision in four key areas: explore membership, grow in maturity, discover your ministry, and engage in mission. Though he admits these are not original, the ways by which his preaching has fleshed them out are unique for this particular congregation. He believes that preaching has brought vision into reality.

Directing Congregational Prayer

Directing others in expectant prayer is essential to generating and sustaining creative tension. "Expect great things from God. Attempt great things for God" was William Carey's mission call. Chapter 7 will emphasize how a preacher/leader's personal spiritual life makes him or her an "ethos giver." Such personal sense of expectancy has to be generated for the whole community. Through prayers of intercession and petition everyone should be opened up to God's "new thing" (Isa. 43:18–19), anticipating together: "What will God's answer be?" Leadership must not leave prayer dependent on individual choice, chance, or pious goodwill, but so practice and preach it that the whole church joins in. In their model, Herrington, Bonem, and Furr advise enlisting an intercessory prayer team to pray for the whole process.

Dealing with Conflict

The formula for change runs: God's vision = transformation = conflict. Human resistance is always predicted whenever God's change process is at work. We noted earlier how difficult it is for situational leaders to deal appropriately with conflict, but deal with it they must. Remember how George Barna goes so far as to claim how valuable conflict is. Surprisingly he calls it "the leader's secret weapon," which is to say, "when you strip it all away, leaders do just two things: They create conflict and they resolve conflict."[11]

Perhaps no skill is more complex to learn. It is intimately tied in with leadership aptitudes as outlined in chapter 4 (see fig. 3). Barna makes interesting generalizations about how each is likely to deal with conflict. Directing leaders will probably force confrontation beyond people's comfort zones, sometimes even enjoying its intensity and energy. Strategic leaders more frequently view conflict dispassionately because their "primary interest is in testing different possibilities, observing the results, and drawing conclusions."[12] In contrast, team-building leaders feel others' pain and seek to deal with conflict by trying to make protagonists see how much they are damaging others and spoiling the common vision. Operational leaders dislike conflict and try to resolve it in a businesslike manner that sometimes may not deal with the root of the problem.

Preacher/leaders need to spend time reading and practicing strategies for managing conflict, working through their own strengths and weaknesses. Among helpful books is Speed B. Leas's advice for leaders to identify and learn about their preferred style(s) from six options: persuading, compelling, avoiding (by several stratagems), collaborating, negotiating, or supporting.[13] The preacher/leader has prime responsibility to preach about conflict and lead God's people to grow through it.

Every Sermon Matters

Scripture discloses truth in practical ways about who God is, what he is saying and doing, and who we are meant to be. It therefore acts as the single most powerful source of transformation, making for "creative tension" in abundance.

Instead of preaching thin-bloodedly, which drains out creative tension and offers generalities to individuals, preacher/leaders must open Scripture expecting to feel the shock of its dynamic, which continuously generates and sustains creative tension—*beginning with them*. This Word will not return to God void (Isa. 55:11). Here, this leadership skill adds an extra dimension to sermon preparation. Alongside traditional skills required for exegesis and interpretation, such as study, listening, imagination, language, performance, and team building,[14] it demands that preachers generate and sustain creative tension in-line with the text's dynamic. Sermons should intentionally say and *do* what the text says and *does* in order to lead congregations.

For 360-degree leading this means preachers immerse themselves in the text, living in its creative tension as God works through them and their hearers. This resonates with homiletical advice that urges preachers to find the "trouble" in the text. For example, Eugene Lowry counsels preachers to read the text out loud.

> Right now we are trying to be impacted by the *whole*. . . . Our present need is to be accosted, confronted. Does this mean that all we can do is wait quietly and prayerfully for the Word to drop by? I think not. There is something we can *do* . . . [to] assist the possibility of our being confronted. *We can look for trouble*. What is there about the text that does not seem to fit? . . . *Trouble* in, around, with, and about the text is often the occasion for a fresh hearing.[15]

In his *Four Pages of the Sermon*, Paul Scott Wilson calls for preachers to look for trouble and conflict in the Bible and relate it to their contemporary situation; then find grace in the text and identify where God is at work today. For him trouble is theological. "In any biblical passage, something is wrong in human affairs because then, as now, sin is present. . . . No matter how positive a text may seem at first, trouble is present and waiting to be discerned."[16] Looking for trouble connects with identifying creative tension within the text.

At this point, much also can be learned from African American emphasis on communal, holistic, socially aware, and celebratory preaching. As noted earlier, E. K. Bailey and Warren Wiersbe analyze some of the differences between black and white preaching. Wiersbe confesses that white preaching too often keeps an individualistic focus rather than seeing the text's community implications. In contrast, black preaching often acts on the text's transformational power to effect behavioral change in community. Preachers should always be alert to ways that God provokes tension and trouble in the text as well as to how to celebrate God's grace which ultimately wins through.

So every sermon matters. For individual sermons, creating tension belongs among the tasks of exegesis and interpretation, design and delivery. Of course, thin-blooded preaching shrinks from creating tension. It takes, for example, Luke 4:42–5:11 and sees its rich material on subjects such as the importance of prayer or Jesus's mandate for mission and preaches generic content that leads no one anywhere. But full-blooded preaching dares to immerse people in the story's rhythm as Jesus leads Simon and all successive disciples. It exposes hearers to the Lord who continually calls *us* to "put out into deep water," racking up tension as the metaphor of "deep water" speaks of risk and opportunity. Preacher/leaders must replicate something of the text's urgent dynamic. It tells out God's creative pull of grace that ever seeks to move us forward, obediently taking risks to seek God happenings.

Importantly, sermon series should also have cumulative impact on community life by God's grace. Sequenced sermons offer a vital strategy for congregational transformation. Over the last twelve months I have interviewed several preachers about sermon series that have led their churches in areas such as: finding God's vision, sustaining church life, dealing with conflict, and bringing healing. Some of these stories will be told to illustrate the change process in chapter 8.

By the power of the Holy Spirit who alone transforms people and communities, preacher/leaders therefore have major responsibility in every sermon to generate and sustain creative tension between present reality and God's future promises.

In summary, *every preacher/leader should—*

- have a clear picture of current reality and preach realistically
- write down a vision for their preaching
- discern, describe, and preach a shared vision
- preach about prayer to direct congregational involvement
- preach about conflict and lead God's people to grow through it
- always preach to generate and sustain creative tension because they have engaged with the tension God has put in the biblical text

2. Harnessing the Power of Mental Models

This second learning discipline challenges mindsets to think in "models." "*Mental models* are the images, assumptions, and stories we use to interpret our world and guide our actions."[17] They simplify complex ideas and dynamics in order to capture people's imagination and spur action. Of course, such models are part of everyday life, as with "cold fronts" on a weather map or "grids" for a city's traffic system. Actually, this book's figures have already visualized models, such as the missional church (see fig. 1), and the congregational transformation model (see fig. 4).

Christian leaders can use mental models to help people understand who they are and how differently they might look as they fulfill God's vision. Such models give shape to the "pictures" that the first learning discipline holds in creative tension, between present and future. Sharpening both reality and vision, they can greatly influence how people make decisions.

Preacher/leaders need to learn how to think with mental models. Inevitably, trying to describe any community to which you belong is fraught with difficulty. Careful discernment is needed, since everyone carries assumptions based on past experiences (good and bad) and present beliefs (true and false). Leaders need mature self-disclosure, daring to examine their own strengths and weaknesses, in order to gain clear mental models of the churches to which they belong.

> The challenge of mental models may be the most significant for Christian pastors. Many have learned in seminary to avoid self-disclosure at all costs. Others have engaged in self-disclosure and had it used against them in unscrupulous ways. Still others enjoy the posture of sitting on a pedestal that far too many church members are willing to encourage.[18]

Thinking through mental models requires developing qualities such as: *empathetic listening* with genuine willingness to listen to others, especially those who seem unsympathetic; *critical thinking* to pare away comfortable assumptions and deal rigorously with hard questions; and *transformational planning* to venture into new ways rather than repeat old patterns. Preacher/leaders must never skimp on developing these qualities through reading and practice.

So, "mental models" can serve to challenge how preacher/leaders think in many ways, as will be seen in some examples below. They can describe a local church's life and character recognizably to its members; they can explain a contemporary culture shift to help people better understand its implications; and they can express vision of how a transformed church might look and work.

To help people understand local church communities better, Aubrey Malphurs offers an overview of six mental models found in American evangelical churches: classroom, soul-winning, social-conscience, experiential, family-reunion, and life-development churches (see fig. 5). The "classroom church," for example, has *information* as its unifying value, the roles of pastor as *teacher* and people as *students*, and its key emphasis *to know*. Its source of legitimacy is *expository preaching*. In contrast, the "life-development church," with its unifying value of

Type of Church	Unifying Value	Role of Pastor	Role of People	Key Emphasis	Typical Tool	Desired Result	Source of Legitimacy	Positive Trait
The Classroom Church	Information	Teacher	Student	To know	Sermon outline	Educated Christian	Expository preaching	Knowledge of Bible
The Soul-Winning Church	Evangelism	Evangelist	Bringer	To save	Altar call	Born-again people	Numbers	Heart for lost
The Social-Conscience Church	Justice	Reformer	Recruiter	To care	Petition	Activist	Cause	Compassion for Oppressed
The Experiential Church	Experience	Performer	Audience	To feel	Handheld mike	Empowered Christian	Spirit	Vitality
The Family-Reunion Church	Loyalty	Chaplain	Siblings	To belong	Potluck	Secure Christian	Roots	Identity
The Life-Development Church	Character	Coach	Ministry	To be	Ephesians 4	Disciple	Changed lives	Growth

Fig. 5. Models of American Evangelical Churches. Taken and adapted from Aubrey Malphurs, *Values-Driven Leadership* © 1996. Reprinted with permission of Baker Books, a division of Baker Publishing Group.

character and roles of pastor and people as *coach* and *ministry*, has as its key emphasis *to be* with its source of legitimacy being found in *changed lives*. Models like this imaginatively visualize present reality and also picture what transformation might mean: "Why yes, we are a classroom church! Is God calling us to be a life-development church?"

Using mental models differently, Herrington, Bonem, and Furr describe complex shifts in culture by contrasting two columns of characteristics. One side describes the "stable institution and context" and the other the "rapidly changing mission field."[19] Older stability is characterized by slow, predictable change; shared values in church and community; pastor as manager; homogeneous target audience; stable strategy; and programs from denominations with a standardization of approaches. In contrast, newer variability is characterized by rapid, discontinuous change; divergent values between church and community; pastor as leader; diverse target audience; continuous adjustments to strategy at a local level; and programs from many different organizations with a customization of approaches.[20] Many churches find themselves in painful transition between these two columns, discovering that old ways do not work and threatened by what might happen next. *ChurchNext*, to use Eddie Gibbs's expression, fills them with dread, but grasping a mental model about change is an important step along the process of transformation.

The last example uses a mental model to envisage how a future church might look, fleshing out God's preferred vision for a particular people in a specific place. Here impatience and presumption are ever-present dangers, for it is especially tempting to identify another model in a successful neighboring church (perhaps included in the Malphurs chart) that leaders then force-feed upon a likely reluctant and frightened congregation. Human desire for success that enforces change by its own strength, albeit in God's name, is doomed to failure. Cutting short the lengthy spiritual process of praying, listening, and thinking through future plans means undeveloped spiritual resources that will fail to cope with conflict in life-giving ways as the community becomes entangled in destructive power plays. Rushing to conclusions rarely brings glory to God.

Always remember when thinking future "models" that churches are not human institutions restricted to human expectations, resourced only by secular leadership principles. Churches belong to God, who gives them preacher/leaders with supreme responsibility to lead their people in discerning and obeying God's will for them. Church futures cannot be cloned. Each community has God's gifting and promise to fulfill specific tasks where it is.

A Flashback

Recall how Jesus modeled preaching/leading in Luke 4:42–5:11. First, he made prayer his priority. Prayer ensures not only dependency on God's power to discern his purposes, but also increases capacity for self-disclosure. As Herrington, Bonem, and Furr comment:

> Studying the Bible and its teaching regarding the nature of God, humanity, and the world is one of the best places to begin. The spiritual disciplines of solitude, meditation, and prayer allow the individual to reflect deeply on the issues of identity.[21]

Prayer forms the primary strategy by which preacher/leaders listen to God's Word and have the courage to discern appropriate "mental models." Authenticity, honesty, and transparency in a preacher/leader's thinking all depend on quality prayer with open Scripture.

Second, by placing "kingdom" central to his message and life, Jesus gives preacher/leaders the principal "mental model" for the future. Jesus breathtakingly generates tension for disciples who thereafter always have to look beyond the present to see his new ways of living. God's kingdom stretches human living into extraordinary possibilities, speaking of God's power breaking into the "now," though "not yet" anticipates its future consummation. By this one expression more than any other, Jesus inspiringly sums up the complex, corporate reality of a new people living for deeper purposes and in greater ways of living. At one stroke "kingdom" magnificently demonstrates the thinking of transformational leadership. And, most importantly, at the same time it remains mysteriously on God's terms. No one should equate it with human programs or local church life. God's kingdom raises the theological and spiritual tempo to create tension as nothing else can.

Writes the British leadership guru John Adair:

> Jesus is a visionary *sans pareil*. His vision was expressed . . . as the *Kingdom of God*. . . . Our general knowledge of leadership now illuminates much of what Jesus does. He communicates the vision and he lives it; he sets a task for himself, calls others, teaches them the leadership appropriate to the Kingdom and he leads them, from in front. He shares their dangers and hardships, and ultimately he gives his life, literally, in the common cause.[22]

Third, Jesus initiates action. As mentioned earlier, his command "put out into deep water, and let down your nets" (Luke 5:4) challenges disciples to act on a new "mental model." Simon will never think the same way about Jesus and his mission. Jesus continually draws disciples forward to new ways of seeing him in order to pursue his mission afresh. Jesus specializes in change dynamics for preacher/leaders and their communities so that they change with him.

Every Sermon Matters

Preacher/leaders must learn how to express a clear picture of current reality so hearers recognize what their community is like. Mental models help people see themselves more as God sees them! But, most importantly, preacher/leaders must learn how to preach powerfully about God's biggest picture—by emphasizing his kingdom.

Tragically, much contemporary preaching lacks any kingdom emphasis. Vic Gordon comments that in spite of scholarly consensus that the kingdom of God formed the main theme of Jesus's preaching and teaching,

> most Christians I run into do not know this! I have asked several thousand Christians in teaching settings in churches all over the United States, "What was the primary subject of Jesus's preaching and teaching?" I am sad to say that I can count on two hands (or maybe even one!) the number who knew. A good number of those who did not know were pastors.[23]

Not only does this silence on the kingdom savage the integrity of Jesus's ministry, it anesthetizes the challenge of preaching/leading by omitting Jesus's greatest "mental model" for transformation. It ruinously thins out preaching's blood.

Preaching the kingdom of God remains the greatest challenge for preacher/leaders. It creates the greatest tension in the New Testament. Preaching the kingdom of God knocks down familiar boundaries and stretches people's thinking. It means big sermons full of creative tension—not just good news to share but a horizon to move towards. You cannot preach kingdom individualistically, cerebrally, or in cowardly fashion. It embraces church, yes, but much more besides as God's reign breaks through barriers of time, space, race, gender, and culture with justice and mercy. It sees God's biggest purposes in a new heaven and a new earth. I recall one respected preacher visiting our seminary when I was a student. "I always preach at least one sermon a year that my people will not understand," he said. Of course many of us may unwittingly do that. But we understood what he meant. He believed in stretching and disturbing hearers for God's sake. Eschatology widens horizons. Hearers can never snuggle comfortably into the status quo when the kingdom of God is proclaimed.

"Mental models" challenge full-blooded preachers to work consistently within Scripture's big picture so the transforming Lord himself leads congregations into appropriate fresh risks in today's time of rapid, discontinuous change. The growing literature about the "missional church" challenges churches to "be in the world as a transforming presence." One of its characteristics, noted earlier, is the "recognition that the church itself is an incomplete expression of the reign of God." Yes, God's kingdom picture for our future is large, full of mystery and promise, yet only by preaching it courageously will people be led into the profoundest places of transformation. Kingdom preaching offers no short-term face-lifts by sensational makeovers. God's future is long-term with qualities that are grown like fruit by the Spirit when preachers and hearers willingly push out into deeper places with God.

So, preacher/leaders have strategic responsibility to assess the mental models that people hold, to evaluate them in the light of current reality, and to help people see God's kingdom implications. Pushing out into deeper waters for the mission of Jesus Christ they refuse to stay in the comfort zone.

To develop the skill of harnessing the power of mental models, *every preacher/leader should*—

- have a clear picture of current reality and preach realistically
- be able to help people understand changing times
- be willing to envisage vision
- powerfully preach the kingdom of God

3. Enabling Team Learning

This third skill concerns a leader's working relationships with others. Though it is a truism that teams are essential for successful leadership, this skill recognizes that teams can produce results that lie far beyond the sole capabilities of the individuals involved and the leader. When J. Robert Oppenheimer successfully created the team of twenty-five hundred scientists who developed the atomic bomb for the Manhattan Project, he was not among the most technically able members of the team. But he knew how to build a team.

Earlier we reflected on how even in the calling of his disciples recorded in Luke 4:44–5:11, Jesus's preaching/leading involves team building. Luke's description places Jesus himself in Simon's boat. But as Simon threw nets into deep water, the overwhelming response required others' assistance: "they signaled to their partners in the other boat to come and help them" (Luke 5:7). Jesus encourages disciples to need each other, to bond together, to belong in a tighter group of three (Luke 9:28), to be sent out in twos (Luke 10), and at every turn to practice team learning.

Teams are often contrasted with committees (though sometimes unfairly, since I have known some committees to work well as teams). While teams have individuals dialoguing to own a common outcome, committees comprise individuals discussing different points of view. Teams encourage group learning with openness to other ideas and a collective willingness to see things differently, but committees allow for maximum individualism, lobbying points of view by persuasion. Teams require close interpersonal relationships to collaborate with honesty and authenticity, but committees work through agendas and argue points. Teams grow as colleagues treat others as equals and exercise the disciplines of dialogue.

Out of his church experience, Michael Slaughter contrasts a team that *dreams*, *develops*, and *deploys* the necessary steps for action together with a typical church committee that meets together once a week or month to *evaluate*, *approve*, and *delegate*. "It is more than the organization of individual pieces. The team travels together through the entire journey. The team also evaluates and 'owns' its own results."[24] However, such groups that dream together are extraordinarily difficult to form, requiring much time, patience, and considerable skill.

Teams form effectively when leaders help people grow past misconceptions, through personality conflicts, and beyond different perceptions so they can focus on new purposes together. Then, instead of defensiveness, dialogue emerges. Indeed, dialogue, defined as the sharing of honest views with mutual listening to form team consensus, also leads to breakthroughs when teams discover fresh understanding. Rather than individuals winning arguments by force of personality or their place in a hierarchy, team members seek to be accountable to each other.

Much team behavior therefore flies in the face of normal human conduct. For dialogue to work, the whole group must agree to practical guidelines and ground rules about its behavior and practice. For example, *performance standards* set up hoped-for outcomes and their time frame. Herrington, Bonem, and Furr warn:

> Establishing performance standards is almost a universal weakness of congregations. Most have chosen to measure only a few basic statistics, such as attendance and finances. . . . Congregations that identify a shared vision and then establish corresponding standards create a dynamic for learning that is potent.[25]

Because of their limited size and commitment, teams have particular advantages in establishing anticipated outcomes and working towards them.

Every Sermon Matters

Perhaps, at first sight, team learning seems the least relevant skill for preacher/leaders. After all, many preachers treat sermons as personal endeavors involving others only as quiescent pew fodder.

Sadly, many pastors have a poor track record with teams. The survey referenced earlier found that 71 percent of the pastors regarded themselves as team players, but only 48 percent of their congregants agreed. Many pastors seem to think teams are overrated and not worth the trouble. Moreover they think that accountability is an overdone concept. We noted how thin-blooded preaching is allergic to team learning, preferring to delve into books and concepts rather than listen to people, who demand time and effort and may strongly disagree. Such preaching deals with "the body of Christ" (1 Corinthians 12) theoretically, managing to avoid costly cut-and-thrust dynamics of people actually working together. Importantly, it misses the power whereby the Holy Spirit enables a prayerful community to discern with "the mind of Christ" (1 Cor. 2:16).

Preacher/leaders must develop team-learning skills to be effective. First, they must play a significant role in the church's key leadership team(s). Their behavior must demonstrate openness to dialogue and accountability under the Holy Spirit. They must answer critical questions such as: How can a group guarantee the importance of each voice to prevent any one person dominating—especially if the preacher is involved? Will preachers willingly learn how to listen properly and respond honestly when others in the group challenge and disagree with them? How can "authority figures" learn the value of openness to different points of view for the sake of something better emerging?

Second, and vitally, preacher/leaders should perceive how every occasion of sharing group dialogue might impact the next sermon in some way. They fully appreciate that their preaching role belongs within the rest of the church's structures, and their sermons relate to all that church leaders are working through. Preaching has a responsibility to sharpen every meaningful aspect of church life. Timothy Peck questions preachers: "Are church leaders twisting your arm to support their ministries from the pulpit?"[26] He recommends that preachers become proactive about which particular aspects of church life need pulpit leadership. Mission priorities, use of premises, strategies of stewardship, development of small groups, and working through worship issues—all these and more are the raw material of sermon application. Preacher/leaders must overcome the divide between sacred and secular to ensure that God's Word addresses the whole of their communities rather than echoes around some pious compartment.

Third, preacher/leaders need to develop team thinking in their preaching role. Some preachers have developed teams formally to aid sermon preparation and evaluation. Earlier I noted John McClure's "roundtable pulpit"[27] where leadership and preaching meet. He commends a process, developed through practical experience, in which groups of ten people meet with him once a week for one and a half hours for a time of feedback/feedforward (ten minutes), engaging the biblical text (twenty minutes), and engaging one another (sixty minutes). Each group operates for a set period of a few months and is succeeded by another group. Over several years a considerable number of the congregation therefore take part in roundtable preaching, learning to bring their insights into sermon preparation and ensuring their collaboration on the final outcome. For McClure this encourages participatory leadership.

Less formally, I have regularly collaborated with other leaders and members of the congregation in planning worship (which includes preaching). For example, a group of leaders helped me develop a celebration service to mark the third anniversary of small groups within the church. Calling the service "20/20 Vision," based on Acts 20:20, their invaluable insights and energy enriched everything about the outcomes. One person wrote a drama entitled: "Bind Us Together, Lord" based on 1 Peter 1, others organized special music, but very significantly their insights about what home groups meant to them and their vision greatly shaped the sermon. Reflecting on some New Testament references to groups in homes such as Colossians 4:15, Philemon 2, 1 Corinthians 16:19, they raised issues that emerged in my preaching:

> These weren't cucumber sandwiches and "Do you like milk in your tea?" meetings. They were learners, debaters, devoted to teaching. A bishop once said: "I wonder why it is that everywhere the apostle Paul went they had a revolution and everywhere I go they serve a cup of tea?" These were men and women who wanted to grow. Frankly, the least effective way you could learn and grow by teaching is for one person to go up to the front, having spent hours in his study, to give a burst of 20 minutes or so, and expect people to learn. It's only in the home that teaching, responding, growing can take place. Where else can you talk about how perplexed and bewildered you are about life and what God has to say to us?[28]

Most strategically, the whole act of worship resulted in many practical commitments and recommitments to the church's small group ministry. In *360-Degree Preaching* I emphasize how the discipline of listening to others is essential for preachers as part of interpreting God's Word for their communities.[29] This is no less true for preacher/leaders.

To develop the skills of team learning, *every preacher/leader should—*

- personally commit to team learning in church life
- discern connections throughout church life with the next sermons
- develop team thinking in their preaching role

4. Practicing Systems Thinking

This last skill concerns the leader's approach towards the whole organization. In the past, leadership studies often specialized in analytical methods that took organizations apart to study different aspects separately. That way unprofitable parts could be axed and productive parts could be resourced. However, leadership studies today advocate *systems thinking*, a holistic approach that treats all the different parts with their complex interactions as belonging together. Each part influences others. Alastair Mant memorably contrasts these two approaches as the bicycle and frog methods.

> Intelligent leaders understand that complex systems are more like frogs than like bikes. You can disassemble a bicycle completely, clean and oil all the separate parts, and reassemble it confident that it will work as before. Frogs are different. The moment you remove any part, *all* the rest of the system is affected instantly, in unpredictable ways for the *worse*. . . . quite a few management consultants really do think that complex organizational systems will respond to the bicycle treatment. They think you can get a realistic picture of the total *system* by simply aggregating its *component* parts. They are not wicked, just dim.[30]

Nobody who takes the New Testament seriously can be dim about complex systems when its primary congregational model is the body of Christ (1 Cor. 12:21–26; Rom. 12:4–5). Not only do all its parts belong together in mutual need, but its unity is found in Christ who is its Head. Organizationally, Christ's body the church is both human and divine. Herrington, Bonem, and Furr claim that

> Christian congregations are the most complicated human organizations that exist. Their mix of the human and the divine, a heritage measured in centuries, and variations in size, context, beliefs, values, and practices make them extraordinarily intricate.[31]

They suggest that an appropriate analogy for a church leader is a physician. It is even more apposite to think of a naturopathic physician whose holistic approach towards healing and wellness seeks to understand how the human body works as a complex whole. Rather than assuming a "pills and scalpel" approach that is sadly typical of so many physicians trained in Western conventional medicine, the naturopathic physician considers the many delicate interactions by which the health or disease of one part impacts the whole body. So too preacher/leaders need to develop holistic understanding of how a congregation's body life functions.

Much of the language of systems thinking is complex and can receive only brief attention here. Within systems of organization, several levels react and interact to change in complex ways, and skill is required to understand how these different levels behave together. Congregations are peculiarly *open systems* because they are open to God with everything affecting every other aspect within them. Beginning with the surface issues, the system becomes increasingly complicated the deeper you look. On the surface and easily discernible are *events* in the congregation's activities and routines; more deeply, *trends* reflect directions taken by a congregation or parts of it that are only detected over time; deeper still, *structure* concerns the pattern of relationships at the congregation's heart, best summed up in the saying "It's just the way we do things around here." Such structure functions below the group's conscious awareness. However, at the deepest level, beneath structure, are *mental models*, which are the ways a congregation understands the nature of the gospel, its mission, its neighborhood, and issues involved in its decision making. We have already encountered this concept, and it forms the core of an organization's working system.[32]

Harnessing systems thinking means deliberate engagement with the complicated relationships between these levels. For example, a change that is easily made at the level of *event* may scarcely affect a congregation's *trend*, let alone impact deeper levels of *structure* and *mental models*. A leader might imagine that much more has been achieved than is the case! But this example is a simple one compared with many other options that can emerge from the potent mix of history, personality, sin, and grace. It lies beyond this chapter's scope to delve deeper into the complicated subsystems of congregational body life. However, some aspects will surface in the next two chapters as I describe the role of spiritual and relational vitality along with the place of mission and vision within the change process.

Every Sermon Matters

Like physicians, preacher/leaders must be aware how the health or disease of one part can impact the whole of church life. All preaching application needs to be thought through holistically to ensure health rather than harm to the congregation's body life.

Jim Nicodem, quoted earlier, names *diagnosing* a key task of preaching/leading. He says: "Like a physician the preacher needs to identify issues affecting the health of the church and to address them." For example, a church can have a group with a critical spirit, which undermines everybody's health. Preaching from the book of Nehemiah to see how Nehemiah works through issues of dealing with a critical spirit enables the preacher to deal directly with the community's Christian quality of life. As Nicodem puts it, "Not a bully pulpit but applying preaching to practical things that face people." Preacher/leaders have the vital spiritual task of directing God's Word deeper than events and trends into structures and mental models for the sake of the body of Christ.

Christian systems remain open to the greatest power of all—God may choose to work with any particular group of people, anytime. In Luke 5 the huge catch of fish overwhelms expectations and brings Simon to his knees and to his Isaiah 6 moment: "Go away from me, Lord, for I am a sinful man!" (Luke 5:8). This testifies to the ultimately impossible-to-manipulate outcome that only God can deliver to preacher/leaders. In Luke 5 God brings it all together—the pushing out into deep water, the spectacular catch of fish, the breakthrough of holiness, and the call to discipleship. Encountering God remains central to genuine spiritual transformation. Spiritual outcomes of preaching/leading depend utterly on God's grace and he promises believers who meet in his name that he will do new things when together they risk trusting in his will.

To develop the skill of systems thinking, *every preacher/leader should—*

- seek to understand how congregations work as complex systems
- diagnose health and disease with spiritual sensitivity
- be open to God's in-breaking power to transform

Unshackled from Thin-Blooded Preaching

When preachers build these learning disciplines into their vocations, they break free from thin-blooded stuff that teaches individuals generic truths without expecting anything in particular to happen. *Generating and sustaining creative tension* brings urgency into sermon preparation and content. *Harnessing the power of mental models* confronts individualism and limited human plans by focusing on the kingdom of God. *Team learning* puts into practice attempts at actually working together as members of the body of Christ. *Systems learning* dares to think through the holistic repercussions of God developing his mission through the church. These disciplines profoundly impact the ways that sermons are prepared and delivered, all relationships a preacher has with other leaders, and the influence of preaching upon the body of believers for the sake of the surrounding community.

7

Growing Character

Remember your leaders, who spoke the word of God to you; consider the outcome of their way of life, and imitate their faith. Jesus Christ is the same yesterday and today and forever.

Hebrews 13:7–8

Rudolph Giuliani, mayor of New York during the attacks of September 11, 2001, considers the two key lessons of leadership "involve the seeing of things with your own eyes and of setting an example."[1] He illustrated this by his response to a fire that broke out at St. Agnes Church in New York in 1992. As a lawyer walking to his office, he noticed smoke pouring out of this historic church. Dashing into the buildings, he ordered everyone out to await the fire brigade, first running up the four floors of the rectory and then entering the burning church to confront some looters. Only later, on returning to his office, did he realize the state of his camel coat. "It was completely black and covered in soot. I later sent that coat to be cleaned but it came back shrunken. To this day, I refuse to part with it. For the events of that afternoon, the Fire Department gave me a medal and I treasure that medal along with my coat as reminders of the St. Agnes fire."[2] Such experiences helped prepare him for leadership.

Personal character lies at the heart of leadership—"the seeing of things with your own eyes and of setting an example." Interestingly, the comedic observer of failed leadership Ricky Gervais says, "Lack of dignity is the biggest failure in leadership. That and vanity. They'll always destroy you in the end."[3] In his seminal systematic and philosophical treatment of persuasive oratory titled *Rhetoric*, Aristotle (384–322 BC) asks the question, "What kind of proof is necessary to convince a listener of truth?" His three answers have stood the test of time. *Logos*, reason, or content convinces hearers' minds; *pathos*, emotion, connects with feelings; *ethos*, ethics, persuades by the speaker's integrity. Aristotle "established personal integrity as the primary proof by which an audience recognizes the authenticity of a public speaker."[4]

Genuine biblical preaching requires a foundational relationship with God, with integrity of thought and behavior manifesting qualities such as authenticity, vulnerability, courage, maturity, and listening to others expressed in genuine relationships.[5] But preachers as leaders find even more is at stake because their ethos, as God's called people, profoundly impacts their communities.

Since it is true that within seconds of any leader's first appearance most people have made up their minds about his or her trustworthiness, how much more significant is a preacher's character?

> Ethos is commonly assessed through what listeners know of the preacher's moral, intellectual, spiritual, emotional, and personal habits, largely through what is learned or signaled of these in the sermon itself.[6]

Bluntly, godly leadership cannot happen without godly ethos. Godly preaching/leading needs godly leader/preachers. Sometimes we speak of the ethos of a church community to describe how it works and feels. I recall early pieces of seminary advice such as: "Young people, be very careful in ministry. Over time your local church tends to grow like you." "No member of your congregation can go to spiritually deeper places than you. Shallow pastors build shallow churches." While such statements oversimplify relationships (for as we have seen, congregational systems are complex mixtures of human and divine), they also contain some truth. Communities *do* tend to grow like their leaders. Contemporary rhetoric similarly speaks of *identity*—a positive identity with the speaker that gives authority.

As preachers immerse in Scripture and walk by the Spirit, they break out of thin-blooded information-giving into full-blooded *ethos-giving*, by

God's grace. A preacher's whole life should lead others. Preachers are called to be ambassadors for Christ, representing Christ not only by their words but also by their presence (2 Cor. 5:18). In Luther's memorable phrase, they become "little Christs." Preaching Jesus means not only preaching about Jesus but also preaching with and for Jesus.

No other form of communication has influence like God-empowered preaching through a godly preacher. Older books emphasized these heady claims. Phillips Brooks for example:

> Truth through Personality is our description of true preaching. The truth must come really through the person, not merely over his lips, nor merely into his understanding. . . . It must come through his character, affections, his whole intellectual and moral being.

He contrasts two kinds of preachers. In one the gospel comes *over* the preacher and "reaches us tinged and flavored with his superficial characteristics, belittled with his littleness." But in the other the gospel comes *through* the preacher and "we receive it impressed and winged with all that earnestness and strength that there is in him."[7] Preacher/leaders are not about littlenesses but about God's transformation—they believe it, experience it, demonstrate it, and preach it indefatigably for their church communities.

Spiritual and Relational Vitality

The transformational model's second part directly relates to the preacher/leader's character. Spiritual and relational vitality is defined as "the life-giving power that faithful people experience together as they passionately pursue God's vision for their lives."[8]

Herrington, Bonem, and Furr describe the stages of spiritual and relational vitality that emerged from fieldwork in one hundred churches, a fourfold process "built on the fundamental assumption that God's people must live as an authentic New Testament community like the one described in Acts 2:42–47."[9] Four aspects have a clockwise dynamic: *encountering God's holiness, experiencing God's grace, embracing unity*, and *engaging community*. (Intriguingly, my 360-degree model for preaching/leading [see fig. 2] also expresses a clockwise dynamic of God empowering the preaching, hearing, and living of preacher and hearers.)

Its clockwise movement depicts spiritual encounter with God's holiness, moving through an experience of grace towards unity and community. But arrows between each element emphasize how, in returning

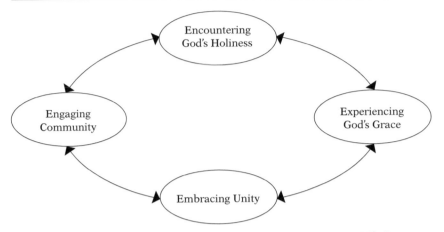

Fig. 6. Elements of Spiritual and Relational Vitality. Taken from Jim Herrington, Mike Bonem, and James H. Furr, *Leading Congregational Change* © 2000. Reprinted with permission of John Wiley & Sons, Inc.

direction, "God's presence in the gathered community leads to a spirit of shared unity, saving grace, and hunger for God."[10] Its spiritual dynamic pushes beyond individual salvation to issues of reconciliation, striving for unity, and building of community.

For preacher/leaders these four elements of spiritual and relational vitality raise very significant ethos issues in two ways. First, they raise personal questions for anyone who would lead through these stages. Second, each stage itself has expectations of the content of practice and preaching.

Personal Ethos Questions

The last chapter warned that the absence of leadership skills reduces preaching to thin-blooded stuff. Likewise, unless preacher/leaders commit to all these elements of spiritual and relational vitality they will fail the ethos test of full-blooded preaching. Certain questions must be answered positively. I couch them in the first person because that is how I have wrestled with them.

Am I willing to preach beyond stage 2, pressing towards unity and community?

The first two elements of encountering God's holiness and experiencing God's grace are foundational, but preaching that is limited to them can so stress the personal dimensions of one's faith-response to God that it severely downplays the vital corporate responsibilities. Amputating love for God from love for neighbor severs Christ's double commandment (Matt. 22:37–40). Playing safe with individualistic truth avoids the hard issues of forgiveness, reconciliation, and community among God's people. Staying at stages 1 and 2 is understandable because it reduces the likelihood of resistance and conflict. But it is cowardly to leave God's corporate demands about embracing unity and engaging community unpreached.

Those who are willing to preach love for God and neighbor by the whole congregation are thrust into the highest ethics, widest action, and deepest commitment. They must trust in the Holy Spirit's promises of guidance and strength. Boldly opening up more of themselves to God, convicted that what they taste and see of him is real, aware of how far they still have to go in their relationship with others, full-blooded preachers bear personal witness to God's gifts of spiritual and relational vitality through community.

Will I let God lead me?

Leaders must never underestimate how much time and effort they must invest in themselves. Bill Hybels claims this is the toughest leadership challenge of all, quoting Dee Hock: "It is management of self that should occupy 50 percent of our time and the best of our ability. And when we do that the ethical, moral, and spiritual elements of management are inescapable."[11] Some call this process self-management, "self-leading," keeping a "spiritual inventory," or maintaining "spiritual fitness."

> Nobody—I mean nobody—can do this work for us. Every leader has to do this work alone, and it isn't easy. . . . Because it's such tough work most leaders avoid it. We would rather try to inspire or control the behavior of others than face the rigorous work of self-reflection and inner growth.[12]

Rigorous self-leadership questions must be asked regularly such as: Is my calling sure? Is my vision clear? Is my passion hot? Am I developing my gifts? Is my character submitted to Christ? Is my pride subdued? Am I overcoming fear? Are interior issues undermining my leadership? Is my pace sustainable? Is my love for God and people increasing?[13] Honest self-questioning keeps preacher/leaders dependent on God.

Will I seek more spiritual wisdom and courage?

Harry Emerson Fosdick no doubt prayerfully wrote these lines:

> Grant us wisdom,
> Grant us courage
> For the facing of this hour.[14]

What an important combination! First, wisdom. Obviously leadership needs intelligence. Alastair Mant calls his leadership book *Intelligent Leadership*. As someone commented: "It doesn't take a great brain to be a Christian but it takes all the brain you've got." But Christian leaders need to use three kinds of intelligence. IQ (Intelligence Quotient) is complemented by EI (Emotional Intelligence), which rates ability to understand and use emotion with self-awareness, self-control, and empathy in handling relationships. Yet, most important is SW—spiritual wisdom. While the church possesses few intellectual geniuses (1 Cor. 1:26), spiritual wisdom is gifted in believers' relationship with God—"these things God has revealed to us through the Spirit" (1 Cor. 2:10).

While IQ and EI focus on individuals and their abilities, spiritual wisdom paradoxically centers upon Jesus Christ and him crucified. Seemingly absurd to the world, the gospel makes sense only in Christ crucified. IQ and EI are God's gifts by genes and nurture, but spiritual wisdom is a supernatural gift utterly dependent on God, who reveals it by his Spirit—"in words not taught by human wisdom but taught by the Spirit, interpreting spiritual things to those who are spiritual" (1 Cor. 2:13). Sometimes people seem to limit the Holy Spirit to roles such as livening up worship (by increasing the loudness of guitars and drums!). Of course worship does register the quality of aliveness to God, but the most profound evidence of the Holy Spirit is found when ordinary men and women are wise about God. For then the Holy Spirit comes to convict, cleanse, purify, but also to inform and teach as well as guide into all truth.

IQ and EI are individual measures of intelligence—it's *my* IQ; however, spiritual wisdom comes in a corporate relationship—"But we have the mind of Christ" (v. 16). It's *our* SW. Preacher/leaders need to grow in dependence on the Spirit of Christ, who works both within individuals and communities of believers. Otherwise, trying to lead others to experience all four elements of spiritual and relational vitality is impossible.

Courage is essential too. Bill Hybels calls his book *Courageous Leadership*. Leadership has always rated the quality of courage highly because, by definition, leaders are exposed and vulnerable out front. Sometimes courage can be publicly and physically heroic as with Giuliani in this chapter's opening story. However, it also properly refers to daily, less obvious, heroic demands of moral courage, like loving in the face of opposition, or being humble before others' pride.

> Leaders of integrity need courage every day as we face decisions, meetings, and challenges that have the potential for loss and pain. . . . We build our leadership and ministry on dozens and hundreds of daily steps of courage: confronting a halfhearted staffer, speaking our vision, making a commitment, reading a critical letter, evaluating our ministry's process. These are the decisive moments that define a courageous ministry.[15]

Regularly Scripture commands "Fear not. Be not afraid." Preacher/leaders need frequently to preach classic courage texts to themselves, such as Joshua 1:1–9 with its repetitive "Be strong and courageous" that confronts each tense—past, future, and present. Facing the past Joshua is given shock treatment: "My servant Moses is dead" (Josh. 1:2). Courage says no to idealized yesterdays that trap by nostalgia. It avoids needless battles when Christians mistake their own church culture with its worship patterns and programs for God's kingdom reality. This insight is found in secular leadership too. As Margaret Wheatley asserts:

> To be responsible discoverers, we need the courage to let go of the old world, to relinquish most of what we have cherished, to abandon our interpretations about what does and doesn't work.[16]

God's courage also looks *forward* to initiate change. Faith language is future language. "Now proceed to cross the Jordan, you and all this people, into a land that I am giving to them. . . . Every place that the sole of your foot will tread upon I have given to you" (Josh. 1:2–3). Leith Anderson has a workshop exercise that invites people to write down what they consider to be the best year in the life of their church. Inevitably, most people look back to past good times, but much more significant are the few who look ahead to say 2010 or even 2025.

Courage also trusts God in the *present*. Discouragement always weighs disproportionately—one negative tends to overwhelm nine positives, but God's core promises remain gloriously current: "I will be with you; I will not fail you or forsake you" (Josh. 1:5). Daily relationship with God, grounded in Scripture, enables spiritual leaders to stay close (Josh. 1:8).

One of my doctoral students wrote honestly about his dealing with "tough issues":

> It's not so much that I am scared of preaching on them but that I failed to recognize preaching as an incredible God-given opportunity to lead. . . . I tend to be a people-pleaser. Rather than being a transactional leader who

avoids risk and conflict, I am developing the traits of a transformational leader, taking the stance of one who is giving life-changing leadership.

When preacher/leaders say yes to these three questions, then leading congregations to spiritual and relational vitality becomes possible.

Practicing and Preaching the Four Elements

Mahatma Gandhi reputedly said, "An ounce of practice is worth more than tons of preaching." Nothing exposes the ounces of a preacher's practice more than leading a congregation towards deeper spiritual and relational vitality through each of its four elements. This is the pulsing heart of Christian leading. As the old challenge asks: Is your public spirituality an overflow or a cover-up? Do God-qualities pervade "all of our attitudes and our actions . . ."? Are they "simultaneously routine and revolutionary"?[17] Preacher/leaders must speak of what they know and do.

1. Encountering God's Holiness

In Luke 5:8–9 Simon's relationship with Jesus dramatically deepened from showing respect, admiration, and obedience to being completely overwhelmed by Jesus's presence: "Master, leave. I'm a sinner and can't handle this holiness. Leave me to myself" (Message).

Transformational leadership begins when leaders recognize their littleness and sinfulness before God's holiness. Here Christian leadership departs radically from secular leadership principles. "Effective change leaders consistently serve as catalysts to help people encounter the holiness of God."[18] Godly leadership cannot happen without godly ethos and that means personal holiness.

Secular leadership in the wake of scandals with Enron, WorldCom, and Martha Stewart has renewed emphasis on ethics in business dealings. Integrity means not cheating and cooking books! But Christian leaders are called not just to honesty but also to holiness. Holiness is God's distinctive quality, utterly separating him from the world by his moral purity. While Old Testament holiness regulations strictly safeguarded God's holiness (remember Uzziah's fate in 2 Samuel 6:7?), the New Testament good news claims "by God's will . . . we have been sanctified through the offering of the body of Jesus Christ once for all" (Heb. 10:10). The church is called to be "saints," literally "holy ones" (1 Cor. 1:2). Once unable to bear Jesus's holiness, Simon Peter, moved by the Holy Spirit, commands: "As he who called you is holy, be holy yourselves in all your conduct; for it is written: 'You shall be holy, for I am holy'" (1 Peter 1:15–16).

Preacher/leaders need to grow in personal worship packed with heartfelt adoration, be broken in humble confession, and be openly pure in spirit. Glimpsing something of God's overwhelming transcendence and gracious immanence, they encounter his holiness. In class recently, one of my students said, "We need more *mysterium tremendum*" and everyone applauded. When preachers take God's holiness seriously, opening up minds and hearts for God's Spirit to move, rebuke, expose, and heal *them*, then new levels of spiritual leadership are possible. "If the leaders of the congregation are not spending significant, consistent time seeking God's direction—through prayer, Bible study, meditation, solitude, and fasting—it will be impossible for meaningful and lasting transformation to occur."[19] Nothing sabotages spiritual leadership more savagely than missing personal worship.

Out of such personal conviction and experience, preacher/leaders are charged to lead public worship, becoming catalysts for the congregation's spiritual and relational vitality. Sometimes preacher/leaders may not be technically responsible for worship details, since many churches appoint "worship leaders." But it is of first importance to remember that worship itself *leads* congregational transformation. How a people see and respond to God in their worship together graphically expresses any church's purpose. When people worship with awe, obedience, confession, trust, generosity, and celebration, it inspires and directs everything else that they do. Only then will they be an awe-inspired, obedient, confessing, trusting, generous, celebrating people on fire for God. Preacher/leaders have critical influence as by their own ethos they share responsibility for worship's quality.

No matter who organizes the details of worship services, preacher/leaders must bring skills of initiating and sustaining transformation right into the center of structuring purposeful corporate worship. Preaching belongs with every other aspect of public worship that is central to a congregation's authentic spiritual relationships. Preacher/leaders must not cede responsibility on this key issue, for nothing should receive more care, skill, and devotion than planning intentional worship in order that people encounter more of God. No other plans and programs, however well-meaning, must be allowed to drain energy away from the priority of worship. Herrington, Bonem, and Furr warn:

> Far too often, congregations assume that they are prepared to deal with the things of God. This can result in making plans and asking God to bless them. . . . When worship is at the heart of planning, we are more likely to focus on aligning all of our lives—individually and corporately—with the ongoing activity of God among us.[20]

Others have commented on this danger in today's church. Art Azurdia, for example, argues that "the greatest impediment to the advancement of the gospel in our time is the attempt of the church of Jesus Christ to do the work of God apart from the truth and the power of the Spirit of God."[21] More disturbing than the powerlessness itself is the fact that few contemporary evangelicals seem bothered, "because the most popular and significant methods and means for doing ministry require little, if any, divine truth and power."[22] Preacher/leaders should know that the only hope for long-lasting change lies in encountering God's power.

The 360-degree leading approach emphasizes that no one is better placed to help worship be genuinely centered on who God is and what God wills than preacher/leaders. They must ensure worship is not some incidental activity on the way to other more relevant plans but *the* rendezvous with God who makes himself known and calls us to himself. Because choices in worship often inflame conflict (some even dubbing contemporary tensions "worship wars"), preacher/leaders must generate and sustain creative tension with spiritual wisdom and courage—so that, at its best, worship might overwhelm, deepen, relate, ignite, unite, and move people onward in their mission for God. While activists and pragmatists urge practical action with short timelines, preacher/leaders know that God first requires worshipers who worship him in spirit and in truth (John 4:24). Worship directs everything else and solid time must be devoted to leading it.

The story of a new pastor arriving at a church in Dallas illustrates this principle well. Finding a demoralized church in decline, he challenged them in one of his first sermons: "If we will seek Jesus and him alone, the concerns we have and the challenges we face will come into perspective."[23] During his first two years he organized a two-day retreat for the church's disheartened leaders, with a sole purpose to provide personal and corporate worship. Toward the retreat's end he said,

> The only agenda I have for now is to repeatedly call us back into the presence of God. Don't misinterpret what I'm saying—I firmly believe God has a plan for us. But I want us to be sure that the plan we commit to is God's, not ours. I don't know when or how he will reveal that plan. Until he makes it clear, I want to ask you as leaders . . . to join me in calling the rest of this body of Christ back to its first love.[24]

Unsurprisingly, this marked the beginning of fresh spiritual vitality for the whole church.

To enable congregations to encounter God's holiness, preacher/leaders must preach on the big themes of holiness, love, sacrifice, service, and reconciliation to help people see God more worshipfully and who they might become through him. Key texts which sound out such big themes include Isaiah 6:1–13, Acts 2:43–47, Romans 11:33–12:2, Colossians

1:13–22, Hebrews 12:18–24, and 1 Peter 2:4–10. Christian leadership
continually preaches God, God, God, not man, man, man. Preaching is
not about racking up great faith in God but proclaiming faith in a great
God. The more a community encounters God's holiness, the more they
know and love the one they worship and the more ready they are to experience congregational transformation. These big themes of Christian
life should ring true because the preacher/leader believes, practices, and
preaches them.

2. Experiencing God's Grace

As people encounter God's holiness, so they are led to experience his
gift of grace in forgiveness. "Effective change leaders help others make
the connection between individual experiences of grace and the need
to extend that grace to all of life's relationships."[25] God's grace breaks
through by sheer love (Isa. 6:5; John 3:16; Eph. 3:2; 1 John 1:9). Spiritual
and relational vitality moves to a deeper level when preacher/leaders help
people together experience and extend grace to others.

Thin-blooded preaching accentuates individualistic grace—"God loves
me, a sinner." But full-blooded preaching requires both personal faith
responses and the relational consequences of grace that practices forgiveness and strives for reconciliation—vertical and horizontal. "God loves *us*
sinners." Just as personal encounter with God is foundational for leading
others to encounter him, so a preacher/leader's personal practice of grace
is essential for community reconciliation. In everyday relationships,
a leader's willingness to practice forgiveness must push out personal
boundaries of grace. Only by such wrestling with the costs of forgiving,
seeking reconciliation, and healing brokenness can they become ethos
givers. Modeling grace is one of the most daunting responsibilities for a
preacher/leader. Christly love is the greatest force for good in the cosmos,
yet it remains one of the most difficult forces to integrate into the rough
and tumble of family and church relationships.

Jim Cymbala at Brooklyn Tabernacle Church provides a striking example of a preacher/leader safeguarding the integrity of a church community. In challenging new members he opens himself up to critique.

And now I charge you, as pastor of this church, that if you ever hear
another member speak an unkind word of criticism or slander against
anyone—myself, another pastor, an usher, a choir member, or anyone
else—you have authority to stop that person in midsentence and say,
"Excuse me—who hurt you? Who ignored you? Who slighted you? Was it
Pastor Cymbala? Let's go to his office right now. He will get on his knees
and apologize to you, and then we'll pray together, so God can restore

peace to this body, but we will not let you talk critically about people who are not present to defend themselves." New members, please understand that I am entirely serious about this. I want you to help resolve this kind of thing immediately. And meanwhile, know this: If you are ever the one doing the loose talking, we will confront you.[26]

Ethos givers always attempt to settle quarrels (Matt. 5:23–24). Yet showing grace in daily pressures of family life and church activities, in sickness and in health, with friends and strangers (often easier with the latter) is much easier said than done. Here an ounce of practice is worth its weight in gold.

Preacher/leaders must therefore take the great themes of love, forgiveness, and reconciliation and apply them to real people in specific community with each other. In particular, 1 Corinthians 13 needs to be preached rigorously. First written to a church replete with spiritual gifts yet missing their whole purpose of love, each line brings creative tension, challenging people's practice of love in relationships, service, and evangelism. During my preaching ministry, I have developed several sermon series that emphasize practicing Christ's love in community. One series entitled "Love Makes the Kingdom Go Round" included these sermons:

"The Fundamental Question" (John 21:15–25)
"Evidences of Love" (1 John 4:7–21)
"Three Loves" (Luke 10:25–37)
"God's Power to Live and Love" (John 14:15–21; Acts 2:1–4; 1 Cor. 12:31–13:3)
"Some Fruit" (Gal. 5:16–26)
"Some More Fruit" (Gal. 5:22–6:10)
"Love That Lays Down Life" (John 15:12–27)
"Love Fulfills the Law" (Rom. 13:8–14)
"Does Love Solve Everything?" (1 Cor. 12:31b–1 Cor. 13:13)

Other series used these and further texts to reinforce God's challenge that we had not yet loved enough.

The practice of forgiveness needs sensitive but courageous preaching. Matthew 6:14–15 and Matthew 18:21–35 require prime time preaching, as do Colossians 3:13 and Ephesians 4:32. Reconciliation requires solid preaching on Romans 5:10–11, 2 Corinthians 5:18–20, Colossians 1:20–22, and Ephesians 2:16.

John Adair in his book on leaders claims that John 13:1–20 is the most extraordinary scene in world leadership as Jesus models his leadership style by washing his disciples' feet. Every preacher/leader should wrestle with the implications of that upper room episode, as with several other texts where Jesus models leadership by serving others.

Cumulative preaching of God's love by preacher/leaders who genuinely seek to express it in their personal lives has incalculable influence on community life. And ultimately, living this out shows that "the greatest of these is love" (1 Cor. 13:13), which presents the most convincing evidence of God's kingdom. As John Killinger comments: "The preacher's first calling, therefore, is to love. . . . We must love people and love God's vision of the community. Then we can preach."[27]

3. Embracing Unity

Stage 3 applies gospel truths of God's grace, forgiveness, love, and service to the whole of a congregation that it might grow in unity. "Effective change leaders continually hold up the mission or purpose of the church as the basis for unity. . . . [Their] focusing on God's mission will challenge the congregation to fully employ its diversity and its creative energies."[28]

Unity requires preacher/leaders to be unswerving peacemakers. No one occupies a more influential place to model and to preach peacemaking. "Making every effort to maintain the unity of the Spirit in the bond of peace. There is one body and one Spirit, just as you were called to the one hope of your calling" (Eph. 4:3–4). Note the relationship between "making every effort" and "the unity of the Spirit." God wins peace and unity through Jesus Christ's sacrifice. "For he is our peace; in his flesh he has . . . broken down the dividing wall, that is, the hostility between us" (Eph. 2:14). Yet this victory requires believers to make every effort to practice peace together. This is not peace in the absence of conflict, concealing disagreement, or evading controversy. Rather, it is costly peace that needs to be waged more zealously than war in order that diverse people might grow into deeper understanding and life together. Sometimes winning peace is more difficult than winning war, and in local church life the need for winning peace never ends.

Jesus's poignant prayer to his Father in heaven remains urgent for unity in the body of Christ: "I ask not only on behalf of these, but also on behalf of those who will believe in me through their word, that they may all be one. As you, Father, are in me and I am in you, may they also be in us, so that the world may believe that you have sent me" (John 17:20–21). Preacher/leaders need to be ethos givers in the spirit of Ephesians 4:1–2: "Live a life worthy of the calling you have received. Be completely humble and gentle, be patient, bearing with one another in love" (NIV). Disunity is 100 percent guaranteed when leaders forget their calling, exercise pride, and express harshness, impatience, and intolerance of others' weaknesses.

Some preacher/leaders inherit obvious situations of need. Eight years ago when Ed Brown, an African American, was appointed pastor of a large, mostly white community church in the village of Skokie outside downtown Chicago, there was considerable surprise. Taken out of his urban African American context he found himself in a fifty-two-year-old suburban church founded by white Swedish immigrants. What would a black preacher do? Reflecting over his ministry so far, Ed Brown says, "I believe preaching has been the heart and core of what has happened here. When we ask new members what brought you here and keeps you here, they say the preaching."[29] His first prayer on arrival was: "Lord, what is it that you want me to do at this church? You've taken me out of my comfort zone—why bring me to this Caucasian church?" In answer, he believes God gave him a vision that he was to lead the church to become a change agent for the community. He shared this vision with his leadership team, went on retreat, held congregational meetings, and found strong endorsement. He preached a series on the church becoming a change agent: reaching out in evangelism (Matt. 28:20), reaching up in discipleship (Ephesians 4), and reaching beyond in mission (Acts 1:8). He preached through each component of this vision, challenging the congregation to see its call not to be a social club but a change agent for community.

Meanwhile the community around the church was rapidly changing. From being a predominantly white church it needed to grow in openness to the diversity of cultures in its surrounding community. First, Ed Brown knew he needed to be accepted as an African American. With care he spent the first four or five years listening to the congregation's expectations of leadership and sought to model gracious character as he preached. "People need to know that I care for them, otherwise there will not be genuine relationships; that I not only 'talk the talk but walk the walk' with consistency and authenticity. Whenever I talk about marriage or raising kids they always look across to my wife and see if she agrees! And that I understand where they live, so my wrestling with the text respects their struggles."

As he preached, so the congregation's diversity increased—African Americans, Jamaicans, Haitians, and Germans began joining in worship in numbers. Now the former white congregation was being pushed out of its comfort zones! Tensions of diversity particularly focused on music in worship with unpleasant conflict between different factions wanting gospel music, traditional hymns, and rock and roll. Tensions led to personal attacks against people, and meetings were convened that Ed Brown led to try to resolve conflict. In this hard time he preached a series of sermons about conflict resolution "without preaching down to people or taking sides." This resulted in the leadership developing a reconciliation policy that the church congregation adopted and agreed to work through. As a result the church lost some people, including two worship leaders. The process took four and a half years.

> I believe that preaching played a significant role. I would look out on Sunday mornings in the midst of the struggle and see people opposed with lines drawn in the sand and I had to lift Scripture to bring healing and reconciliation. I'll be honest, in many instances we didn't succeed. Some people were willing, some were not. But what happened ultimately is that we came through a stronger church.

Throughout Ed Brown knew his role as preacher/leader was strategic.

> People were looking at me to see in the midst of the conflict. People always look at leadership more intensely in difficulty to see how we're going to re-spond. Are we going to respond biblically with Christian integrity or attack people and take sides in an unchristian manner? I don't like conflict, but I grew and the church grew, and I know I look at the conflict differently now. As a result people have opened up in genuine fellowship and are listening to God's Word in a different way. Conflict is a part of life, part of ministry. Accept it. You don't grow without it. Not all conflict is bad. You may lose some friends but if you remain faithful to God, genuine fellowship and community can come out of it. Actually good things happened to people that wouldn't have come without conflict.

This is full-blooded preaching born out of integrity when a preacher/leader practices grace.

4. Engaging Community

Stage 4 is closely linked with embracing unity—"Unity must be trans-lated into community if God's people are to have an ongoing impact in the world."[30] Spiritual and relational vitality should always expand into mission to others.

Most evangelical preachers do not need persuasion about the priority of evangelism. They warm to stories, such as that told by Rick Warren when he started Saddleback Church in California. He took six months of extensive personal Bible study on what the Bible says about church that also led to a series of sermons. Just in Matthew's Gospel alone he worked on Matthew 5:13–16, 9:35, 11:28–30, 16:15–19, 18:19–20, 22:36–40, 24:14, 25:34–40, and 28:18–20. However, he concluded that two statements from Jesus summarize it all in Matthew 22:37–40 and Matthew 28:19–20. "I believe that every church is defined by what it is committed to, so I came up with this slogan: 'A Great Commitment to the Great Commandments and the Great Commission will grow a Great Church.'"[31] He claims this belief controls every church activity and program.

However, as we have seen, thin-blooded preaching focuses exclusively on *individuals* responding to this mission challenge, restricting leadership to the micro level. But spiritual and relational vitality raises the stakes to a higher level of mezzo-leadership that leads believers *together* to embody outcomes of new life in Christ. In terms of the missiological model (see fig. 1) the community operates along two axes: the *reciprocal relationship axis* between gospel and church, so that the local church community develops communal responsibilities, and the *missionary dialogue axis* between church and its surrounding culture. Engaging community means that congregations take missional responsibility to model God's truth for the sake of what is often an alien and hostile local culture. God's mission leads people to worship, witness, and serve together in contrast with the world.

One pastor reflecting on this challenge wrote to me about his fresh commitment:

> The church I serve is blinded by our society's obsession with individualism. We have designed and scheduled our ministries to match up with the desires of the individuals within our congregation. We are offering our people the choice of different styles, times, focus, etc., to meet the needs of the individual consumers. . . . We have catered to the individual to the neglect of the body. Our members must begin to experience a unity that translates into community. I am making a commitment to begin preaching "body, body, body." The first and most difficult step will be helping them see the difference between God's vision for community and the present reality. They have little comprehension of the community experienced within the first-century Christian church. This journey will require some instruction, but victory will only be possible if engaged with leadership through preaching. They have to "get it" and then apply it in our new world.

Unless a people have embraced unity and engaged in community, a church comprises individual believers who acculturate to culture, making no impact for God because such a church has no discernible contrast with its surroundings. Preacher/leaders must intentionally work towards nurturing their congregation's spiritual and relational vitality in a way that both experiences God's grace—"until we all reach unity in the faith and in the knowledge of the Son of God and become mature, attaining to the whole measure of the fullness of Christ" (Eph. 4:13 NIV)—yet also expresses God's grace urgently through the Great Commandment (Matt.

22:37–40) and the Great Commission (Matt. 28:19–20). God's purpose in transforming congregations is that they might transform the world.

Thinking through Core Values

To aid this process of developing spiritual and relational vitality, some preacher/leaders have used "core values" in order to sharpen essential values and beliefs.

Aubrey Malphurs advocates such "values-driven leadership," drawing on insights from business studies:

> A ministry's key values or beliefs are the shaping force of the entire institution. They beget attitudes that specify behavior. They affect everything about the organization, the decisions made, the goals set, the priorities established, the problems solved, the conflict resolved, and more.[32]

Core values differ from "vision" (describing the "what" of the future) because they answer the question "Why?" and they are not to be confused with strategies (that answer the question "How?") or doctrinal statements. Rather, sourced by Scripture, they sum up the spiritual and relational convictions that drive the rest of ministry. Malphurs urges churches to begin by defining core values before anything else. Lyle Schaller agrees: "The most important single element of any corporate, congregational, or denominational culture . . . is the value system."[33] Preacher/leaders as ethos givers therefore have a vital role in identifying both their own and their congregation's core values. They share responsibility for "discovering them, making them clear, and ensuring that all live up to them in the decision-making process."[34]

Though it lies beyond this book's scope to deal with the practical issues of undertaking audits and establishing agreed values, I commend this process as a method of developing spiritual and relational vitality. Malphurs suggests different ways to undertake a "values audit" and offers two sets of questions to discover core values—first for individuals and then for organizations. Out of twenty-nine values for individuals, the twelve highest ranked are to be selected and graded in order. The values are:

1. godly servant leadership
2. a well-mobilized lay ministry
3. Bible-centered preaching/teaching
4. the poor and disenfranchised
5. creativity and innovation

6. world missions
7. people matter to God
8. an attractive facility
9. financial responsibility
10. the status quo
11. welcoming visitors
12. cultural relevance
13. intercessory prayer
14. sustained excellence/quality
15. fellowship/community
16. evangelism
17. strong families
18. a grace-orientation to life
19. praise and worship
20. a Christian self-image
21. social justice
22. committed Christians (discipleship)
23. giving/tithing
24. counseling
25. civil rights
26. Christian education (all ages)
27. the Ordinances
28. equal rights
29. other[35]

Selected values should be tested biblically, for each core value must be supported by a scriptural principle. For example, Malphurs links "creativity and innovation" (fifth in list) with God's creativity in Genesis 1 and 2.

Malphurs mentions preachers only briefly, but clearly regards them as having a crucial role in auditing and communicating values. He sees the sermon as the most obvious place to inspire values, though other communication avenues should also be used. Indeed, he pleads for a new paradigm of ministry—a "professional pastor at the head of its ministry not at the feet of its board."[36] In addition to a church's shared core values, identifying personal core values is also a vital part of preacher/leaders investing time in their own leadership. This and working with congregations to develop fresh values through spiritual and relational vitality involves much spiritual wisdom and courage. E. K. Bailey ruefully reflects on his experience:

Changing the core values of a congregation is a process and it takes patience. I would identify the movers and shakers in the church and . . .

meet with them every week, either one-on-one or in small groups. I would talk to them about changing the core values where the church is called to match what God says in the Scriptures. . . . But before you can make some significant progress, God may have to take some of them to heaven.[37]

In full appendixes Malphurs provides some credos developed by churches, parachurches, and marketplace organizations. Interesting examples reflect how different organizations express what really matters to them about values such as balance, prayer, love, community, and lay ministry.

Balanced Christianity. You need a balanced Christian experience which includes meaningful worship, life-related biblical teaching, significant relationships with other Christians, and serving others according to your gifts, abilities, and interests.[38]

A commitment to prayer. We believe that God desires his people to pray and that he hears and answers prayer (Matt. 7:7–22; James 5:13–18). Therefore the ministries and activities of this church will be characterized by a reliance on prayer in their conception, planning, and execution.[39]

Love Jesus Christ. No one can love God for us. We must individually stay connected to Christ through an abiding relationship (John 15). Through the Word of God, prayer, personal worship, and obedience we can love God with heart, soul, mind and strength.[40]

Be connected through a small group. Community groups help us develop caring relationships with one another. In this small-group context we can get to know people, hold each other accountable, and offer newcomers a place to begin.[41]

Build friendships with non-Christians. We can always be on the lookout for ways to reach out with the love of Christ to those who are teetering on the edge of a Christless eternity. By building relationships with non-Christians we may eventually be able to communicate the life-changing message of salvation through Jesus Christ.[42]

A commitment to lay ministry. We believe that the primary responsibility of the pastor(s) and teachers in the local church is to "prepare God's people for works of service" (Eph. 4:12). Therefore, the ministry of Lakeview Community Church will be placed as much as possible in the hands of nonvocational workers. This will be accomplished through training opportunities and through practices which encourage lay initiation, leadership, responsibility, and authority in the various ministries of the church.[43]

We believe that loving relationships should permeate every aspect of church life.[44]

Different churches will necessarily express their beliefs and values in various ways, but defining and writing down core values ensures that spiritual and relational vitality does not peter out as pious vague hope but thrives in honest specific practice.

Not to Rush the Process

To conclude this chapter I turn to one story in progress from Jon Stannard, who is a Baptist pastor in Newbury, England. After a year or two as new pastor to this well-established church, he introduced the idea of core values in November 2003 as the first step in developing a vision for the church. He invited a select team of six people representative of church life to work through issues involved with core values. Only one member had theological training and two were under twenty years old. From the group's many ideas, consultation of other documents, and much prayer, Jon worked on a draft core values statement that could be placed before church leaders and the whole church in written form. Meanwhile he preached on the importance of this process. As the core values were initially focused into six statements, he preached on each of them one week at a time, produced a Bible study for each one, and a daily reading program for fifty days leading up to Easter 2005, which linked each core value to a Scripture with a meditation. Finally, the core values were once again brought before the whole church to be launched on Pentecost Sunday 2005.

At the same time a process began of putting the whole church into small groups, initially fourteen in number, tasked with teaching, pastoral care, service, mission, and prayer as well as offering friendship. Leaders were selected and trained with an ongoing training program to identify new leaders. Jon aims to preach again on core values each year and to ask the groups to work through each of the values in turn, asking how all group members might implement them in their lives. "This I pray will enable them to be 'lived' out rather than noted, and ignored." He reflects further on this experience thus far.

The primary way of communicating core values has been through preaching and my own personality, I guess. Speaking about the vision somehow seems to touch people more. Preaching is, I believe, firmly at the heart of drawing people together and leading them to new places. That and a strong desire to ensure that *everyone* knows I care even if I can't do all the caring. We will need to repeat the core values again and again. Preaching on them once a year will be the minimum.

I guess the most important lesson I learned about core values is not to rush the process and just announce them, but to ensure that the whole church is on board rather than just forge ahead. The sermon, Bible study and daily reading series will lead up to the launch rather than follow it. It's taken some time to formulate but we are in a good strong position, and *all* the church will be on board by the time we come to formally adopt them. The period of time from starting the process to launch will be just under a year.

The written statement reads:

Core Values for NBC

We as Newbury Baptist Church with all our variety of backgrounds, ages and cultures, will endeavor to demonstrate creatively our LOVE for GOD, Father, Son and Holy Spirit, and for ONE ANOTHER by striving to:

- *Worship* and praise God in all that we are and do in loving obedience to His will.
- *Grow* in our love for, and our understanding of, God through faithful prayer and Bible study, so that we might become more Christ-like in all that we think, say and do.
- *Deepen* our relationships with one another through regular fellowship in Sunday worship and in small groups.
- *Support* one another by giving and receiving encouragement, hospitality, forgiveness and pastoral care.
- *Serve* in the church and in the world in unity with other Christians, through sacrificially giving of our time, energy, gifts and money.
- *Witness* to the gospel of Jesus through our attitudes and actions and by relevant evangelism and mission, welcoming the stranger and challenging injustice.[45]

Whether or not core values are used, the four elements of spiritual and relational vitality sum up the spiritual center that drives every congregation. And placed slap-bang at its core are preacher/leaders. At every turn they need to practice what they preach and preach what they practice: practice spiritual wisdom and preach spiritual wisdom; practice courage and preach courage; practice holiness and preach holiness; practice prayerfulness and preach prayerfulness; practice love and forgiveness and preach love and forgiveness; practice peacemaking to resolve conflict and preach peacemaking to resolve conflict; practice the Great Commission and preach the Great Commission. There is no substitute for preacher/leaders doing and saying God's Word as Christ's ethos givers for their communities.

8

Initiating Process

One of my heroes is the frontier scout and pioneer Daniel Boone. Once, returning from the uncharted forests beyond the Kentucky river, he was asked by a lady if he was ever lost. "I can't say that I was ever lost, ma'am," he replied, "but I was once sure bewildered for three days." We need to be bewildered as a prelude to finding the way ahead.

John Adair, *Creative Church Leadership*[1]

Lynn Cheyney reminds me of Daniel Boone. When she was interviewed in 2000 to become senior pastor of a large church in the south Chicago suburbs, she startled the search committee. Asked, "What would be your vision for the church?" she replied: "I have no idea. I don't know you yet. Discerning the vision for the church is something we would do together. We would first need to get to know one another and learn to love God together. Only then can we effectively listen for what it is that God is asking of us."[2] She was the first candidate who hadn't said flat out, "Here's what we need to do!" and presented a program. Of course, Lynn Cheyney was passionate about the big vision of loving God and neighbor and sharing in Christ's mission. It was the more specific vision for that particular church that she didn't know yet. As she put it, "Clarity of vision is crucial but the process for the unfolding of a vision will be different in different church contexts." Coming to a traditional "country club" church that had gone through a church split and leadership difficulties during the 1990s, she said: "Part of my work was to spend two years learning this particular church's story and language. When I came, my language was not the language of this particular family of faith. Their story was complex and layered with both richness and pain. It would have been a mistake for me to come in and announce 'Here's where we need to go.' First, I needed to experience their uniquenesses and fall in love with them. Two, I'd hoped they could fall in love with me and that together we could fall in love with Jesus Christ." Four years later she says, though they have accomplished a great deal of healing and growth, they are still not at that place of absolute clarity about God's specific vision. "Perhaps it is two years away, but it is beginning to take shape—I look forward to a vision that has been birthed in their hearts and isn't shaped only by my nudging from behind or dragging from in front."

Lynn Cheyney has several convictions about preaching/leading. First, preaching's supreme importance to leadership: "I cannot imagine accomplishing anything apart from preaching. Preaching is the catalyst for transformation." Like many traditional churches the move to blended worship brought resistance, but "a sermon I preached on worship—'it's not about you, it's about God'—began the change process." Similarly, the church, which had known generous donors in the past and therefore hadn't needed to take offerings through its formative years, required key lessons on stewardship. She preached a month of sermons on stewardship in her first year and immediately saw an enormous increase in giving which has continued each year. She claims that preaching is unparalleled in its power to shape and define the church's mission and ministry. As the church continues to make extraordinary demands on her time and energy, chipping away at her prayer, study, and preparation, she is mindful of "making sure I am giving every ounce of due to preaching because it is the most important thing I do."

Second, the preacher's character matters vitally. She learned very early on how much her people needed to be able to trust her because of their recent history—was she going to be reliable, to stay with them, and to love them? In each of her three churches she has found particular character issues such as integrity and spirituality that needed to be modeled by the preacher/leader. Third, she believes in relational leadership—everything of value comes out of relationship including vision. For her, it is essential to be connected with people by learning their story both as individuals and as a local church. And she believes that loving the people is crucial. "If they know they matter to you, that you genuinely care about them and want to be with them, that leading and being in relationship with them is important to you, it makes all the difference!"

Lynn Cheyney's insights neatly introduce this final chapter that seeks to integrate the preacher/leader's skills (chap. 6) and the ethos responsible for nurturing spiritual and relational vitality (chap. 7) with a process that initiates change. Her experience highlights four important issues. First, it shows the unique character of each congregation's story. She rightly recognized that no generic, one-size-fits-all program could be satisfactorily grafted onto her particular congregation. Little of spiritual value could happen and no authentic visions could be dreamed unless the congregation itself became vitally alive to God and to each other. She dared to place herself at a critical place as preacher/leader with love and integrity in order for a congregation to understand itself and God's will for its future.

Second, and linked with each situation's uniqueness, any church's change process rarely follows a straightforward pattern. Notice that though the specific vision for the church was not clear after four years (and probably needs another two years), she has already initiated very significant changes in worship to introduce blended worship and has also challenged the church effectively about stewardship. Those issues arose in early months of addressing the congregation's spiritual and relational vitality and were dealt with as they emerged. For other churches these issues of worship and stewardship might have belonged within the longer process of discerning the specific vision. There are no hard-and-fast rules for how and when leadership issues are tackled.

Third, she brings an emphasis with which women have been particularly identified. As women have developed and reflected upon their growing role in exercising leadership they have emphasized the critical importance of relationships. Earlier I mentioned Alice Mathews, who, though cautious about gender stereotypes, claims that most women leaders employ a more collegial leadership style than most men. As a woman preacher she describes a type of leadership "from the middle," where leaders bring people face-to-face with their problems in order to resolve them. For her, preaching/leading means bridging the gap between the realities of where people are and the values they espouse. "When women lead, much of the focus is on listening to understand the issues and then educating in ways that transform situations."[3]

Fourth, and closely bound up with relational leadership is the need for patience about the amounts of time involved. Perhaps Cheyney's interviewers were disappointed she did not seem to be a fired-up visionary with ready plans for immediate operation in their timeline. In truth she was a fired-up preacher/leader committed to initiate spiritual and relational vitality in God's timeline. Nothing wrecks church life faster than leaders' impatience that pushes their agendas of change ahead of God's pacing. The fruit of the Spirit are long-term fruit (Gal. 5:22–23) that include patience, faithfulness, and self-control.

Change Process

The third part of the congregational transformation model comprises eight stages that integrate and place in order the many challenges facing preacher/leaders. Not intended to be prescriptive, they guide through the change process, showing the vital importance of an intentional sequence of leadership actions. Congregational transformation does not originate out of vague wishful thinking. Because each congregation is unique, it will tell its story of transformation in different ways using various terms, but this outline provides a general guide to the kinds of issues that must be tackled. It is like a river map for whitewater rafting.

Stage 1: Making Personal Preparation

Stage 2: Creating Urgency

Stage 3: Establishing the Vision Community

Stage 4: Discerning the Vision and Determining the Visionpath

Stage 5: Communicating the Vision

Stage 6: Empowering Change Leaders

Stage 7: Implementing the Vision

Stage 8: Reinforcing Momentum through Alignment

Earlier, in chapter 5, these stages were briefly introduced with connections drawn between the weekly preaching task and stages 1, 2, and 5. Now they must be dealt with as a whole, showing how different skills and various aspects of spiritual and relational vitality fit in to one process. Jim Herrington, Mike Bonem, and James Furr cluster the stages together, linking stages 1 through 3 as *laying the groundwork for change*, stages 4 and 5 as *discerning and communicating the vision*, and stages 6 through 8 as *achieving and maintaining widespread impact*.

Laying the Groundwork for Change

Less visible than the later stages, the first three are all about developing a congregation's "inner life," making it ready for change. Lynn Cheyney's story well illustrates her care to lay solid groundwork by first understanding her church's story and language. Of course, an older, well-established (and declining) church needs much more patience than a new church plant or a congregation that recognizes it is in crisis, when more immediate actions may be both needed and possible.

Stage 1: Making Personal Preparation

Making personal preparation entails "carving out the time and space to discern God's voice and direction for the leader's own ministry and for the church, and living with the tension this creates."[4] Adequate preparation is always the secret of effective preaching/leading. Preachers can only lead as far as their personal devotion, self-awareness, accountability, and courage will let them.

Personal devotional life has already been strongly emphasized as prerequisite to preaching/leading (Luke 4:42). Rick Warren uses memorable surfing imagery to capture its spiritual dynamic. While surfers have much to learn about how to recognize, ride, and get off "surfable" waves, they cannot, of course, create the waves themselves.

> Only God can create waves—waves of revival, waves of growth, and waves of spiritual receptivity. Our job as church leaders, like experienced surfers, is to recognize a wave of God's Spirit and ride it. It is not our responsibility to make waves but to recognize how God is working in the world and join him in the endeavor.[5]

For Warren this means offering a daily prayer: "Father, I know you're going to do some incredible things in your world today. Please give me the privilege of getting in on some of what you're doing."[6] Leaders should stop asking God to bless what they are doing and commit to do what God is blessing.

Practically, preacher/leaders can "get in on some of what God is doing" by reflecting personally on great biblical texts of God leading his people forward. Spending quality time considering Moses's leadership in the exodus, Ezra's reforming, Nehemiah's building, Jesus's calling of disciples for kingdom living, the apostles' bold preaching of Jesus, and the early church's expansion described in Acts helps leaders live in these stories of God's waves. Of course, preachers can be guilty of manipulating stories to their own end, turning Nehemiah, for example, into some poster figure for a pet project. But preacher/leaders, authentically inspired by stories of God in action, can retell them so that people can "catch God's wave." Whenever preacher/leaders live expectantly and prayerfully within Scripture's story, bringing their own aptitudes and skills, they belong within God's great continuing contemporary story. This is one of preaching's greatest opportunities.

Complementing great Scripture stories, preacher/leaders need also to imbibe good biographies. Jim Nicodem, senior pastor of Christ Community Church, advises preacher/leaders to "go to school on good leaders."[7] However, rather than reading leadership books, he recommends biographies of noted leaders. Most recently he has read about Abraham Lincoln, Andrew Carnegie, and Martin Luther King Jr.

Maturing self-disclosure is also vital because those called to be ethos givers need to understand themselves as well as possible. They will be exposed to others' evaluations like no one else and therefore need to know *who* they are, secure in God's call. Whether checking if they have abused Nehemiah as a poster figure, are trapped with an inaccurate picture of present reality, or have failed to deal with conflict positively, preacher/leaders continually need to develop self-awareness. Various forms of spiritual inventory can help in this process. For example, in the last chapter preacher/leaders were challenged to undertake both an individual and an organizational "values audit" which can help identify "core values."

To help self-understanding, *accountability* is also essential. Since one leader cannot possess all the necessary aptitudes and skills, he or she needs to recognize strengths and limitations and balance them by developing accountability, whether with a formal group, a peer or peers in ministry, or a trusted mentor. Again, Jim Nicodem has taken this responsibility seriously, involving himself in a peer group of three other senior pastors in comparable church situations, who therefore share very similar pressures, problems, and joys. Meeting periodically for three days at a time, they worship, pray, talk, and share with as much honesty and transparency as possible. "They can challenge me about anything—about my devotional life or my fantasy life. They really understand my temptations and needs—we can be real together."

And throughout, *courage* is needed to keep at the tasks of honest self-disclosure and accountability. Unless problems of hurt, brokenness, and defensiveness are dealt with responsibly in the preacher/leader's personal life, they can fester insecurities and fatally damage hopes of transformation for community. Only by openness to the Holy Spirit, who grants self-disclosure and guidance, who authenticates call and gifting, and who grows his fruit of love, joy, peace, patience, kindness, generosity, faithfulness, gentleness, and self-control (Gal. 5:22–23), can spiritual leaders discern and ride surfable spiritual waves.

Stage 2: Creating Urgency

Creating urgency means "creating energy for change: being clear and explicit about current reality in contrast to God's ideal."[8] Urgency is a recurring leadership theme, but it is included at this point *only* after expending time on personal preparation. For preacher/leaders, urgency is energized by God's vision in Scripture of who they and their people might become. But it needs to be based upon honest portrayal of the current situation, warts and all.

Occasionally, preachers find themselves primed to create urgency from the outset. For example, Herrington, Bonem, and Furr describe a pastor who was called to a church in their area that was in massive decline. On his first Sunday, presenting each person with a graph of past attendance trends, he said:

> This congregation has been in decline for thirty-five years. We must face that reality squarely. If there is any possibility that God is going to use us to bring hope to this city, we must be very clear about our reality.[9]

That first Sunday began a turnaround as the congregation stopped pretending and started urgently working through the implications of living out God's mission.

But for most congregations much more time is needed to assess data and communicate a helpful picture of their current situation. Hard data in the form of surveys, demographic studies, feedback and interviews should be complemented by individual stories. Congregational surveys require great care not only about asking appropriate questions and quantifying results but also ensuring that feedback visibly values each person's concerns. Sadly, surveys can do as much harm as good. Sometimes leaders fail to repeat the details enough or make little effort to interpret them responsibly, just assuming that everyone immediately gets the point. Not so. Preacher/leaders have to keep using skills of generating and sustaining creative tension in order to keep the facts before people so that, alongside Scripture's stories and mandate for mission, a congregation becomes increasingly aware of the gap between current reality and God's ideal for them. Without overkill or manipulation, such a picture of reality becomes part of the preaching process, developing the congregation's inner life so that "speaking the truth in love, we . . . grow up in every way into him who is the head, into Christ" (Eph. 4:15).

Stage 3: Establishing the Vision Community

Establishing the vision community means "creating an environment in which challenge and diversity lead to genuine collaboration and commitment."[10] Vision has cropped up many times already. No one should underestimate its importance. A Chinese proverb runs: "If we don't change the direction we're going, we're likely to end up where we are headed." But how exactly do churches find vision?

Of course, churches differ greatly in their organizational methods at this point. This model suggests one possibility—that each church creates a vision community, a new group of key members who genuinely represent the wider congregation. Comprising about 10 percent of the average attendance and (ideally) comprising no more than twenty-five in number, this vision community then becomes part of the change process. They should be passionately concerned to seek God's will and willing to invest heavily in developing genuine dialogue.

Such a process demands much of the preacher/leader, for establishing such a group is itself a major leadership task. In many cases the pastor also becomes this group's leader, though each church's polity determines how such a group fits within a church's structure. Always, group members need to be of good standing, demonstrate spiritual maturity, show ability to dialogue, and exhibit openness to appropriate changes. Representing the church's diversity in age, gender, and ethnicity, they must learn to grow as a team, with the preacher helping to lead the way—remember to employ the skill of enabling team learning discussed in chapter 6. A vision community must be allowed time and space to develop with integrity, and the wider congregation needs to understand and trust the group as it toils on its behalf.

There are other ways of developing vision. For example, Bill Hybels recommends a process that he claims has been effective in hundreds of churches across the world. First, the leader brings together the senior leadership team comprising people such as key staff members, lay leaders, elders, and deacons. He or she challenges them to give clarity to God's vision for the church and asks them to meet for the next eight Saturday mornings

> and figure out together, under the direction of the Holy Spirit, where God wants us to lead his church. We'll start by studying Acts 2 and asking God to give us the pictures, ideas, and words that capture his vision for this church. Then when we present it publicly we will be of one heart and one mind, and hopefully, the rest of the congregation will buy into it.[11]

Hybels warns leaders how much time and energy is needed for this process to unfold and how vital it is that the whole leadership core is united and clear about its vision.

Some church traditions, like my own, involve regular congregational meetings in decision making and this allows other variations of practice for choosing a group and sharing in its work. In my own story, told at the end of the chapter, the midweek prayer meeting resembled a vision community that enabled the change process to develop. But in whatever ways vision is identified within a congregation, preacher/leaders should be in the thick of the process, for they bear major responsibility not only to listen to God's Word for the congregation but also to listen to the congregation as they interpret and respond to God's purposes.

Discerning and Communicating the Vision

The next stages of the change process build upon the congregation's inner life and move towards its outer, public life.

Stage 4: Discerning the Vision and Determining the Visionpath

Discerning the vision and determining the visionpath means "producing a written description of God's preferred future that is broad and exciting in its direction but clear and explicit in its details."[12]

Already distinctions have been made between *mission*, the mandate given the church at large; *vision*, the clear, shared, and compelling picture God gives a specific church; and *visionpath*, an immediate objective within the vision. Each level moves down towards greater detail. At the mission level, God's great purposes inspire expansive language, such as—"To know Christ and to make him known." At the vision level, the broad-brush mission statement is distilled down to something unique—"God's vision for you is like a fingerprint: there is no other one like it in the world."[13] And while a vision statement may be a few sentences, a visionpath may require several pages.

All three—mission, vision, and visionpath—require similar leadership steps. *Seek input* is the vision community's first task, as its members listen to each other as well as to the rest of the congregation. Prayer remains central to discerning God's will and preachers will particularly focus on directing congregational prayer at this stage. *Write first draft* is probably the preacher/leader's responsibility, which provides a starting point after having worked carefully through many initial ideas. *Seek private feedback* safeguards the preacher/leader's accountability as others provide honest feedback and help, especially when there may be little experience in writing such statements. *Revise second draft* assumes, rightly, that the preacher/leader can improve on initial work. *Obtain public feedback* involves full discussion within the vision community, leading to presentation before the whole congregation for feedback. *Develop consensus* is the desired outcome as a form of words is ultimately accepted by the whole group with excitement and anticipation.

Preacher/leaders cannot escape huge responsibilities here. Inevitably involved in the initial stages of praying and thinking through God's vision for congregations, they must commit to work through every part of this process. Perhaps, as situational leaders who feel like "fish out of water" (to use George Barna's description), they feel uneasy about the practicalities of developing mission, vision, and visionpaths. But, with tuned-up aptitude and applied learning disciplines (chaps. 5–6), their vocation as preacher/leaders demands their utmost for his highest.

Yes, this sequence of activities is time-consuming, labor-intensive, and can be spiritually draining. Engaging with others, writing and rewriting, presenting and receiving feedback, all in God's name, asks much of preacher/leaders who might otherwise be locked into traditional sermon-making mode. For example, writing out a vision statement to do justice to God's specific call on a congregation is a difficult exercise. Only a particular group of people can discern the right vision in the right words for their situation. Beware of thoughtlessly adopting language from another church situation. Also, much confusion is possible between broader mission statements and more specific vision, or between vision and goals. Barna calls "To preach the gospel to the whole world" a partial mission statement, but he describes "To build a church of 5,000 people by 2010" a goal statement and a very human one at that![14] Sometimes visions can be also confused with "core values."

And yes, on top of all the potential confusion it can be an uncomfortable process. One pastor described how sharing his vision with the wider group was like "giving birth in a room full of people, and then surrendering the baby to the audience's custody, all the while worrying that they will not even like the child."[15]

Yet, in spite of all these demands, this process strategically discerns and expresses God's will. Preachers should, of all people, be passionate about discerning and expressing God's will, because they are purposefully set aside to listen to Scripture and then preach its challenge week by week. They should be on fire for this task. This should not be an extra chore undertaken reluctantly, but grasped as of prime importance to leadership through preaching. By this process, people grow into God's vision of who they might become together and how they might act for him.

Hybels calls the vision statement the "main thing," and even suggests (agreeing with Peter Drucker) that it should be able to fit succinctly and memorably on the front of a T-shirt. Twenty-seven years ago he formulated nine words that have focused the "main thing" at Willow Creek ever since: "Turning irreligious people into fully devoted followers of Christ."[16] He claims that such crisply stated vision increases energy and ownership, provides focus, and smoothes the process of leadership succession. "Vision. It's the most potent weapon in a leader's arsenal. It's the weapon that unleashes the power of the church."[17]

Earlier I argued how much preaching needs leadership insights (chap. 3). Stage 4 offers a critical example of how preachers need to use leadership techniques (along with other people in their churches) to bring intentionality to their role. Instead of thin-blooded preaching trotting out individualistic, generic truths with no vision for community, full-blooded preaching commits preachers and hearers to specific action for God. Repetitive, well-meaning pious truths just do not lead. But preacher/leaders who are committed to discerning God's vision within the change process do lead.

Stage 5: Communicating the Vision

Communicating the vision involves "finding creative ways that enable the entire congregation to thoroughly understand God's vision for their future and its implications."[18] Of all the eight stages, this relates most obviously to the preacher's public role. As the vision emerges through prayer and dialogue, within the small group and wider congregation, the preacher/leader has prime responsibility to preach it. Of course communicators can use letters, papers, small group discussion, audiovisual resources, drama, music, and special events. But God's empowering of his Word through preacher/leaders communicates like nothing else. The sermon is easily the most powerful communication tool ever devised when God chooses to bless it.

Stage 5 involves explanation, motivation, and feedback. This sounds similar to how 360-degree preaching/leading works (see fig. 2). As preacher and people are caught up hearing God's vision to experience greater spiritual and relational vitality so they are mobilized to act, God's Word returns to him fulfilled (Isa. 55:11). Without manipulation or browbeating, by a sensitively paced preaching process, congregations should be brought to points of decision and fresh action. Preacher/leaders should involve others in sharing the vision, especially members of the vision community. They can help answer questions such as: How can creative tension be generated to challenge a congregation to face change? What stories need to be told? Where will there be resistance and how can it be dealt with maturely? What are the mental models that best sum up the vision and its implications? What terms, phrases, and analogies work for the local situation, like "Saddleback Sam" and "Unchurched Harry and Mary"?

Vision must therefore be an integral part of weekly preaching. Some high-profile leaders have even developed rules for its inclusion. Rick Warren, for example, restates Saddleback's vision and purpose every twenty-six days in order to keep the church moving in the right direction.[19] Bill Hybels warns how vision leaks for even the most committed hearers and insists that people need nonstop reminders. However, he always begins each new ministry year with a vision talk in early September, followed by another vision talk in January. He describes one such talk called "The Soul of Willow Creek."

> I delivered it at our weekend services because I wanted everyone, including seekers, to know who we are and where God is leading us. I wanted

to give them a glimpse into the soul of Willow. People loved it. Two weeks later, at our midweek New Community services, we had our formal Vision Night where I recast the vision in greater detail.[20]

Jim Nicodem practices *vision casting* in his preaching. We have noted that his church mission "To know Christ and to make him known" has a fourfold vision: Membership, Maturity, Ministry, and Mission. He designs his preaching seasonally along themes within these four *M*'s, ensuring that each is given high profile within church life over a few months. For example, promoting maturity involves issues such as discipleship and stewardship. Ministry directs the church with special challenges. He cites a recent sermon series in which he challenged the church about "finding a way out of the grandstands onto the playing field. . . . It takes a team to win a world."[21] His preaching series outlined six spiritual gifts needed to build a team.

In every congregation, whether large or small, preacher/leaders should bring intentional leadership into weekly preaching. I uncovered a delightful example through an interview with Dr. Vic Gordon.

Not Nearly Living Up to Its Potential

Vic Gordon, currently senior pastor for First Baptist Church of Huntington Beach/Fountain Valley in California, is passionate about preaching's role in leadership.

Preaching is the most important leadership task of the pastor. Every Sunday as I preach I see it as an act of leadership—calling people to understand who God wants us to be and what he wants us to do. Every Sunday I am in the pulpit I am an advocate for God's vision. I get more leadership punch in preaching than anything else I do.[22]

When he moved to Huntington Beach Church in Southern California in 2000, he found "a solid church but not nearly living up to its potential for God." It is placed within a suburban beach community that he describes as "hedonistic, materialistic—a wonderful place to live but a difficult place to follow Jesus in many ways."

Within two months of arrival he began to preach about the importance of understanding vision biblically—"a word from the Lord about who he wants us to be and what he wants us to do." He believed it was vital to teach people that vision is found by a *community* listening to God, rather than by a few people expressing opinions or engaging in brainstorming. He wanted to develop a theology of church in which community discernment of vision would be taken seriously. He undertook a preaching series entitled: "Seeing and Hearing Christ's Vision for His Church."

"The Greatest Commandment: Worship" (Matt. 22:34–40)

"Why Should We Be a Vision-Led Church?" (Matt. 22:34–40)

"The New Commandment: Community?" (Matt. 22:34–40)

"The Great Commission: Mission" (Matt. 28:16–20)

"What the World Needs Now" (Matt. 28:16–20)

"Mission Jesus Style" (John 17:15–18)

"Checking In on the Vision" (Matt. 22:34–40; John 13:34–35; Matt. 28:18–20; John 17)

"Christ's Ultimate Concern" (John 17)

"What Do We Need to See the Vision?" (Phil. 1:27–2:11)

"The Call of the Beach" (Luke 12:1–3)

"Focusing on the Vision" (Rom. 12:1–3)

"The Total Body Concept" (1 Cor. 12:1–27)

"Grounded in the Gospel" (1 Cor. 15:1–11)

"The Final Week" (Mark 14:43–52; Mark 11:1–11; John 20:19–29)

After each of these sermons a large group met each Wednesday night for one and a half hours' dialogue with him to follow up on issues that the sermons were raising. The group was charged to discern what God was saying to them in community so that together they would grow in God's purpose. After three to four months a smaller group of people took responsibility for sorting out the main issues that had emerged from all the preaching, dialogue, and praying. Vic Gordon demonstrated real skills as preacher/leader tying in his sermons with an intentional structure for congregational response and feedback. Here was creative tension as people worked and prayed together.

After a further three to four months of dialogue, a one-page vision emerged that took the form of a prayer. Titled "God's Direction for First," it begins with a purpose statement: "To be authentic followers of Jesus Christ, loving God, one another, and the world." A description of the vision follows. It is summarized below with each paragraph beginning with the same words:

We hear you calling . . .

To be a people of substance—to move beyond the knowledge of the Bible and the truth of the Gospel to living out that knowledge and truth . . . authentic disciples.

To love you completely, to genuinely worship you both in our individual lives and together as a group of believers.

To follow Christ's example to lay down our lives for each other with sacrificial love, a love that flees divisiveness and appreciates the diversity of the body and the uniqueness of each person . . . to reach out intentionally to those both younger and older than ourselves.

To go, taking the Gospel of Christ to a broken world, to enfold people into our church family, to pursue peace and justice.

To live out this balanced Christian life in our unique setting of Orange County and Southern California, a setting that fosters images of materialism and shallowness . . . to cultivate genuine relationship and sound ministries that stand against these images.

To live out this vision, not only here at home but everywhere we go.

For Vic Gordon the most important aspect of this process was the necessity of the whole congregation affirming this vision in unity. It took eight to ten months of preaching, praying, and dialogue for the entire congregation to be unanimous, but visible unity was paramount. The content of this prayer could also be said to describe "values" (chap. 7) as it lays foundations for the kind of community they believe God calls them to be.

While striving for unity, Vic inevitably had to deal with resistance. The Ephesians 4:15 phrase "speaking the truth in love" became another key theme. Believing that Christian leadership should be exercised in love, kindness, and with affirmation, he responds to critics: "We love you and we want you to come with us but we cannot let the church's lowest denominator determine where we go." Several people unhappy, for example, with the personal implications of being an "authentic follower of Jesus Christ," or encouragement given to women in leadership, did opt out of the church. But the early months of preaching for God's vision to be clear to the whole congregation ensured a solid base on which the church has continued to grow.

Achieving and Maintaining Widespread Impact

The last three stages all bring action out into the open. But this public impact is only achieved and maintained by all the elements that contributed to the process—hidden and public, detailed and broad—being brought "into alignment." Everything else that has happened up to this point is intimately involved in its continuing success.

Stage 6: Empowering Change Leaders

Empowering change leaders means "cultivating a broader base of committed leaders and removing the barriers that would prevent them from serving effectively."[23] Making sure that vision actually makes measurable difference requires leaders to bring others alongside them and ensure that change goes deeper into church systems.

What a challenge to thin-blooded preaching that is not only content to be a solo activity conducted in a separate "spiritual" compartment apart from others but also settles for low compliance rather than costly involvement. Preacher/leaders must address both of these needs.

First, their preaching must release others' gifts of leadership. So often preaching seems to isolate or elevate the person at the front to the detriment of others, who are excluded from dialogue and genuinely sharing responsibility. Many preachers have a poor track record even of mentoring apprentice preachers. Not only should they identify and inspire the next generation of preachers, but also empower new leaders throughout the church. Preacher/leaders should lead the way in mentoring and coaching others.[24] God gives each church all the resources needed to do his will where they are, calling a unique group of people together whose spiritual gifts need to be matched with their responsibilities. Preacher/leaders must preach about discerning body gifts, practice identifying individuals whose latent gifts need special care and attention, and encourage them to come alongside in leadership.

Second, they must impact deeper structures of church systems rather than just scratch the surface. Initial change can leave most people untransformed, especially where die-hard committees and strong personalities are obstructive. Applying skills of "systems thinking," preacher/leaders must discern how vision should affect deeper levels of structure, identifying main sources of conflict and helping communities move to a culture of openness and accountability. Unless preacher/leaders, with others, understand current structures realistically and work courageously towards reducing barriers for change, little worthwhile will happen.

As throughout the entire change process, God's gift of spiritual and relational vitality provides the only source of hope and energy for longlasting change. Only as a community deepens in worship, reconciliation, unity, and mission can God's will be fleshed out. By identifying priorities through visionpaths and by working sensitively and prayerfully one objective at a time, each preacher/leader should recognize fellow visionaries and bring them alongside. This part of the change process is costly and sometimes harrowing, testing a preacher/leader's spirituality to the limit.

Stage 7: Implementing the Vision

Implementing the vision means "coordinating multiple, concurrent action plans and achieving the right pace for the process—in consideration of resource limitation, congregational attitudes, and urgency."[25]

Notice how late in the process vision really begins to bite. But without all the prayer, skill, and hard work of six earlier stages leading up to this point, the sheer complexity of implementing vision can easily become bogged down in failure. Without authentic spiritual and relational vitality or preacher/leaders committed to practicing leadership disciplines to implement vision, congregations are going nowhere.

Visions have a time span envisaged in terms of three to five years that are implemented along several visionpaths, each involving much more detailed one-year projects. These visionpaths require action plans setting out specific activities in order to reach goals with measurable outcomes. Preacher/leaders must share with others in "frog thinking" systems thinking (chap. 6), which envisages how each piece belongs together and plans a realistic implementation process with "follow through" that manages the many different action plans. Implementing action that achieves results is the nitty-gritty center of leadership.

Much has been written advising leaders about how to prioritize and plan for implementation. For example, when facing barriers to change, such as strong hostile personalities, leaders are advised to term each new initiative as an "experiment." As Herrington, Bonem, and Furr suggest, "An experiment signals that the leaders do not claim to have all the answers. Experiments give people more room to innovate, learn and improve with less risk of repercussion."[26]

At every point, preacher/leaders have responsibility to see how Scripture nurtures visions and visionpaths, and how its practical application relates to specific nitty-gritty action. Action plans can be legitimate sermon applications, allowing full-blooded preaching to apply God's specific purpose by God's grace. Part of the Holy Spirit's work through preaching is to make connections in the minds and hearts of people in ways that add up to a community response. Of course there is an attendant danger that the sheer intensity of "getting things done" can turn sermons into illegitimate motivational tools in order to hit action plan goals. Any preacher who thoughtlessly bends Scripture to such ends endangers its integrity. Sermons should never be reduced to organizational motivation talks.

By full-blooded preaching God leads people to genuine long-term transformation through spiritual and relational vitality. I witnessed an interesting sermon application when Jim Nicodem, concerned about social initiatives in his church, preached on the responsibility of loving neighbors. In order to ensure practical implementation, he encouraged "market stalls" from a number of local organizations (secular as well as Christian) to be set up in the church foyer so that afterwards, church members could sign up for specific neighborhood action. Large numbers of people committed to action and fleshed out a visionpath for community service.

Stage 8: Reinforcing Momentum through Alignment

Reinforcing momentum through alignment means "creating an environment in which widespread commitment to follow God's vision routinely overshadows fears of continuous change."[27]

Preacher/leaders must never lose sight of the larger picture where all things are working together for good—God's alignment of all the parts of his community where "worship, small group activities, ministries and programs, budgets, decision making, organization, and attitudes of individual members all reflect the vision."[28]

But because congregations in transition are fragile, their progress can easily be blocked by what Herrington, Bonem, and Furr call "momentum killers," such as when people try to limit change by treating it as a finite program, which can quickly lead to self-satisfaction and stagnation. Momentum can also be blocked by fatigue, especially if a few people have carried the burden of change without significant, wider sharing in the congregation. And, of course, resistance from individuals and groups can also seriously disrupt any hope of progress.

Preacher/leaders should resolutely set their faces against momentum killers with a passion to keep telling out the bigger picture of God's kingdom. Of course, preacher/leaders are just as liable to misread God's direction as anyone else, and they need to resist stubborn self-will that masquerades as implementing God's plan. Yet when they remain humble, open to God's way, they play a major role in encouraging "alignment" every time they preach God's Word, as the Holy Spirit brings unity that only God can foster. He is the integrator of vision and community, the inspirer of action, the sustainer of implementation, and the giver of sheer grace. One great contribution of African American preaching has been its emphasis on designing sermons to end with community praise excitedly celebrating God's grace. Such a conclusion ensures congregations focus on God rather than themselves. Stage 8 involves complex leadership responsibilities, working with different goals within varying visionpaths, creating a continuing role for the vision community and especially of coping positively with conflict. But, through it all, preacher/leaders must keep the whole community sensitive to the big picture of God's purpose and glory.

In chapter 6 I referred to a sermon I preached to celebrate the third anniversary of a small group ministry. Some four years before that date, the vision for small groups was first raised. With the deacons, I realized that the growing congregation needed a structure of house groups. At a church weekend conference a vision for small groups was presented with some initial enthusiasm but also much confusion. A task group began working through the implications, trying to learn from other church experiences as much as possible. So many questions were posed: Would they involve everyone? How often would they meet? What would be their prime purpose—Bible study, prayer, pastoral concerns, evangelism? Who would lead them? Who would oversee the leaders? How would present church members be integrated? How would newcomers join in?

Over a year with almost weekly meetings, and wider monthly congregational meetings, along with support by prodding sermons, many of the above questions were resolved. Visionpaths were identified to ensure that timely implementation could occur. Yes, everyone would be included in an initial fifteen groups (though we knew from others' experience that less than 60 percent of the congregation would participate). The groups were designed to radiate out from the church like a bicycle wheel. Everybody was placed in their "sector group," which brought together people across gender, age, and race. Meeting weekly on Tuesday nights (apart from the monthly congregational meeting), their focus would be pastoral with a solid content of Bible study and prayer. Each group would care for those who could not (or would not) attend. Content would be linked with the previous Sunday sermon through questions provided on the bulletin. Leaders would be trained and overseen by four couples acting as area leaders who would maintain close contact, ensuring integration of old and new members.

All the time through this long and detailed process, my preaching continued to share progress and excitement. The launch was planned very carefully and made within Sunday worship that was designed in collaboration with the task group. In response, well over 50 percent of the congregation committed to their designated groups. But from that point on, I found there was never any time within the church's life and system that I could relax reinforcing momentum for small groups. Conflict, misunderstandings, entropy, and poor group leadership were ever ready to ambush progress. Preaching/leading had to keep the big picture in mind.

The particular sermon, mentioned in chapter 6, marked part of the intentional desire to keep the whole church focused, three years after the vision was first implemented. Small groups became a critical part of life, providing hospitality on Sundays after worship, participating in worship, and undertaking pastoral and evangelistic responsibility. At Christmas, and other significant times, they reached out imaginatively to absent members. They integrated seekers and new Christians with aplomb. Their impact was everywhere. Maintaining alignment required committed leading/preaching through the rest of my ministry that continually encouraged everyone to participate, empowered other leaders, and confronted "momentum killers."

Every Sermon Matters

I believe that all the stages of change process belong within the preaching task. Urgency, values, mission, vision, implementation, and alignment are not terms to be smuggled in like illegal aliens into the sermon-making process or treated as some trendy twenty-first-century fashion that has no biblical place. No, these leadership concepts should be recognized as legal residents that have always been there and are vital to the full-blooded process of preaching/leading. They impact how individual sermons are prepared and how sermon series are planned.

In *360-Degree Preaching* I commended "the preaching swim" as a model for sermon preparation and delivery (see fig. 7). It expresses how a preacher immerses into and belongs within the mysterious and powerful spiritual dynamic of God—Father, Son, and Holy Spirit—empowering Scripture, interpretation, design, and delivery. Preachers are charged to discern and respond to what the text *says* and *does*—to engage with the dynamics of God's Word which not only addresses heads but also transforms lives. After all, God's Word is God's act (Gen. 1:3). As preachers identify what it says and does by exegesis, they dare, by God's Holy Spirit, to interpret it relevantly so their sermons *say* and *do* what the text *says* and *does*. This is preaching/leadership's core—that the sermon *does* God's Word to help shape new creation in Christ by his Spirit. Preaching's best outcome occurs when both hearers and preacher are immersed in the outcomes of living out Scripture's challenge. The two questions that confront preachers from the beginning—"So what?" and "Yes, but how?"—are resoundingly answered as a congregation experiences God's will. And many classic aspects of leadership belong within this preaching process.

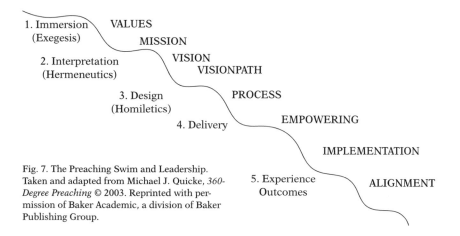

Fig. 7. The Preaching Swim and Leadership. Taken and adapted from Michael J. Quicke, *360-Degree Preaching* © 2003. Reprinted with permission of Baker Academic, a division of Baker Publishing Group.

A Brief Summary

Stage 1: Immersion (Exegesis)

Immersion into Scripture is the way to begin doing exegesis. In exegesis preachers pay prayerful attention to what God's Word means in its original context in order to ground their sermons on God's authoritative Word. When church leaders speak of "core values" and "mission" for congregational identity and purpose, they must relate them directly to scriptural authority and careful exegesis—nowhere else does God make it clearer what it means for preacher/leader and people to belong together as God's people. Aubrey Malphurs underlines the fact that the early Jerusalem church identified its values: "They devoted themselves to the apostles' teaching and fellowship, to the breaking of bread and the prayers" (Acts 2:42).

> Their values were evident in their actions. People could see what the church was devoted to by what they did. . . . If the early church knew and operated on their values, wisdom dictates that today's churches should follow suit.[29]

Preacher/leaders have a crucial role to help people discern and articulate their core values based on scriptural exegesis.

Similarly, when Christian leadership uses the word *mission* to indicate the big picture of what God calls a people to be and to do, Scripture provides its basis. Imperatives about loving God and neighbor (Matt. 22:34–40) and reaching the world for discipleship (Matt. 28:16–20) give mission its dynamic for all subsequent visions and visionpaths. By responding to Scripture's commands, preacher/leaders keep churches sensitive to living out its mission's three directions—between gospel and culture, gospel and church, and church and culture (see fig. 1). The Blackabys' definition of leadership as "moving people onto God's agenda" requires preacher/leaders to discern God's agenda through prayerful listening to Scripture. This is the source of God's vision and direction, and by preaching its message, hearers can become kingdom people living out God's counterstory of new creation in Christ.

Stage 2: Interpretation (Hermeneutics)

Interpreting Scripture for today involves using hermeneutical principles coupled with faithful listening to the ancient text. As each preacher listens to God's Word, many other "voices" can drown out, conflict, or resonate with what God is saying. Alongside Scripture's "voice," the "voices" of preacher, culture, congregation, and the worship context all bear upon how God's Word sounds out its contemporary significance. The *focus*—the saying of Scripture in contemporary words—is accompanied by *function*—the doing of Scripture in contemporary ways and means. The "voices" that a preacher heeds (of which Scripture should be dominant) must crystallize into specific words for specific actions. Identifying the text's *focus* and *function* is central to interpretation so that the sermon re-presents what God says and does today. Scripture never presents flat, neutral text—it always expects some kind of response. Therefore, the pivotal moment of preparation, and of preaching/leading, is the identification of the sermon's main impact—"what by the grace of God the sermon will say and do." Here the sermon impacts lives and leads people on God's authority.

Stage 2 also involves fleshing out vision. "When a church needs a God-honoring, kingdom-advancing, heart-thumping vision it turns to its leaders. . . . Vision is a picture of the future that produces passion."[30] Only by interpreting the biblical text can preacher/leaders discern vision for their particular congregations. Specific directions for individuals and community, grounded upon their values and living out their mission, depend on interpreting Scripture today. Also, visionpaths, which describe the more immediate implications of a larger vision, are closely connected to how a preacher/leader applies a sermon. Each sermon should give unambiguous application so that a congregation can translate its passion for mission and vision into practical action.

Stage 3: Design (Homiletics)

Designing the sermon calls for another set of skills (homiletics) to shape content with clarity and integrity. All sermons must answer two questions: "So what?" and "Yes, but how?" Thin-blooded preaching can dodge both questions and design sermons that appeal to individuals by informing them without disturbing them. Figure 3 gave a range of options for heralds, teachers, inductive, and narrative preachers, depending on Scripture genre, preacher's personality, and context. Each kind of preaching presents different ways of re-presenting the text's main impact, but preacher/leaders know the vital importance of collaborating with the Holy Spirit to design their best form of full-blooded preaching that gives glory to God and inspires missional response.

Stage 4: Delivery

Delivery of the sermon is the critical stage when all the hard work of discerning God's message, his mission, vision, and goals becomes public.

Only the Holy Spirit convicts, renews, and energizes sermon outcomes, but the quality of sermon delivery can greatly help or hinder his work. Every sermon event risks false persuasion and unworthy dullness, yet in preaching, God promises "treasure in clay jars, so that it may be made clear that this extraordinary power belongs to God and does not come from us" (2 Cor. 4:7). Authenticity guards against hypocrisy, integrity avoids manipulation, and good listening prevents boredom. Issues of empowering others and of implementing the change process are vitally involved with the ways that preacher/leaders are heard.

Stage 5: Experience Outcomes

Experience the outcomes is the cutting edge of preaching/leadership. In the "preaching swim" I envisage a massive splash as the congregation "jumps into God's Word and will." Preaching God's Word should always make a difference—there should be as much action *after* the preaching event as before it. Sermons can move individuals and communities forward more powerfully and permanently than any other way of leading people. Preachers, who first immersed themselves in Scripture and sensed God's values, mission, and vision for themselves and their people, should so preach by Holy Spirit power that hearers willingly commit themselves too. Here specific applications that implement transformation belong within God's process of alignment as people embrace the outcomes of values, mission, vision, and visionpaths. God's involvement in 360-degree leading makes transformation happen when preacher/leaders act on scriptural authority and flesh out its impact in the context of particular communities.

A Postscript

At times I have dipped into the experiences of well-known preacher/leaders as well as other colleagues whom I have interviewed. But throughout this entire project of leadership through preaching I have been writing out of personal experience. As I shared in chapter 1, how I began ministry is best summed up by John Killinger's book title *The Centrality of Preaching in the Total Task of the Ministry*. For twenty-one years of pastoral ministry this remained true. Especially looking back on my Cambridge ministry I see so much that resonates with the outworking of the "congregational transformation model." A few pages back I gave a taster about the implementation of small group ministry.

In chapter 1 I described how reluctant I was when I arrived as pastor to St. Andrew's Street Baptist Church in 1980. The church was dying before my eyes. I had little trouble portraying current reality but great difficulty in seeing any vision. I knew that spiritual and relational vitality was crucial to any God happening, though I had no clue then, of course, about the leadership model in this book. From the outset two priorities gripped me: preaching and prayer. I know my inadequacy drove me to spend longer in the Scriptures, holding onto the bigness of God's promises, glimpsing the breadth of the kingdom of God, to work through the implications of the Lord's call upon me and my people on this main street in Cambridge. Like others mentioned in this book I kept asking: What is God calling us to do together? With honesty, trying to live as close as I could be with Jesus, I majored first on prayer.

It is intriguing to reflect back on the role of preaching in those first months of new ministry as issues of values, prayer, and vision were presented. On my first Sunday I preached my heart out with a sermon entitled "Glory in the Cross" (1 Cor. 2:1–5; Gal. 6:11–16). I called people to go with me to the cross—God's greatest action for us. Directing others into a lively corporate prayer life seemed to be a priority, and I pleaded with the congregation to come to the Tuesday prayer meeting to make an urgent start with God. To my surprise, fifty out of seventy people came that first week. Luke 11:5–13 became our theme story, when Jesus dares to liken God to a man asleep in bed who refuses at first to answer the door and help his neighbor. Only as the neighbor keeps knocking and asking with nagging persistence is there a happy outcome. This is a challenge to persistence in intercession. I introduced an idea that would give rigor to our congregational prayer life—we made a prayer agenda of issues that would focus daily, individual, and corporate prayers. Specific issues were prayerfully identified (no more than five or six at a time) and written down in a large book that we would maintain for many years as a record of our asking and God's answering. This battered and dog-eared book, with a mixture of handwriting and styles, remains one of the most important records of church life through the 1980s. It is no exaggeration to say that every major breakthrough is found in its pages, anticipated, prayed through, and rejoiced over. Every hope, disappointment, financial problem, meeting decision, and nut-and-bolt issue is here.

Accompanying this community commitment to prayer, I preached within the rhythm of the Christian Year, a sermon series exulting in gospel reality:

"Great Joy" (Luke 15:1–7; John 15:5–11)
"Great Rewards" (Mark 10:28–31; Luke 17:7–10)
"Great Confidence" (Acts 2:38–42; 3:1–8)
"Great Love" (1 John 4:7–21)

"Great Liberty" (John 8:31–40; Rom. 6:15–18)
"Great Life" (John 10:7–16)

Focusing on a great God who makes great promises, the preaching emphasized corporate responsibilities in these "values" thrust upon us by
God's grace. For example, preaching on "Great Love" I used a three-
sided triangle from God to me, from me to my brother, and from God
to my brother.

> Already God loves my brother, my neighbor. He calls me to form the third
> side of the triangle and make that love all the more evident. The particular
> people around us here in this city are the first recipients of love.

Reinforcing the importance of corporate prayer, I preached a series
of eight sermons called "With Jesus in the School of Prayer." In the
prayer diary we continued to focus on specific issues. On that first list
at number four we wrote: *Let us pray for a clear vision of God's will for
our city center strategy—particularly the use of our premises.* I believe
that out of this, continuing prayer vision came. I had been there three
or four months when I arranged to meet someone outside the front of
the church on a weekday. I don't remember who it was, but the person
never showed up. As I was standing outside I suddenly realized how many
hundreds of people were passing the church front doors. Shoppers laden
with bags from the large superstores nearby, formally dressed business
people, groups of tourists with cameras round their necks, foreign students dangerously wobbling on rented bicycles, local students noisily in
groups, young mothers with strollers, young people looking bored, and
the homeless looking hungry. For the first time it hit me how busy our
street was during the week.

Up until then I had only been on the premises for Sunday worship,
evening business meetings, and occasional women's meetings. I had only
been at the church building when downtown was quiet. Now I saw it for
real. Oh the irony! The only times we were open for business, downtown
was closed (and easier for us to park). While the city bustled with life we
were closed. We had so organized ourselves in a city of 110,000 people
we had become invisible. Suddenly I was overwhelmed by a vision of
who we should be—open 24/7 to live out God's mission in the heart of
the city. I returned home overwhelmed by my experience. Was this an
answer to our prayer request for our use of the premises?

My sermons continued to focus on mission and vision through these
months. For example, that first summer I preached on "Making Links"
(Matt. 28:16–20). The whole church family was present (by now the congregation was growing), and we used brightly colored streamers to tell

the story of Jesus's first links with his disciples, and then with his church family, and then through *us* to new disciples. Children took streamers, crisscrossing the church so that every person could take hold of one. I called them God's lifelines linking disciples with Jesus as Savior. As we held streamers I challenged them about belonging to Jesus, together and reaching out beyond to make more disciples, especially those who lived and worked near us. I longed for the front doors to be opened and the streamers to be taken out there and then!

As prayer combined with vision, my preaching continued to generate and sustain creative tension about our part within the bigger picture of God's mission. Very soon there came a possibility of taking a little shop with a janitor's house above it to create a small coffee shop as an outreach. Just thirty-six feet by seventeen feet, this offered an opportunity for creative mission. Some of us were so excited that God seemed to be answering us. However, the church congregational business meeting said no but agreed to set up a team to examine the vision more closely. Three questions were posed for the team and whole congregation: Who are the people we want to reach? What would attract these people? Can we foresee the resources being available, for whatever we do is likely to need more people and more money?

This group became the equivalent of a vision community. I shared in every meeting though I did not convene it. As we pursued these questions, so we began the change process that would occupy the next ten years of working and planning. Team meetings, congregational meetings, church retreats, daily prayer, and weekly sermons created a tumultuous mix, resonating at every turn with elements of the congregational transformation model. As preacher/leader I was in the thick of it, yet God was working through my role in subtle ways as pastor and encourager, developing my learning disciplines of generating and sustaining creative tension, mental models, team learning, and systems thinking. Take any single sermon preached back then and you will find it was immersed in developing spiritual and relational vitality within a change process that would eventually implement the vision.

When I tell this story I speak of a series of elements, each of which was growing: Growing Prayer, Growing Vision, Growing Preaching, Growing Debate, Growing People, Growing Faith, Growing Giving, and Growing Pain. When I am asked what I learned through this process, I confess that some of the most difficult lessons concerned hostilities and hurts provoked by those who disagreed with the steps we were taking. Expressing themselves with verbal anger, resignations, and destructive letters, a relatively few people caused mighty waves of negatives. When things went wrong, which they seemed to do regularly, some of us interpreted them as hurdles the Lord wanted us to leap over by faith, but others saw them as signs of God's displeasure at our disobedience. All talk of life-giving conflict seemed wishful thinking at the time it was occurring. But looking back, the maturity of the whole congregation did deepen and the eventual outcomes did give God glory.

This is not the place to expand on the ultimate conclusions as the church grew from a handful or so of tens to many hundreds, from closed front doors to a seven-day-a-week mission, from one minister to a team of fourteen full-time staff, from a traditional inward structure to an outward mission structure. People gave generously nearly two million dollars to open a mission center, alongside the main church building, breaking through the church sidewall to integrate Sunday worship with weekly witness. Instead of a shut worship building, our mission center was reaching thousands every week through a restaurant open to the general public, counseling services for families and individuals, and job clubs for the unemployed. The homeless slept the nights during the winter months in our main hall, young people occupied the top floor, and members of the congregation committed themselves to work through every one of these activities to live out kingdom good news.

Whenever people ask me about large faith projects, I always say:

Don't do it unless the Lord gives you no choice—it must begin with his vision for his glory.

Only do it by prayer and keep praying for his guidance.

Seek God's unique plan for your church because of your community's need.

Keep preaching and communicating—every step forward must be scripturally based and courageously shared.

Expect opposition—every step forward for God will be under attack.

Expect rising costs—every project always seems to at least double original estimates.

Attempt great things for God, expect great things from God.

You can see why I believe in leadership through preaching. By full-blooded preaching, God quickens people, offers salvation, gives vision, energy, and faith, and leads them forward into transformation, with deeper worship and greater mission for his glory. May God inspire a new generation of preacher/leaders who are open to the Holy Spirit to lead congregational transformations everywhere they are called to preach/lead for him.

Appendix A

"Leadership 101"

The world church in the twenty-first century lives in tumultuous times. Never has the church grown as fast. Statisticians estimate that every hour there are over three thousand new Christians born again in God's kingdom. That's a Pentecost every hour. But most of this growth is in the southern church—Latin America, Africa, and Asia. I had lunch with Luis Bush of the Lausanne Covenant a little while ago. I asked him, "What is the most stirring spiritual event you have been to recently?" He paused and said, "In Indonesia, where over one million people gathered to pray and pray and pray."

But every hour in the northern church, where we are, in Western Europe and North America, we are hemorrhaging. Thomas Reeves analyzed seven main denominations in North America to find they had all lost between one-fifth and one-third of their members since 1960. Methodist research in 1995 showed that over the previous thirty years they had lost on average one thousand church members every single week.

Part of the exuberance in the southern church is that it appears to worship and live closer to Jesus. There is an immediacy of living for him, of trusting and obeying. It seems to me possible that we in the northern church have let our history, traditions, organizations, and structures

Stereo draft of sermon preached on Luke 4:22–5:11 by Michael Quicke at First Baptist Church, Wheaton, Illinois, May 29, 2005.

put a barrier between us and Jesus! We are no longer as close as we once were.

Tonight let's say it. *Jesus is the world's only Savior and the world's greatest leader, and that he has done it all for you and me.* He has saved us once and for all. We cannot add to it or improve on it. He has given us all that we need to belong and grow. He took thirty years to prepare for his ministry and his mission of three years was the most clearly focused mission in the world. Calling him "Lord" means putting him in control. Staying close to the dynamics of being with him.

So, we need a reality check. One of the New Testament stories that has been so influential on my own understanding of leadership comes in Luke's account of the call of the first disciples (Luke 4:42–5:11). Stay close to the story and you can feel the pulse, the rhythm of Jesus's leadership. Let's enter its dynamic.

1st—Prayer

Leadership with Jesus begins at daybreak at prayer in a solitary place. It's not incidental that we call devotions our "Quiet Time." Christian happenings begin in prayer . . . always.

Prayer in the quiet precedes noisy action.
Private prayer precedes public prayer.
Personal relationship with the Father precedes public relationship.
Words to God precede words for God.
Time with God precedes time for God.

Who we are in secret with God is the test of authenticity. One of the greatest lies we have been sold is that prayer is very important but that our plans and actions are even more important. Such is our pride that we believe we did it. We sprinkle a prayer or two on our business meetings but we know what we can achieve. And we miss the larger part—what might have been achieved if we had first prayed and kept praying.

My father died two summers ago, aged eighty-eight. A retired pastor, he had deliberately reduced his possessions to the minimum. But I shall never forget finding by the side of his armchair his worn leather briefcase full of all his prayer commitments. Page after page about so many needs, individuals, and organizations. Each one marked right up until the morning he went into the hospital. He refused to have TV because he said that it interfered with his quiet time with God. I found so many of his prayer notebooks and journals, and I marveled how much was accomplished in that little room for eternity. And I also thought (because this crosses your mind at a time like that) what my boys would find of my private life of prayer with God.

Nothing worthwhile is accomplished for God without prayer. "Apart from me you can do nothing" (John 15:5). Andrew Murray provocatively commented that God only answers prayers when they are asked for his glory. When we petition and intercede it is "your kingdom come, your will be done on earth as in heaven. . . . yours is the power and the glory for ever and ever." Prayer is central for each preacher/leader and all who hear them.

2nd—Preach

The people want Jesus to stay but his mission is to preach. It is strong language: *I MUST preach to others, because that is why I was sent* (Luke 4:43). And *he kept on preaching* (v. 44). We must never lose the centrality of preaching to the leadership of Jesus. Jesus has a world to love and save and he does it by preaching/leading to the cross and beyond. It is his preferred method. Yes, pragmatists allow leadership to pull strings and push preaching to one side to do devotional duty. There are books out there: *21 Irrefutable Laws of Leadership*—follow these and people will follow you. *12 Steps to a Successful Church*. Beating that—*10 Steps to a Very Successful Church*.

But Jesus does his mission by this one mode . . . preaching, proclaiming, pouring out good news. But as he preaches he also leads—note this carefully—preachers and listeners.

Among the skills that leadership books say leaders should have are the skills to "generate and sustain creative tension." Jesus Christ was the master of generating and sustaining creative tension. His message is summed up: "I must preach the good news of the kingdom of God" (v. 43 NIV). He always looks beyond and sees new ways of living. God's kingdom, now present yet not fully vindicated. Present future. From the beginning Jesus was about deeper purposes and greater ways of living. And ever since we carry two passports. One is stamped with our country of citizenship, an awful looking photograph, place of birth, height, color of eyes, and expiry date. The other we carry as children in the kingdom of God, sons and daughters of the Most High, royal priests; to all who received him, who believed in his name, he gave the right to become children of God. . . . children born not of natural descent, nor of human decision . . . children born of God (John 1:12–13). No expiry date. Jesus says "I am the way, the truth, and the life" (John 14:6). I am your journey, and your purpose, and your Savior. Everything is found in me. So keep following, keep growing.

Can you find any single example where his preaching did not cause tension? When he allowed people to sit back comfortably? He called people into kingdom—to cross the gap between how things are now and how they might become by the grace of God. Always creating and sustaining tension. Keeping people in kingdom torque (spelled T-O-R-Q-U-E!), never arriving, always pressing on. Never having loved enough, forgiven enough, or lived enough. As Oswald Chambers put it: "He puts crowns just above our heads and expects us to grow into them." Never complacent, never bland, never predictable. Luke 4 is the locus of prophetic preaching when Jesus intentionally self-fulfills Isaiah 61. And the rest of the Christian story is living in tension between the now and not yet.

Only by a gross act of myopic self-indulgence can preachers and congregations be self-congratulatory. It's a travesty that much church culture has forsaken kingdom tension for instant market attractiveness. There has been a massive sellout on the tension of Christian life, of sanctification, radical love, and mission.

Preacher/leaders have the responsibility of keeping the tension between present reality and God's future promise ever alive so that creatively the Holy Spirit can transform people and communities. Positively, it begins with a preacher's personal vision that is open to God in daily relationship and weekly preaching, which flows through worship into the business life and mission life of the church. Every one of us is being stretched. Jesus's way does not work like anything else. He calls us to preach and live kingdom possibilities, to be stretched in faith.

3rd—Push Out

(If you want a point that begins with another "p"!) In the pulse of Jesus's leadership, just see what he does next. He is still preaching (what a surprise), and he sees two boats not being used by fishermen who are *washing* their nets. Not incidental detail. We happen to know they are washing them after a tough night when they didn't catch a thing. Wash, stretch out, repair any holes—the worst part of the job. Every job has a downside.

Jesus chooses one boat, belonging to Simon—it has his Galilee registration number on the side. He tells Simon to put it close to the shore so that people can hear him. First there is more preaching (Luke 5:3). *When he had finished*, he asks Simon, "Put out into deep water, and let down the nets for a catch." This is what is called an acted parable. The time for hearing words is over. And you don't need any imagination to hear the weariness in Simon's voice: "Master, we've worked hard all night and haven't caught anything."

You notice how this is all on Jesus's terms. In a way it seems rather trivial. All his great kingdom preaching and then getting into a boat to fish. But you see, the last time they tried it didn't work. Now in deep water he wants them to show that they trust him. They've only just washed and repaired nets after futile effort. But Jesus leads by command and from the beginning to the end of our lives we should keep saying what Simon says: "But because you say so, I will."

I'm weary and fed up with everything right now. *But because you say so, I will.*

I'm a realist and I found that doesn't work. *But because you say so, I will.*

I just don't see how that could work in this situation with these people. *But because you say so, I will.*

I have been giving of my best to this relationship, within this church, and nothing seems to be happening. *But because you say so, I will.*

Every Christian community lives with one of two dynamics:

One is **PULL IN.** Stay where I am, as I am. Safe in my "comfort zone." In Luke 5 terms, it means staying near the beach. It's the specialty of transactional leaders to seek what is mutually comfortable and avoid what is uncomfortable. To avoid cost, sacrifice, the threat of the new, radical change. Its slogan is: *Because we say so*. And many of us practice it skillfully in church life—what someone called the Dead Sea syndrome, with everything flowing in and nothing flowing out.

The other is **PUSH OUT**. Trust Jesus in new places. Go out of my "comfort zone" because he says so. Go to what is uncomfortable. Trust Jesus to do the work. Only those who *PUSH OUT* and take risks with Jesus discover who Jesus really is. Only when we risk can God do something new and others share in the astonishment. Fishing is the paradigm for mission, of course. Jesus is leading them into faith action.

[Need to see the story move forward.]

4th—Power in the Midst

Only when they push out and let down nets can there be a God happening. Jesus does need them to play their part. He's not going to make the fish jump into the boat. It is no good staying on the beach and expecting fish to land themselves gratefully ashore, waddling out of the water like some happy Nemos flopping around with smiles on their faces. They have to act. But when they do, in spite of their weariness and bad past experience, they find so many fish that they fill one boat, filling everything, slithering all around, under their arms, in their ears, jumping all over the place. And they notice that the level of the water is the same as the top of the boat. *They began to sink.* How about that? The previous night not one tiny fish. Not one. Now, so many they are going to sink.

Fishing is the paradigm for mission. And God happenings always surprise. They are never predictable and they can overwhelm our mediocre expectations. This is the sign of the kingdom. This will hold them, like the transfiguration, and healings, and words in the fragile journey to the cross, and beyond, blazing in Spirit glory in the Spirit's birthing of the church. God is in this story as he is in ours. Never forget that he writes the script.

To use contemporary jargon, he is being missional. Jesus is giving them a new way of seeing their mission and recognizing his power.

Note in passing how Jesus is in one of the boats and identifies with Simon in the task. But so great is that response that "they signaled to their partners in the other boat to come and help them" (v. 7). Teams are universally endorsed by leadership studies. It has become a truism that for any organization to be effective there must be teams, and Jesus shows us from the very beginning as he calls disciples that working with others is vital in his work.

5th—Presence

As Simon witnesses all this he realizes how he cannot cope with this person, Jesus. "Master, leave. I'm a sinner and can't handle this holiness. Leave me to myself" (v. 8 Message). Until we have encountered the real God we shall never understand how holy he is. How utterly unholy we are. And that experience of inadequacy and depth is the ground rock for Christian leadership and eventfulness. Simon came in with respect and admiration for Jesus, but meeting Jesus in power means overwhelming worship. We come into worship seeking to express as best we can our devotion to God; but when we are shocked by God's power then worship is for real. We should never become too familiar, too casual, too arrogant. Who God is, whose ways are not our ways, holds us dependent and needy from beginning to end. Yet always with awesome expectation that God happenings can occur right here, in the midst, anytime we do his will.

6th—Personal Call

Out of this experience comes Jesus's call to Simon and the others to catch people. The rhythm of staying close to Jesus pulses through prayer, preaching, pushing out in faith, daring to act on God's good news, into fresh God happenings and renewed call into mission. Jesus says: "Do not be afraid; from now on you will be catching people" (v. 10). Of course he's afraid. He's seen again how big God is, so holy, so powerful. But this is the single most important call humankind ever hears. And they leave everything and follow him.

I believe that Christian communities need to know the pulse and rhythm of Christ's command. And one reason why I believe this so strongly is my own experience of leadership through preaching. It's personal and it needs corroboration.

My last church was in downtown Cambridge, through the 1980s and into the 1990s. It had a proud history and possessed a large building, but when I was called, the elderly congregation was down in number to around seventy in the morning and twenty in the evening. I couldn't always see them because the mist would roll in and they sat far back. But they had a core of pray-ers who wanted to stay close to Jesus. Frankly, the church seemed to be dying—perhaps burial was going to be my ministry. As someone said to me, "There are already too many churches in Cambridge!"

I had been there a few months when I arranged to meet someone outside the front of the church on a weekday. I don't remember who it was and which day. But as I was standing outside I suddenly realized how many hundreds of people were passing the church front doors. Shoppers, tourists, university students, moms with toddlers, businesspeople, and a few homeless begging. On the sidewalk they kept coming by, five-deep. Hundreds of them. For the first time it hit me how busy our street was during the week and how totally we ignored these people. We only met when the city was quiet and empty and it was easy to park. And it seemed to me that the Lord was calling us, weak though we were, to push out into deep water. To open our doors to mission on our high street.

We made it an urgent matter for prayer. Prayer that was organized so that every member of the congregation had the same topics to pray for every day and together in corporate prayer. We kept a book to record these prayers and God's answers. We prayed about the use of our premises, our finances, our missionaries, our vision.

We suffered disappointments. One or two early possibilities didn't work out. We kept praying. And then at a congregational meeting one person said why didn't we open our church doors right now. Say, at Christmas. We could sing carols (which seemed risky, knowing some of the singers), we could offer coffee and cookies, we could tell out the Christmas message. Some expressed worries. Might people drop drink or crumbs in the church building? But come to think about it there would be no one left to use the church building unless God did something!

When the day came there was much nervous excitement. Would any-body actually come in? How would we deal with total strangers in our space? How many do you think actually came in that day? By four o'clock in the afternoon over five hundred people had come in to lay down weary burdens of Christmas shopping to hear something of the true people of Christmas. We sang and talked. "I've been passing here for years, and didn't know you existed," said one person. "I'll come back for your services," said another. An international singer, Wanda Jackson, who was in concert in Cambridge that night, came in, with her bodyguard. "Please would someone pray with me," she said. "I was so hoping to find a church open today." We could hardly believe how many people and how many needs. Pushing out: God was showing us what he could do even with us. And that became the story of the next twelve years as the church pushed out into the deep waters of mission and we were transformed to be a seven-day witness on the main street.

Do you want to join me in the pulse of staying close with Jesus? (Brief challenge left unworded).

Appendix B

Some Leadership Definitions

A leader is a person with certain *qualities* of personality and character, which are appropriate to the general *situation* and supported by a degree of relevant technical knowledge and experience, who is able to provide the necessary *functions* to guide a group towards the further realization of its purpose, while maintaining and building its unity as a team; doing all this in the right ratio or proportion with the contributions of other members of the team.

John Adair, *Action-Centred Leadership*
(London: McGraw-Hill, 1973), 15.

Leadership involves a person, group, or organization who shows the way in an area of life—whether in the short or the long term—and in doing so both influences and empowers enough people to bring about change in that area. From a Christian point of view it is only when the direction and the method are in-line with God's purposes, character, and ways of operating that godly leadership takes place.

Robert Banks and Bernice M. Ledbetter,
Reviewing Leadership (Grand Rapids: Baker, 2004), 16–17.

A Christian leader is someone who is called by God to lead and possess virtuous character and effectively motivates, mobilizes resources and directs people toward the fulfillment of a jointly embraced vision from God.

George Barna, *The Second Coming of the Church*
(Nashville: Word, 1998), 107.

Leadership is
- —knowing what to do next
- —knowing why that's important, and
- —knowing how to bring appropriate resources to bear on the need at hand.

> Bobb Biehl, *Increasing Your Leadership Confidence*
> (Sisters, OR: Questar, 1989), 13.

The manager is the classic good soldier; the leader is his own person. The manager does things right; the leader does the right thing.

> Warren Bennis, *On Becoming a Leader*
> (Reading, MA: Addison-Wesley, 1989), 45.

Spiritual leadership is moving people on to God's agenda.

> Henry Blackaby and Richard Blackaby, *Spiritual Leadership*
> (Nashville: Broadman & Holman, 2001), 20.

Leadership over human beings is exercised when persons with certain motives and purposes mobilize, in competition or conflict with others, institutional, political, psychological, and other resources so as to arouse, engage, and satisfy the motives of followers.

> James MacGregor Burns, *Leadership*
> (New York: Harper & Row, 1978), 17.

Leadership is a dynamic process in which a man or woman with God-given capacity influences a specific group of God's people toward His purposes for that group.

> J. Robert Clinton, *The Making of a Leader*
> (Colorado: NavPress, 1988), 14.

Leadership is the process of persuasion or example by which an individual (or leadership team) induces a group to pursue objectives held by a leader or shared by a leader and his or her followers.

John W. Gardner, *On Leadership* (New York: The Free Press, 1990), 1.

The great leader is seen as servant first, and that simple fact is the key to his greatness.

Robert K. Greenleaf, *Servant Leadership* (New York: Paulist, 1977), 7.

Leadership is critically concerned with establishing and coordinating the relationships between four things: the *who*, the *what*, the *how* and the *why*:

- Who are you?—An identity.
- What does the organization want to achieve?—A strategic vision.

- How will they achieve this?—Organizational tactics.
- Why should followers want to embody the identity, pursue the strategic vision and adopt the organizational tactics?—Persuasive communication.

Keith Grint, The Arts of Leadership
(Oxford: Oxford University Press, 2000), 27.

Leadership is a process that helps direct and mobilize people and/or their ideas. Leadership within a complex organization achieves this function through three subprocesses: establishing direction, aligning people, motivating and inspiring.

John P. Kotter, A Force for Change (New York: Free Press, 1990), 5.

What enabled leaders to get extraordinary things done. They:
1. Challenged the process
2. Inspired a shared vision
3. Enabled others to act
4. Modeled the way
5. Encouraged the heart

James M. Kouzes and Barry Z. Posner, The Leadership Challenge
(San Francisco: Jossey-Bass, 1987), 8.

Leadership is the process of bringing people to a point of having to face their problems and to deal with them. And that is what preaching is about.

Alice Mathews, Preaching That Speaks to Women
(Grand Rapids: Baker, 2003), 132.

Leadership is influence.

John C. Maxwell, Developing the Leader within You
(Nashville: Thomas Nelson, 1993), 1.

Leadership appears to be the art of getting others to want to do something that you are convinced should be done.

Vance Packard, quoted in Kouzes and Posner,
The Leadership Challenge, 1.

Powerful leaders of the past and present were dreamers and visionaries. They were people who looked beyond the confines of space and time to transcend the traditional boundaries of either their positions or their organizations.

John E. Roueche, George A. Baker III, and Robert R. Rose,
Shared Vision: Transformational Leadership in American Community
Colleges (Washington, DC: Community College Press, 1989), 109.

Leadership is influence, the ability of one person to influence others.

> J. Oswald Sanders, *Spiritual Leadership*
> (1967; repr. Chicago: Moody, 1994), 31.

The only thing of real importance that leaders do is to create and manage culture. . . . The unique talent of leaders is their ability to work with culture.

> E. H. Schein, *Leadership and Organizational Culture*
> (San Francisco: Jossey-Bass, 1985), 5.

We are coming to believe that leaders are those people who "walk ahead," people who are genuinely committed to deep change in themselves and in their organizations. They lead through developing new skills, capabilities, and understandings. And they come from many places within the organization.

> Peter Senge, quoted in Frances Hesselbein, Marshall Goldsmith,
> and Richard Beckhard, eds., *The Leader of the Future*
> (San Francisco: Jossey Bass, 1996), 45.

The Christian leader is a person of integrity who is generative, compassionate, and who communicates hope and joy; who listens to people, creates a vision with those people, responds to the needs of the Christian community, especially the alienated and marginalized, works collaboratively with others in responding to those needs, expands the concept of ministry, and supports the gifts and ministries of the laity and those who influence their values.

> Loughlan Sofield, *The Collaborative Leader*
> (Notre Dame, IN: Ave Maria, 1995), 40.

Leadership in action is "perceiving and articulating the vision of the kingdom of God and effectively defining and communicating its incarnation, following Christ's example of service."

> Benjamin Williams and Michael McKibben, *Oriented Leadership:*
> *Why All Christians Need It* (Wayne, NJ: Orthodox
> Christian Publications Center, 1994), 22–23.

Leadership is a relationship—a relationship in which one person seeks to influence the thoughts, behaviours, beliefs or values of another person.

> Walter C. Wright Jr., *Relational Leadership*
> (Carlisle, UK: Paternoster, 2000), 2.

Appendix C

Personal Credo about Preachers as Leaders

I believe that preachers are leaders:

- *I believe that preaching is God's primary way of transforming individuals and communities because he empowers it.* Every spiritual surge in the church's story since the first century has owed its life to God's presence and action. Leander Keck puts it: "Every renewal of Christianity has been accompanied by a renewal of preaching. Every renewal of preaching, in turn, has rediscovered biblical preaching." From Jesus (Mark 1:14), we see that this is God's preferred method of working. It may seem foolish—spoken words to groups of Galileans—but it pleases God to use the foolishness of preaching. At every turning point in Acts there's a preacher. Preaching has always been God's way of confronting people with truth, salvation, and renewal.

- *I believe that preachers have been leaders at every breakthrough in the Christian story.* It happens to be the case that the church's greatest thinkers and leaders did their thinking and their leading through preaching. Often without realizing it, preachers today build on the work of preaching giants such as Origen (who united exegesis and preaching), Augustine (who brought together a careful use of rhetoric with exegesis and preaching), and Luther (who concentrated on one passage with a passion for simplicity and doctrinal truth). In my own story, Spurgeon was sixteen when he started to preach. He died aged fifty-seven, having planted 198 churches—most still going strong—a seminary, large orphanages, and a legacy of extraordinary writing. How he lived out God's timeless truths in his time!

- *I believe that preachers as leaders arise out of God's calling and gifting.* Now, it is God who raises up an Origen, Augustine, Luther, and Spurgeon. He does it in his own time. Sometimes little seems to happen—"In those days the word of the LORD was rare; there were not many visions" (1 Sam. 3:1 NIV). "Where there is no vision, the people perish" (Prov. 29:18 KJV). But at other times, God raises new preachers, harnessing hearts, souls, minds, and strength to speak and to lead for him. There *are* preachers, leaders, and visions.

- *I believe that preaching needs to recover its prophetic voice today.* I believe that preaching needs to be renewed in holy boldness, courage, insight, and passion. Sometimes the term *prophetic preaching* is used loosely and extravagantly as when a preacher appears to have particular intensity or deals with justice issues. Someone said to me that its two characteristics are sweat and noise. But the word *prophetic* goes back to the todayness of Jesus preaching Luke 4:21. Closely associated with the work of the Holy Spirit (Luke 4:14; 4:18) it is about communities being grasped by divine reality (1 Thess. 1:5).

- *I believe that preaching brings the whole church under God to see his vision and hear his Word for his mission.* When the church is born Peter sees Joel's prophecy fulfilled: "Your sons and daughters will prophesy, your young men will see visions, your old men will dream dreams. Even on my servants, both men and women, I will pour out my Spirit in those days, and they will prophesy" (Acts 2:17–18 NIV). This is a threefold vision. First, of God whose glory they have beheld in Jesus. Second, of themselves as a new people, with all barriers down of gender, race, and class, now able to participate in new creation. Third, it's a vision for the world—this is a whole new way of seeing life and its future. Vision is essential for the people of God. And how can God's vision be communicated without preaching?

- *I believe that preachers have to reclaim the preaching/leading task with prayer, humility, energy, and collaboration.* Twenty-first-century preachers need many qualities. Prayer sustains dependency upon God's grace, and humility shows necessary reliance. Yet, with deep confidence in the power of God's Word and his call, preachers are called to give their best energies. Hearers need to be involved with preachers in new ways of living by God's vision. For God's sake, and his church's sake, we need a new generation of preacher/leaders today.

Notes

Introduction

1. Michael J. Quicke, "Preaching with Purpose: The Pulpit Is More Than Something to Lean On," *Spotlight on Northern* (2003): 8–9.

2. Michael J. Quicke, *360-Degree Preaching: Hearing, Speaking, and Living the Word* (Grand Rapids: Baker, 2003), 27.

3. James Black, *The Mystery of Preaching* (London: Marshall, Morgan & Scott, 1977), 38.

Chapter 1: A Great Divide

1. Quicke, *360-Degree Preaching*, 36.

2. See comments of Cinthia Richie, "Why Men Hate Going to Church," *Chicago Tribune*, April 24, 2005.

3. George Barna, *The Second Coming of the Church* (Nashville: Word, 1998), 107.

4. Bill Hybels, "Creating a Leadership Revolution" (address at Leaders' Gathering, Willow Creek Community Church, South Barrington, Illinois), May 27, 2004.

5. Christopher Idle, "Who's Who in the Forest: New Perspectives," *Baptist Times* (September–November 1999).

6. John Killinger, *The Centrality of Preaching in the Total Task of the Ministry* (Waco, TX: Word, 1969).

7. Walter Brueggemann, *Texts under Negotiation: The Bible and Postmodern Imagination* (Minneapolis: Fortress, 1993), 25.

8. Eric Reed and Colin Hansen, "How Pastors Rate as Leaders," *Leadership* 24, no. 4 (Fall 2003): 30–34.

9. Thomas G. Bandy, *Coaching Change: Breaking Down Resistance, Building Up Hope* (Nashville: Abingdon, 2000), 148–53.

10. Kennon L. Callahan, *Twelve Keys to an Effective Church* (New York: Jossey-Bass, 1983), 29.

11. Christian A. Schwarz, *Natural Church Development: A Guide to Eight Essential Qualities of Healthy Churches* (Carol Stream, IL: ChurchSmart Resources, 1996), 30–31.

12. Leith Anderson, "Iron Sharpens Iron—Culture, Church and Leadership" (seminar, Northern Seminary, Lombard, Illinois), September 24, 2003.

13. Henry Blackaby and Richard Blackaby, *Spiritual Leadership: Moving People on to God's Agenda* (Nashville: Broadman & Holman, 2001).

14. Rick Warren, *The Purpose Driven Church: Growth without Compromising Your Message and Vision* (Grand Rapids; Zondervan, 1995).

15. Jim Herrington, Mike Bonem, and James H. Furr, *Leading Congregational Change: A Practical Guide for the Transformational Journey* (San Francisco: Jossey-Bass, 2000).

16. Aubrey Malphurs, *Values-Driven Leadership: Discovering and Developing Your Core Values for Ministry* (Grand Rapids: Baker, 1996), 111. Citations are to the 1996 edition.

17. Interview with Bishop Vaughn McLaughlin, "The Wizard of Odds," *Leadership* 24, no. 2 (Spring 2003): 24–29.

18. John Maxwell, "Thinking, Leading, and Preaching," in *Preaching* 19, no. 4 (January/ February 2004): 19.

19. John McClure, *The Roundtable Pulpit: Where Leadership and Preaching Meet* (Nashville: Abingdon, 1995), 50.

20. John P. Kotter, *Leading Change* (Boston: Harvard Business School Press, 1996).

21. Andy Stanley, *Visioneering* (Sisters, OR: Multnomah, 1999).

22. For more detailed discussion of culture shift, see Quicke, *360-Degree Preaching*, 36–54.

23. See especially Lesslie Newbigin, *Foolishness to the Greeks: The Gospel and Western Culture* (Grand Rapids: Eerdmans, 1986). Also see websites such as The Gospel and Our Culture, http://gospel-culture.org.uk/ and The Gospel and Our Culture Network, http://www.gocn.org/.

24. George R. Hunsberger, "The Newbigin Gauntlet: Developing a Domestic Missiology for North America," in George R. Hunsberger and Craig Van Gelder, eds. *The Church between Gospel and Culture: The Emerging Mission in North America* (Grand Rapids: Eerdmans, 1996), 6–7.

25. Terri Schiavo became a national cause in January 2005 over her husband's right to remove her feeding tube.

26. For example, Willow Creek chooses "teaching" as its first value. Warren also writes of the primary importance of teaching to win souls.

27. Kennon Callahan is credited with developing this concept.

28. Kennon L. Callahan, *Effective Church Leadership: Building on the Twelve Keys* (San Francisco: Jossey-Bass, 1990), 23–26.

29. Blackaby and Blackaby, *Spiritual Leadership*, 10.

30. George Barna, *A Fish Out of Water: 9 Strategies to Maximize Your God-Given Leadership Potential* (Nashville: Integrity, 2002), 5–6.

31. Lee G. Bolman and Terrence E. Deal, *Leading with Soul: An Uncommon Journey of Spirit*, new and rev. ed. (1995; repr., San Francisco: Jossey-Bass, 2001).

32. Russ S. Moxley, *Leadership and Spirit: Breathing New Vitality and Energy into Individuals and Organizations* (San Francisco: Jossey-Bass, 1989).

33. Peter B. Vaill, *Spirited Leading and Learning: Process Wisdom for a New Age* (San Francisco: Jossey-Bass, 1998).

34. Robert Banks and Bernice M. Ledbetter, *Reviewing Leadership: A Christian Evaluation of Current Approaches* (Grand Rapids: Baker, 2004), 58–60.

35. Stephen Pattison, "Recognizing Leaders' Hidden Beliefs," in *Faith and Leadership: How Leaders Live Out Their Faith in Their Work and Why It Matters*, ed. Robert Banks and Kim Powell (San Francisco: Jossey-Bass, 2000), 169–81.

36. Stephen R. Covey, *The Seven Habits of Highly Effective People: Restoring the Character Ethic* (New York: Simon & Schuster, 1989).

37. Banks and Ledbetter, *Reviewing Leadership*, 63.

38. Robert E. Quinn, *Deep Change: Discovering the Leader Within* (San Francisco: Jossey-Bass, 1996), xii.

39. Malphurs, *Values-Driven Leadership*, 101.

40. Tim Stafford, "The Third Coming of George Barna," *Christianity Today*, August 5, 2002, 33–38.

41. Reed and Hansen, "How Pastors Rate as Leaders," 30–34.

42. Ibid., 32.

43. E. K. Bailey and Warren W. Wiersbe, *Preaching in Black and White: What We Can Learn from Each Other* (Grand Rapids: Zondervan, 2003), 55.

44. Ibid.

45. Alice P. Mathews, *Preaching That Speaks to Women* (Grand Rapids: Baker, 2003), 131.

46. Ibid., 132.

47. Ibid., 133.

48. Peter Senge, *The Fifth Discipline: The Art and Practice of the Learning Organization* (New York: Doubleday/Currency, 1990), 219–20.

49. Hunsberger, "The Newbigin Gauntlet," 9.

50. Ibid.

51. Ibid., 10.

52. Walter C. Hobbs, "Faith Twisted by Culture: Syncretism in North American Christianity," in Craig Van Gelder, ed., *Confident Witness-Changing World: Rediscovering the Gospel in North America* (Grand Rapids: Eerdmans, 1999), 96–97.

53. Stanley Hauerwas and William H. Willimon, *Resident Aliens: Life in the Christian Colony* (Nashville: Abingdon, 1989), 41.

54. Lesslie Newbigin, quoted in Hunsberger, "The Newbigin Gauntlet," 15.

55. Eddie Gibbs, *ChurchNext Quantum Changes in How We Do Ministry* (Downers Grove, IL: InterVarsity, 2000), 52.

56. Ibid., 64.

57. I am grateful to Craig Williams for letting me read his unpublished Doctor of Ministry Report. Craig Williams, "The Impact of Preaching on Developing the Character of a New Church Development," (D.Min., Columbia Theological Seminary, 2003).

58. Ibid.

Chapter 2: Together in Scripture

1. Vic Gordon (pastor, First Baptist Church of Huntington Beach/Fountain Valley in California), in interview with the author, May 27, 2004.

2. Ralph Earle, *1 Timothy*, ed. Frank E. Gaebelein (Expositor's Bible Commentary 11; London: Pickering and Inglis, 1978), 380.

3. Leighton Ford, *Transforming Leadership: Jesus' Way of Creating Vision, Shaping Values, and Empowering Change* (Downers Grove, IL: InterVarsity, 1991).

4. David Baron, with Lynette Padwa, *Moses on Management: 50 Leadership Lessons from the Greatest Manager of All Time* (New York: Pocket Books, 1999).

5. Laura Beth Jones, *Jesus CEO: Using Ancient Wisdom for Visionary Leadership* (New York: Hyperion, 1995).

6. Warren Bennis and Burt Nanus, *Leaders: Strategies for Taking Charge* (New York: HarperCollins, 1997), 4.

7. James MacGregor Burns, *Leadership* (New York: Harper & Row, 1978), 2.

8. Blackaby and Blackaby, *Spiritual Leadership*, 21.

9. Warren Wilhelm, "Learning from Past Leaders," in Frances Hesselbein, Marshall Goldsmith, and Richard Beckhard, eds., *The Leader of the Future: New Visions, Strategies, and Practices for the Next Era* (San Francisco: Jossey-Bass, 1996), 226.

10. Blackaby and Blackaby, *Spiritual Leadership*, xi.

11. John Adair, *Great Leaders* (Guildford, Surrey, UK: Talbot Adair, 1989), 16.

12. Ibid., 47.

13. Blackaby and Blackaby, *Spiritual Leadership*, 24.

14. Banks and Ledbetter, *Reviewing Leadership*, 35.

15. Quicke, *360-Degree Preaching*, 48.

16. Ibid., 27.

17. Barna, *A Fish Out of Water*, 7.

18. Blackaby and Blackaby, *Spiritual Leadership*, 75–83.

19. See Sidney Greidanus, *The Modern Preacher and the Ancient Text: Interpreting and Preaching Biblical Literature* (Grand Rapids: Eerdmans, 1988), 8.

20. Walter Brueggemann, "Prophets, Old Testament," in William H. Willimon and Richard Lischer, eds., *Concise Encyclopedia of Preaching* (Louisville: Westminster John Knox, 1995), 389.

21. Richard J. Skylba, quoted in Stephen Vincent DeLeers, "Sunday Prophecy," in *Papers of the Annual Meeting of the Academy of Homiletics* (San Antonio, TX: Academy of Homiletics, 2004), 106.

22. John Stott, *Basic Christian Leadership: Biblical Models of Church, Gospel, and Ministry* (Downers Grove, IL: InterVarsity, 2002), 36.

23. Hudson Taylor, *China's Millions* 1, no. 5 (1875): 55.

24. Stott, *Basic Christian Leadership*, 49.

25. Ibid., 63.

26. Ibid., 68.

27. Ibid., 69.

28. Quicke, *360-Degree Preaching*, 59.

29. See ibid., 29–32.

Chapter 3: Both Need Each Other Today

1. Dietrich Bonhoeffer, *Life Together* (London: SCM, 1954), 17–18.

2. Stott, *Basic Christian Leadership*, 113.

3. Alvin Toffler, *Future Shock* (Toronto: Bantam Books, 1970).

4. Leonard Sweet, *Soul Tsunami: Sink or Swim in New Millennium Culture* (Grand Rapids: Zondervan, 2003).

5. Herrington, Bonem, and Furr, *Leading Congregational Change*, 10.

6. Quinn, *Deep Change*, xiii.

7. Herrington, Bonem, and Furr, *Leading Congregational Change*, 95.

8. Ibid., ix.

9. Ibid., 8.

10. Lyle E. Schaller, *The Change Agent: The Strategy of Innovative Leadership* (Nashville: Abingdon, 1972), 23.

11. Herrington, Bonem, and Furr, *Leading Congregational Change*, 3.

12. Paul Borden, "Leading and Preaching," *Preaching Today* audiotape 183 (Carol Stream, IL: Christianity Today International, 2001).

13. Herrington, Bonem, and Furr, *Leading Congregational Change*, 3.

14. Gibbs, *ChurchNext*, 16.

15. Ibid., 11.

16. Malphurs, *Values-Driven Leadership*, 10.

17. Ibid., 34.

18. Ibid., 42.
19. Herrington, Bonem, and Furr, *Leading Congregational Change*, 50.
20. Ibid.
21. Wilhelm, "Learning from Past Leaders," 223.
22. James MacGregor Burns, *Leadership* (New York: Harper & Row, 1978).
23. Abraham Maslow arranged a hierarchy of human needs: first, physical needs of food, health, and survival; second, safety needs of personal security; third, love needs of belonging to a group; fourth, esteem needs of being respected and appreciated; and last, need of self-actualization.
24. Herrington, Bonem, and Furr, *Leading Congregational Change*, 96.
25. Warren Bennis and Burt Nanus, *Leaders: The Strategies for Taking Charge* (New York: HarperCollins, 1985), 21, quoted in ibid., 11.
26. Herrington, Bonem, and Furr, *Leading Congregational Change*, 11.
27. Bill Hybels, *Courageous Leadership* (Grand Rapids: Zondervan, 2002), 67.
28. Borden, "Leading and Preaching," *Preaching Today* audiotape.
29. Ibid.
30. Jim Nicodem, "Preaching with a Leader's Heart," *Preaching Today* audiotape 228 (Carol Stream, IL: Christianity Today International, 2002).
31. Jack Hayford, "How Preaching and Leadership Intersect," *Preaching Today* audiotape 215 (Carol Stream, IL: Christianity Today International, 2001).
32. Ibid.

Chapter 4: Fulfilling Vocation

1. Malphurs, *Values-Driven Leadership*, 111.
2. Barna, *A Fish Out of Water*, xv.
3. Thomas J. Peters and Robert H. Waterman Jr., *In Search of Excellence: Lessons from America's Best-Run Companies* (New York: Harper & Row, 1982).
4. William Diehl, *In Search of Faithfulness: Lessons from the Christian Community* (Philadelphia: Fortress, 1987), quoted in Banks and Ledbetter, *Reviewing Leadership*, 92.
5. Banks and Ledbetter, *Reviewing Leadership*, 92.
6. Schaller, *The Change Agent*.
7. Ibid., 12–13.
8. See Quicke, *360-Degree Preaching*, 97–104. I have since changed "pastor preacher" into "inductive preacher," which allows for a wider range of inductive preaching. See also Michael Quicke, "Preaching in History: Assessing Today's Preaching in Light of History," in Haddon Robinson and Craig Brian Larson, eds., *The Art and Craft of Preaching: A Comprehensive Resource for Today's Communicators* (Grand Rapids: Zondervan, 2005), 64–69. In figure 3, I have placed herald first so the sequence of types of preaching lines up with leadership aptitudes.
9. Barna, *A Fish Out of Water*, 23.
10. Ibid., 41.
11. Ibid., 43.
12. Ibid., 45.
13. Ibid., 48.
14. Ibid., 49.
15. Ibid., 42.
16. Ibid., 58.
17. Ibid., 28.
18. Ibid., 139.
19. Peter F. Drucker, quoted in *The Leader of the Future*, xiii–xiv.
20. T. R. Glover, *The Jesus of History* (London: Student Christian Movement, 1917), 213.

Chapter 5: Developing a Model

1. Jim Herrington, Mike Bonem, and James H. Furr, *Leading Congregational Change: A Practical Guide for the Transformational Journey* (San Francisco: Jossey-Bass, 2000).
2. Ibid., 1.
3. Henry T. Blackaby and Claude V. King, *Experiencing God: Knowing and Doing the Will of God* (Nashville: Broadman & Holman, 1990).
4. Ibid., 8.
5. Herrington, Bonem, and Furr, *Leading Congregational Change*, 2.
6. Ibid., 12.
7. Ibid., 5.
8. Ibid., 34.
9. Ibid., 7.
10. Ibid., 16.
11. Ibid., 10.
12. Ibid., 11.

Chapter 6: Learning Skills

1. Herrington, Bonem, and Furr, *Leading Congregational Change*, 160–61.
2. Rick Warren, *The Purpose Driven Church: Growth without Compromising Your Message and Vision* (Grand Rapids: Zondervan, 1995), 57, 60.
3. Ibid., 60.
4. Herrington, Bonem, and Furr, *Leading Congregational Change*, 100.
5. See, for example, Kennon L. Callahan's diagnostic approach in *Twelve Keys to an Effective Church* and Christian Swartz's eight vital signs in *Natural Church Development: A Guide to Eight Essential Qualities of Healthy Churches* (Carol Stream, IL: ChurchSmart Resources, 1996).
6. Herrington, Bonem, and Furr, *Leading Congregational Change*, 50.
7. Barna, *A Fish Out of Water*, 71.
8. Ibid.
9. See Covey, *The Seven Habits of Highly Effective People*, 66–94.
10. Barna, *A Fish Out of Water*, 67–92.
11. Ibid., 139.
12. Ibid., 143.
13. Speed B. Leas, *Discover Your Conflict Management Style* (Bethesda, MD: Alban Institute, 1997).
14. Quicke, *360-Degree Preaching*, 92–93.
15. Eugene L. Lowry, *How to Preach a Parable: Designs for Narrative Sermons* (Nashville: Abingdon, 1989), 32–33.
16. Paul Scott Wilson, *The Four Pages of the Sermon: A Guide to Biblical Preaching* (Nashville: Abingdon, 1999), 74.
17. Herrington, Bonem, and Furr, *Leading Congregational Change*, 113.
18. Ibid., 118.
19. Ibid., 116.
20. Ibid.
21. Ibid., 118.
22. John Adair and John Nelson, eds., *Creative Church Leadership* (Norwich, UK: Canterbury, 2004), 8.
23. Vic Gordon, "The New Testament in the New Millennium," in Scott M. Gibson, ed., *Preaching to a Shifting Culture: 12 Perspectives on Communicating That Connects* (Grand Rapids: Baker, 2004), 45.

24. Michael Slaughter, *Out on the Edge: A Wake-Up Call for Church Leaders on the Edge of the Media Reformation* (Nashville: Broadman and Holman, 2000), 128.

25. Herrington, Bonem, and Furr, *Leading Congregational Change*, 139.

26. Timothy Peck, "Pressured to Promote," *Preaching Today* audiotape for January–March 2003, (Carol Stream, IL: Christianity Today International, 2003).

27. McClure, *The Roundtable Pulpit*.

28. Sermon preached at St. Andrew's Street Baptist Church, Cambridge, England, May 18, 1986.

29. See Quicke, *360-Degree Preaching*, 160–61.

30. Alastair Mant, *Intelligent Leadership* (St. Leonards, NSW, Australia: Allen & Unwin, 1997), 54.

31. Herrington, Bonem, and Furr, *Leading Congregational Change*, 145.

32. Ibid., 143–57.

Chapter 7: Growing Character

1. Rudolph W. Giuliani, *Leadership* (New York: Hyperion, 2002), xiv.

2. Ibid., xvi.

3. Ricky Gervais, quoted in Brian Appleyard, "The Maverick Art of Leadership," *The Sunday Times*, January 9, 2005, news review, 3.

4. David M. Brown, *Transformational Preaching: Theory and Practice* (College Station, TX: Virtualbookworm.com, 2003), 242.

5. Quicke, *360-Degree Preaching*, 93–95.

6. Paul Scott Wilson, *The Practice of Preaching* (Nashville: Abingdon, 1995), 30.

7. Phillips Brooks, *Lectures on Preaching* (New York: E. P. Dutton & Co., 1877), 8.

8. Herrington, Bonem, and Furr, *Leading Congregational Change*, 16.

9. Ibid., 18.

10. Ibid.

11. Dee Hock, "The Art of Chaordic Leadership," *Leader to Leader* (Winter 2000): 22.

12. Hybels, *Courageous Leadership*, 184.

13. Ibid., 182–97.

14. Refrain of Harry E. Fosdick's hymn "God of Grace and God of Glory" (1930): "God of grace and God of glory, on Thy people pour Thy power."

15. Craig Brian Larson in David Goetz et al., eds., *Leadership Devotions: Cultivating a Leader's Heart* (Wheaton: Tyndale, 2001), 39.

16. Margaret J. Wheatley, *Leadership and the New Science: Discovering Order in a Chaotic World*, 2nd ed. (San Francisco: Berrett-Koehler, 1999), 6.

17. Herrington, Bonem, and Furr, *Leading Congregational Change*, 18.

18. Ibid., 19.

19. Ibid., 31.

20. Ibid., 20.

21. Arturo G. Azurdia III, *Spirit Empowered Preaching: Involving the Holy Spirit in Your Ministry* (Fearn, Scotland: Christian Focus, 1998), 29.

22. Herrington, Bonem, and Furr, *Leading Congregational Change*, 30.

23. Ibid., 21.

24. Ibid.

25. Ibid., 22.

26. Jim Cymbala, *Fresh Wind, Fresh Fire: What Happens When God's Spirit Invades the Heart of His People* (Grand Rapids: Zondervan, 2003), 160.

27. John Killinger, *Fundamentals of Preaching* (London: SCM, 1985), 164.

28. Herrington, Bonem, and Furr, *Leading Congregational Change*, 24–25.

29. Ed Brown (senior pastor, Skokie Valley Baptist Church), in interview with the author, June 15, 2004. Subsequent quotations are also from this interview.

30. Herrington, Bonem, and Furr, *Leading Congregational Change*, 25.

31. Warren, *The Purpose Driven Church*, 103.

32. Malphurs, *Values-Driven Leadership*, 20–21.

33. Lyle Schaller, *Getting Things Done* (Nashville: Abingdon, 1986), 152.

34. Malphurs, *Values-Driven Leadership*, 60.

35. Ibid., 185–86.

36. Ibid., 102.

37. Bailey and Wiersbe, *Preaching in Black and White*, 43.

38. Fellowship Bible Church of Dallas, Texas, in Malphurs, *Values-Driven Leadership*, 167.

39. Lakeview Community Church, Cedar Hill, Texas, in ibid., 170.

40. Carroll Community Church, Westminster, Maryland, in ibid., 165.

41. Ibid.

42. Ibid.

43. Lakeview Community Church, Cedar Hill, TX, in ibid., 170.

44. Willow Creek Community Church, South Barrington, Illinois, in ibid., 174.

45. Core Values, Newbury Baptist Church, http://newburybaptist.org.uk/core/core.htm (accessed April 5, 2006).

Chapter 8: Initiating Process

1. Adair and Nelson, *Creative Church Leadership*, 214.

2. Lynn Cheyney (senior pastor, Flossmoor Community Church), in interview with the author, June 15, 2004. Subsequent quotations are also from this interview.

3. Mathews, *Preaching That Speaks to Women*, 133.

4. Herrington, Bonem, and Furr, *Leading Congregational Change*, 34.

5. Warren, *The Purpose Driven Church*, 14.

6. Ibid., 15.

7. Jim Nicodem (pastor, Christ Community Church, St. Charles, Illinois), in interview with the author, June 1, 2004.

8. Herrington, Bonem, and Furr, *Leading Congregational Change*, 40.

9. Ibid., 37.

10. Ibid., 48.

11. Hybels, *Courageous Leadership*, 42.

12. Herrington, Bonem, and Furr, *Leading Congregational Change*, 61.

13. Barna, *A Fish Out of Water*, 74.

14. Ibid., 72–78.

15. Herrington, Bonem, and Furr, *Leading Congregational Change*, 57.

16. Hybels, *Courageous Leadership*, 45.

17. Ibid., 50.

18. Herrington, Bonem, and Furr, *Leading Congregational Change*, 68.

19. Warren, *The Purpose Driven Church*, 111, quoted in ibid., 62.

20. Hybels, *Courageous Leadership*, 44.

21. Nicodem, interview.

22. Gordon, interview. Subsequent quotations are also from this interview. See note 1 (chap. 2).

23. Herrington, Bonem, and Furr, *Leading Congregational Change*, 77.

24. See, for example, Bandy, *Coaching Change*.

25. Herrington, Bonem, and Furr, *Leading Congregational Change*, 84.

26. Ibid., 82.

27. Ibid., 94.
28. Ibid., 87.
29. Malphurs, *Values-Driven Leadership*, 63.
30. Hybels, *Courageous Leadership*, 31–32.

Figure Credits

The diagram (fig. 1) on page 40 is taken from George R. Hunsberger, "The Newbigin Gauntlet: Developing a Domestic Missiology for North America," *Missiology: An International Review* 19, no. 4 (1991): 395. Reprinted with permission of the American Society of Missiology.

The diagram (fig. 2) on page 52 is taken from Michael J. Quicke, *360-Degree Preaching: Hearing, Speaking, and Living the Word* (Grand Rapids: Baker, 2003), 51. Reprinted with permission of Baker Academic, a division of Baker Publishing Group.

The diagram (fig. 4) on page 94 is taken from Jim Herrington, Mike Bonem, and James H. Furr, *Leading Congregational Change: A Practical Guide for the Transformational Journey* (San Francisco: Jossey-Bass, 2000), 13. Reprinted with permission of John Wiley & Sons, Inc.

The diagram (fig. 5) on page 113 is taken and adapted from Aubrey Malphurs, *Values-Driven Leadership: Discovering and Developing Your Core Values for Ministry* (Grand Rapids: Baker, 1996), 54. Reprinted with permission of Baker Books, a division of Baker Publishing Group.

The diagram (fig. 6) on page 128 is taken from Jim Herrington, Mike Bonem, and James H. Furr, *Leading Congregational Change: A Practical Guide for the Transformational Journey* (San Francisco: Jossey-Bass, 2000), 18. Reprinted with permission of John Wiley & Sons, Inc.

The diagram (fig. 7) on page 165 is taken and adapted from Michael J. Quicke, *360-Degree Preaching: Hearing, Speaking, and Living the Word* (Grand Rapids: Baker, 2003), 132. Reprinted with permission of Baker Academic, a division of Baker Publishing Group.

Index

Aaron, 49
abortion, 31
Abraham, 80
accountability, 43, 152
action, 115
Adair, John, 49–50, 83, 115, 136, 147, 181
African American preaching, 110, 163
Alexander the Great, 49
Alfred the Great, 49
alignment, 163, 165
ambition, 50
Anderson, Leith, 28, 131
Andrew, 78
anemic preaching. *See* thin-blooded
    preaching
apostles, 48, 151
Aquila, 78
Aristotle, 126
Atkinson, David, 77
Augustine, 83, 185, 186
authenticity, 115, 126
authority, 50
Azurdia, Art, 133

Bailey, E. K., 35, 110, 142
Baker, George A., III, 183
balanced Christianity, 143
Bandy, Thomas, 28
Banks, Robert, 32, 51, 79, 181
Baptist tradition, 24
Barna, George, 24, 31, 34, 53, 72, 78, 82–
    86, 87, 104, 106, 109, 155, 156, 181
Barnabas, 78

Baron, David, 46
Beatitudes, 64
Bennis, Warren, 46, 70–71, 182
BHAG (big hairy audacious goal), 27
Bible
    conflict in, 110
    immersion in, 166
    interpretation, 166–67
    on leadership, 45–48, 54
    as normative, 42
    nurtures visions and visionpaths, 162
    power of, 48
    studying, 115
Biehl, Bobb, 182
"big dog syndrome", 15
biographies, 151
Black, James, 18
Blackaby, Henry and Richard, 28, 31, 48,
    50, 53–54, 70, 92, 108, 166, 182
Blackburn, Lancashire, 25–26, 79
black preaching, 110, 163
body of Christ, 121
boldness, 39, 42
Bolman, Lee, 32
Bonem, Mike. *See* Herrington, Bonem,
    and Furr
Bonhoeffer, Dietrich, 64, 69
Boomers, 65
Borden, Paul, 67, 72
boredom, 24
Brooks, Phillips, 127
Brown, Ed, 138
Brueggemann, Walter, 26

Burns, James MacGregor, 46, 70, 182
Bush, Luis, 173
business models, 63

Callahan, Kennon, 28
calling, 17, 19, 78, 129, 178, 186
Calvin, John, 83
care, 32
Carey, William, 108
Carnegie, Andrew, 152
CEO, pastor as, 16, 28
Chambers, Oswald, 176
change, 65–66, 72, 93–95, 101
    groundwork for, 150–54
    initiating, 131
    mental models of, 114
    preparation for, 95
    process, 94–96, 149, 150, 161
    resistance to, 80, 109
change agents, 80, 89, 96
change leaders, 160–61
character, 125–27
Cheyney, Lynn, 35, 147–49
Christian leadership, 17, 24, 27, 47, 49,
    57, 59, 71
Chrysostom, John, 83
church, 40, 41–42, 53, 58, 140
    corporate dimensions of, 18
    decline, 92
    as marketing organization, 63
    as transforming presence, 117
Churchill, Winston, 49
classroom church, 112, 113
Clinton, J. Robert, 182
coaching, 28
cold war, 24
collaboration, 17, 109, 186
collaborative preaching, 29
collegial leadership, 35, 149
comfort zones, 109, 177
commitment, 38
committees, 118
communicating the vision, 157–60
community, 18, 29, 40, 42, 58–59, 126,
    127, 128, 129, 139–40
compelling, 109
compliance, 38
conflict, 19, 66–67, 87, 129
    avoidance, 37, 66
    as life-giving, 97
    as life-threatening, 96–97
    resolution, 138–39, 145

congregational leadership, 100
congregational prayer, 108–9
congregational transformation, 11, 16, 27,
    38, 60, 92, 93, 99, 104, 112, 133–34,
    150
congregations
    as complex systems, 121–22
    unique character, 149, 150
consensus, 155
control, 32
conversion encounter axis, 40, 41
core values, 68–69, 141–44, 145, 152, 156,
    166
corporate personality, 58
corporate worship, 133
correction, 54
counterstory, 26, 31, 34, 40, 60, 166
courage, 60, 126, 130–31, 142, 145, 152
covenant, 58
Covey, Stephen, 32, 106
cowardice, 39, 129
creating tension, 110–11
creating urgency, 96, 152–53
creative tension, 98, 104, 105–11, 123,
    153, 157
creative thinking, 91
critical thinking, 112
criticism, 97
cross-over thinking, 91
culture, 26, 40, 41–42
Cymbala, Jim, 135
David, 46, 78
deacons, 59
Deal, Terrence, 32
Deborah, 78
default vision, 86
defensiveness, 105
delegating, 118
denial, 80
devotional life, 151
diakonia, 32
dialogue, 40–42, 118, 119
Diehl, William, 78–79
dignity, 126
directing leader, 84
discerning the vision, 155–57
disciplines, 98
discouragement, 131
Drucker, Peter, 88, 156
Du Pree, Max, 33

Earle, Ralph, 46
efficiency, 32
emotional intelligence, 130
emotions, 36
empathetic listening, 112
empowerment, 32, 96, 160–61, 165
energy, 17, 186
eschatology, 116
ethos, 126, 128, 133. *See also* godly ethos
ethos givers, 79, 97, 108, 135–37, 141, 152
evaluation, 68, 105–6, 118
evangelism, 30–31, 39, 41
evangelists, 48
events, 122
excellence, 78
exegesis, 54–55, 59, 104, 110, 166
exhortation, 34
experiential church, 112, 113
experiment, 162
explanation, 157
Ezra, 151

faith, 131, 135
faithfulness, 78
fame, 56
family-reunion church, 112, 113
fatigue, 163
fear, 131
feedback, 155–56, 157
Finney, Charles, 83
First Baptist Church (Huntington Beach, CA), 158
foolishness, of preaching, 57–58, 79, 185
Ford, Leighton, 46
forgiveness, 63, 129, 135, 136, 145
Fosdick, Harry Emerson, 130
friendships, with non-Christians, 143
full-blooded preaching, 17, 25, 43–44, 52, 60, 98, 104, 111, 124
Furr, James. *See* Herrington, Bonem, and Furr
future, 65, 114, 131

Gandhi, Mahatma, 49, 132
Gardner, John W., 182
Generation X, 65
Generation Y, 65
generic application, 37, 60, 66
Gervais, Ricky, 126
Gibbs, Eddie, 42, 68, 114
gifting, 17, 79, 186

Giuliani, Rudolph, 125, 130
Glover, T. R., 89
goals, 32
God
  agenda, 53–54, 166
  creativity, 142
  glory, 15–16, 172
  holiness, 127, 132–35
  judgment, 55
  will, 63, 96, 107, 156
  Word, 48, 73
godly ethos, 126, 132
Gorbachev, Mikhail, 24
Gordon, Vic, 45, 93, 116, 158–60
gospel, 40, 41, 53, 127
grace, 127, 135–37, 140
Great Commandment, 140, 145
Great Commission, 27, 140–41, 145
Greenleaf, Robert K., 182
Grint, Keith, 183

habitual leaders, 82–83, 84, 87, 88
Hauerwas, Stanley, 41
Hayford, Jack, 73
herald preachers, 81, 84, 87–88
hermeneutical circle, 41
hermeneutics, 166–67
Herrington, Bonem, and Furr, 29, 65, 66, 67, 68, 69, 91–98, 103, 113, 115, 118, 121, 127, 133, 150, 153, 163
Hock, Dee, 129
holiness, 101, 127, 132–35, 145
holistic preaching, 60
Holy Spirit, 11, 17, 36, 53, 59, 89, 112, 119, 130, 176
  dispensing with, 62
  fruit of, 152
  ministry of, 57–58
  power, 93
  and unity, 163
homiletics, 167
honesty, 115
hope, 55
hospitality, 43
human glory, 15–16
humanistic models, of leadership, 62
humility, 17, 186
Hunsberger, George, 30, 39–41
Hybels, Bill, 16, 24, 29, 71–72, 83, 92, 129, 130, 154, 157

identity, 126
Idle, Christopher, 24
imagination, 84, 110
immersion, in Scripture, 166
implementation, 165
incarnational preaching, 18
inclusive preaching, 18
individualism, 35–36, 40, 66, 118, 129, 135, 140
inductive preachers, 82, 85, 88, 193n8
influence, 31–32, 56
innovation, 142, 162
input, 155
intelligence, 130
intentionality, 67
intercessory prayer team, 109
interpretation, 54–55, 59, 110
intuition, 85
IQ, 130
Isaiah, 78

Jackson, Wanda, 180
James, 78
Jeremiah, 78
Jesus
  and business models of leadership, 64
  calling disciples, 151, 178
  death and resurrection, 62
  as head of body, 59
  leadership model, 46, 49–50, 53, 115–16, 136–37, 176
  as missional, 178
  prayer, 137, 174–75
  preaching, 50, 100, 115–16, 175
  as transformational leader, 89, 99–101
Joel, 186
John, 78
Jones, Laura Beth, 46
Joshua, 78, 131

Keck, Leander, 185
Killinger, John, 25, 137, 168
King, Claude, 92
King, Martin Luther, Jr., 152
kingdom of God, 100–101, 115, 116–17, 137
koinōnia, 32
Kotter, John, 29–30, 92, 183
Kouzes, James M., 183

LaCugna, Catherine Mowry, 33
lay ministry, 143

leader
  as physician, 121–22
  vs. manager, 70–71
leadership
  aptitudes, 83–86
  "from the middle", 85, 149
  levels of, 86–88
  needs preaching, 62–65, 71
  practical aspects of, 11
  separated from preaching, 23–25, 60
  as skillful shepherding, 16
  through preaching, 11, 17
leadership literature, 19, 29–30, 31, 32
learning disciplines, 93–95, 98
Leas, Speed B., 109
Ledbetter, Bernice, 32, 79, 181
life-development church, 112, 113
Lincoln, Abraham, 49, 152
listening, 110, 120, 126
local churches, 24–25
Lord's Supper, 58
love, 32, 134, 136, 137, 145, 176
  for God, 129, 143
  for neighbor, 129, 162
low compliance, 37–38, 66, 71, 96
Lowry, Eugene, 110
Luther, Martin, 83, 127, 185, 186

macro level of leadership, 86–87
maintenance, 31
"main thing", 156
Malphurs, Aubrey, 29, 33, 69, 77, 112, 141–43, 166
managers, vs. leaders, 70–71
Manhattan Project, 117
Mant, Alasdair, 121, 130
Maslow, Abraham, 70
Mathews, Alice, 35, 85, 149, 183
Matthias, 78
maturity, 18, 108, 126, 154
Maxwell, John, 29, 183
McClure, John, 29, 85, 120
McKibben, Michael, 184
McLaughlin, Vaughn, 29
membership, 31, 108
mental models, 98, 100, 104, 111–17, 122, 123, 157
mentoring apprentice preachers, 161
metanoia, 33
mezzo level of leadership, 86–88, 140
micro level of leadership, 86–88, 140

Microsoft, 33
Millennials, 65
mind of Christ, 59
ministry, 108
mission, 32, 55, 69, 108, 165, 166, 170–71,
    177, 178
missional church, 39, 42–43, 55, 117
missional preaching, 39–43, 60
missionary dialogue axis, 41–42, 66, 87,
    140
mission priorities, 119
mission statement, 25, 33
models. *See* mental models
modernity, 41
momentum, 163
money, 31, 56
Moses, 48–49, 53, 56, 64, 78, 151
motivation, 84, 157
Moxley, Russ, 32
Murray, Andrew, 175
Murrows, David, 24
mystical metaphors, 32

naïveté, 67
Nanus, Burt, 46, 70–71
narrative preachers, 81, 82, 85, 88, 167
needs, 70
negotiating, 109
Nehemiah, 123, 151, 152
New Age spirituality, 32
Newbigin, Lesslie, 30, 39, 41
Newbury Baptist Church (Newbury,
    England), 144–45
new creation, 66, 97
Nicodem, Jim, 72–73, 106, 108, 122–23,
    151–52, 158, 162
noncompliance, 38
northern church, 173
nostalgia, 105, 131

obedience, 80
online resources, 37
open systems, 122
operational leaders, 85, 109
Oppenheimer, J. Robert, 117
Origen, 185, 186
outcomes, 168

Packard, Vance, 183
paradoxes, flattening of, 63–64
participatory leadership, 120

passion, 129
pastor preacher, 193n8
pastors, 11, 48, 72
patience, 97
Pattison, Stephen, 32
Paul, 45, 78, 83, 89
peace, 66
peacemaking, 137, 145
Peck, Timothy, 119
preferred future, 69
performance, 110, 118
personal preparation, 151
persuading, 109
Peter. *See* Simon Peter
Peters, Thomas, 78
Posner, Barry Z., 183
Post-Boomers, 65
postmodernity, 65
power, 32, 50, 177–78
    ambiguity of, 56–57,
    paradox of, 59
    in weakness, 56, 59, 64
    practice, 132, 145
pragmatism, 31, 64, 73, 175
prayer, 17, 100, 115, 143, 145, 155, 169–
    72, 174–75, 179, 186
preaching, 100
    causes tension, 176
    foolishness of, 79
    leadership through, 11, 17
    needs leadership, 65–66, 71
    as pejorative term, 88
    separated from leadership, 23–25
    and transformation, 148
    as vision casting, 158
    without leading, 60
"preaching swim", 93, 165–68
Pre-Boomers, 65
presence, 178
present, 131
pride, 15, 64–65, 129
Priscilla, 78
process, 68, 85, 165
proclamation, 51
prophetic preaching, 17, 18, 186
prophets, 48, 55
prosperity gospel, 36
public witness, 43
pulling in, 177
purpose, 56
pushing out, 176–77, 180

Quicke, Michael J., 11, 23
quiet time, 174
Quinn, Robert, 33, 65

realistic preaching, 18
reciprocal relationship axis, 41, 140
reconciliation, 42, 129, 134, 135, 136
Reeves, Thomas, 173
relational leadership, 148
relational vitality, 93–95, 96–97, 127–28
relationships, 126
relevance, 55, 59
reproof, 54
righteousness, 54
rituals, 32
Rose, Robert R., 183
Roueche, John E., 183
"roundtable pulpit", 120

sacrifice, 134
Saddleback Church, 16, 139, 157
salvation, 52, 63
sanctification, 176
Sanders, J. Oswald, 184
Schaller, Lyle, 67, 80, 141
Schein, E. H., 184
Schiavo, Terri, 31
Schmidt, Wayne, 34
Schwarz, Christian, 28
secularism, 64
secular leadership, 31–33, 46–47, 62–64,
    131, 132
self-disclosure, 152
self-interest, 68
self-leading, 129
self-management, 129
Senge, Peter, 37, 71, 92, 98, 184
sermon
  delivery of, 167–68
  designing of, 167
  preparation, 104, 110, 120
  series, 111
servants, servanthood, 32, 46, 48, 50
service, 32, 134, 137
shepherding, 16, 46
Silas, 89
Simon Peter, 59, 78, 83, 101, 115, 117,
    132, 176, 177–78, 186
sin, 63, 67, 132
situation, 100
situational leaders, 83, 86–87, 99, 104, 155

skills, 98
Skylba, Richard, 55
Slaughter, Michael, 118
slave, 50
smaller-scale ministry, 16
small groups, 38, 67, 119, 120, 143,
    163–64
social-conscience church, 112, 113
social issues, 31
Socrates, 49, 83
Sofield, Loughlan, 184
solitary place, 100
soul-winning church, 112, 113
southern church, 173
spineless theology, 36–37
spiritual growth, 78, 93
spiritual inventory, 129, 152
spiritual leadership, 28, 47, 53
spiritual vitality, 93–95, 96–97, 127–28
spiritual wisdom, 57, 63, 130, 142, 145
Spurgeon, Charles Haddon, 83, 84, 186
Spurgeon's College, 27
St. Andrew's Street Baptist Church (Cam-
    bridge), 26–27, 168–72, 179–80
stagnation, 163
Stanley, Andy, 30
Stannard, Jon, 144–45
stewardship, 32, 119
stories, 153, 157
Stott, John, 56, 57, 64–65, 84
Stowell, Joseph, 34
strategic leaders, 84
strategies, 141
strength, 57
structure, 122
study, 110
success, 32
surveys, 153
Sweet, Leonard, 65
systems thinking, 98, 104, 121–23, 161

Taylor, Hudson, 56
teacher preachers, 81–82, 88
teaching, 30–31, 33, 34, 39, 41, 48, 54
team-building, 85, 109, 110
team learning, 98, 104, 117–21, 123
teams, 101, 178
techniques, 32
tension. See creative tension
Thatcher, Margaret, 24
theological spine, 60

theology, 63
thin-blooded preaching, 26, 27, 30, 33–39, 66, 71, 104, 110–11, 123–24
Toffler, Alvin, 65
transactional leaders, 70, 177
transformation, 17, 29, 60, 92. *See also* congregational transformation
transformational leadership, 70, 71, 99–101, 132
transformational planning, 112
transformational preaching, 17
transparency, 115
trends, 122
Trinity, 51
trust, 32

unity, 127, 128, 137–39, 160
urgency, 96, 165

Vaill, Peter, 32
values, 68–69, 165, 170–71
values audit, 141–42, 152
values-driven leadership, 141
vanity, 126
vision, 56, 69, 106–8, 141, 165, 170, 186
  communicating, 38, 96
  discerning, 155–57
  implementing, 38, 161–62
  of leaders, 32, 34, 129
vision community, 96, 108, 153–54, 171

visionpath, 69, 70–71, 96, 155, 162, 164
vision statement, 25, 156
vocation, 78–80, 89
vulnerability, 126

Warren, Rick, 16, 29, 79, 92, 103, 139, 151, 157
Waterman, Robert, 78
weakness, 56
Welch, Jack, 34
Wesley, John, 83
Wheatley, Margaret, 131
white preaching, 110
Wiersbe, Warren, 35, 110
Wilhelm, Warren, 47, 69
Williams, Benjamin, 184
Willimon, William, 41
Willow Creek, 16, 156, 157
Wilson, Paul Scott, 110
wisdom, 23, 97, 130
women, leadership style, 35, 149
Word and sacrament, 27
Word of God, 48, 53–54, 73
words, and leadership, 47–48
worldly wisdom, 57, 63
worship, 27, 28, 64, 119, 133
  and transformation, 133–34
worship leaders, 133
worship wars, 134
Wright, Walter C., Jr, 184

Michael J. Quicke is Charles W. Koller Professor of Preaching and Communication at Northern Seminary in Lombard, Illinois. He is the author of *360-Degree Preaching: Hearing, Speaking, and Living the Word*, awarded 2003 Book of the Year by *Preaching* magazine. Former principal of Spurgeon's College in London, he regularly preaches and lectures on preaching worldwide.

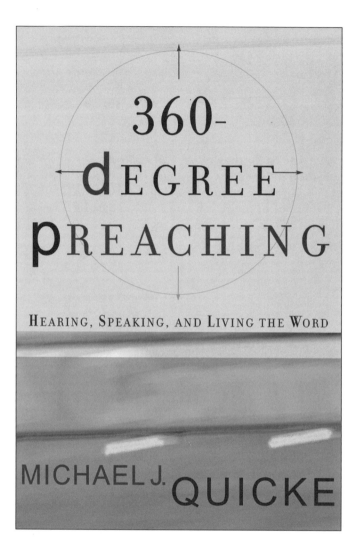